C000171226

797,885 Books

are available to read at

www.ForgottenBooks.com

Forgotten Books' App
Available for mobile, tablet & eReader

ISBN 978-1-332-16068-6
PIBN 10292826

This book is a reproduction of an important historical work. Forgotten Books uses
state-of-the-art technology to digitally reconstruct the work, preserving the original format
whilst repairing imperfections present in the aged copy. In rare cases, an imperfection in
the original, such as a blemish or missing page, may be replicated in our edition. We do,
however, repair the vast majority of imperfections successfully; any imperfections that
remain are intentionally left to preserve the state of such historical works.

1 MONTH OF
FREE
READING

at

www.ForgottenBooks.com

By purchasing this book you are eligible for one month membership to ForgottenBooks.com, giving you unlimited access to our entire collection of over 700,000 titles via our web site and mobile apps.

To claim your free month visit: www.forgottenbooks.com/free292826

English
Français
Deutsche
Italiano
Español
Português

www.forgottenbooks.com

Mythology Photography **Fiction**
Fishing Christianity **Art** Cooking
Essays Buddhism Freemasonry
Medicine **Biology** Music **Ancient
Egypt** Evolution Carpentry Physics
Dance Geology **Mathematics** Fitness
Shakespeare **Folklore** Yoga Marketing
Confidence Immortality Biographies
Poetry **Psychology** Witchcraft
Electronics Chemistry History **Law**
Accounting **Philosophy** Anthropology
Alchemy Drama Quantum Mechanics
Atheism Sexual Health **Ancient History**
Entrepreneurship Languages Sport
Paleontology Needlework Islam
Metaphysics Investment Archaeology
Parenting Statistics Criminology
Motivational

BENGAL DISTRICT GAZETTEERS.

NADIA.

[*Price*— *In India, Rs. 3; in England, 4s. 6d.*]

BENGAL DISTRICT GAZETTEERS.

NADIA.

BY

J. H. E. GARRETT,

INDIAN CIVIL SERVICE.

CALCUTTA:

BENGAL SECRETARIAT BOOK DEPÔT.

1910.

PLAN OF CONTENTS.

TABLE OF CONTENTS.

CHAPTER I.

PHYSICAL ASPECTS.

CHAPTER II.

HISTORY.

CHAPTER III.

THE PEOPLE.

CHAPTER IV.

PUBLIC HEALTH.

CHAPTER V.

AGRICULTURE.

CHAPTER VI.

NATURAL CALAMITIES.

CHAPTER VII.

RENTS, WAGES AND PRICES.

CHAPTER VIII.

OCCUPATIONS, MANUFACTURES AND TRADES.

CHAPTER IX.

MEANS OF COMMUNICATION.

CHAPTER X.

LAND REVENUE ADMINISTRATION.

CHAPTER XI.

GENERAL ADMINISTRATION.

CHAPTER XII.

LOCAL SELF-GOVERNMENT.

CHAPTER XIII.

EDUCATION.

CHAPTER XIV.

CHRISTIAN MISSIONS.

CHAPTER XV.

THE NADIĀ RĀJ.

CHAPTER XV.

GAZETTEER.

GAZETTEER

OF THE

NADIA DISTRICT.

CHAPTER I.

PHYSICAL ASPECTS.

THE district of Nadiā forms the north-eastern portion of the Presidency Division, and lies between north latitude 24° 11' and 22° 53', and east longitude 89° 22' and 88° 9'. It extends over an area of 2,793 square miles, and has a population, according to the Census of 1901, of 1,667,491 persons. It takes its name from the town of Nadiā or Nabadwip, situated at present on the west bank of the Bhāgirathi, but the administrative head-quarters and chief city of the district (although not the most populous) is Krishnagar, on the Jalangi river, in latitude 23° 24' N. and longitude 88° 31' E.

The district is separated on the north from the districts of Pabnā and Rājshāhi by the Padmā or Ganges; on the north-west, from the district of Murshidābād, for about three-quarters of this boundary, by the Jalangi or Khariā; and on the west from the districts of Bardwān and Hooghly by the Bhāgirathi or Hooghly. On the remaining sides of the district there are no natural boundaries, but it is bounded on the south by the 24-Pargannahs district, on the south-east by Jessore, and on the east by Faridpur. On the western boundary there were two strips of land included in the district, though they lie, at present, on the west bank of the Bhāgirathi. On the southernmost of these, which has an area of about 11 square miles, lies the town of Nadiā or Nabadwip; it is probable that this strip would have been transferred to the district of Bardwān, within the natural boundary of which it now falls, had it not been for the previous history of the river and the anomaly which would have been caused by including within another district the town from which the Nadiā district derives its name : indeed the order for transfer

2 NADIA.

was actually passed by Sir George Campbell, but was rescinded in the following year by his successor, Sir Richard Temple. The other strip is the island of Agradwip, which lies about 15 miles north of Nadiā: this, however, was transferred to the district of Bardwān with effect from 1st April 1888. There seems no doubt that at one period the main channel of the Bhāgirathi passed to the west of both these strips.

Natural configuration.

The Nadiā district is a large alluvial plain stretching southwards from near the head of the delta formed by the successive rivers into which the Ganges has from time to time distributed itself. As to the formation of this delta, the following remarks of Dr. Thomas Oldham recorded in the proceedings of the Asiatic Society of Bengal, 1870, page 47, may be quoted :—

"I suppose no one will hesitate to acknowledge that the whole of the country, including the Sunderban proper, lying between the Hooghly on the west and the Meghnā on the east, is only the delta caused by the deposition of the débris carried down by the rivers Ganges and Brāhmaputrā, and their tributaries. It is also equally well known that in such flats the streams are constantly altering their courses, eating away on one bank and depositing on the other, until the channel in which they formerly flowed becomes choked up, and the water is compelled to seek another course. It is also certain that in this peculiar delta the general course of the main waters of the Ganges has gradually tracked from the west towards the east, until of late years the larger body of the waters of the Ganges have united with those of the Brahmāputrā and have together proceeded to the sea as the Meghnā. Every stream, whether large or small, flowing through such a flat, tends to raise its own bed or channel by the deposition of the silt and sand it holds suspended in its waters, and by this gradual deposition the channel bed of the streams is raised above the actual level of the adjoining flats. It is impossible to suppose a river continuing to flow along the top of a raised bank, if not compelled to do so by artificial means, and the consequence of this filling in and raising of its bed is that, at the first opportunity, the stream necessarily abandons its original course, and seeks a new channel in the lower ground adjoining, until after successive changes it has gradually wandered over the whole flat and raised the entire surface to the same general level. The same process is then repeated, new channels are cut out, and new deposits formed.

"Bearing these admitted principles in mind, look to the delta of the Ganges and Brāhmaputrā The Ganges river emerging from its upper levels round the Rājmahāl Hills, and prevented by their solid rocky barrier from cutting further to the west, sought its channel in the lower ground adjoining, and originally the main body of its waters flowed along the general course now indicated by the Bhāgirathi and Hooghly. But gradually filling up this channel, it was again compelled to seek a new course in the lower, because as yet comparatively unfilled-in, ground lying to the east. And the same process being repeated, it wandered successively from the rocky western limit of the delta-flat towards the eastern. If this progress eastwards was allowed to be sufficiently slow to admit of the gradual filling in of the country adjoining, the delta was formed continuously up to the same general level, and the larger streams or channels passing through this flat to the sea became unavoidably diminished in size, and in the quantity and force of the water they carried, the main body passing around further to the east, and having its course in the channels successively formed there. I need not here point out the successive stages in the formation of the delta, or shew how these have been exactly paralleled by similar change in the course and deposits of the Brāhmaputrā and the other rivers which unite with the Ganges."

Revd. J. Long, in an article entitled "The Banks of the Bhāgirathi," and published in volume VI, December 1846, of the *Calcutta Review*, writes thus: "We name this article the banks of the Bhāgirathi, though some Europeans call the river as far as Nudiyá the Hugly; but Hugly is a modern name given to it since the town of Hugly rose into importance; the natives call it Bhāgirathi, because they say it was the channel Bhāgirath cut in bringing the Ganges from the Himālaya to Ganga Sāgar. This name recalls, what is believed to be a fact, that the Ganges itself formerly ran by Katwa, Tribeni, and not as it does now into the Padmā; our reasons are, the natives attribute no sanctity to the waters of the Padmā, thinking the Bhāgirathi to be the true bed of the river; hence the water flowing by Bishop's College is not esteemed holy, as they say that the site of Tolly's Nala was the ancient bed; there are no places of pilgrimage along the banks of the Padmā, while on the Bhāgirathi are Tribeni, Sāgar, Nudiyá and Agardip. Dr. Buchanan states on that subject: 'I think it not unlikely that on the junction of the Kosi with the Ganges, the united mass of water opened the passage now called Padmā, and the old channel of the Bhāgirathi from Songti (Suti) to Nudiyá was then left comparatively dry. In this way we may account for the natives considering that insignificant channel as the proper continuation of their sacred river, as they universally do, a manner of thinking that, unless some such extraordinary change had taken place, would have been highly absurd.' The names of places near the Bhāgirathi ending in *dvrip* island, *dāngā* upland, *daha* abyss, *sāgar* sea, seem to indicate that a large body of water formerly flowed near them."

The country is flat and the general aspect is that of a vast level alluvial plain, dotted with villages and clusters of trees and intersected by numerous rivers, back-waters, minor streams and swamps. The soil is agriculturally classed as high land, and bears cold weather crops as well as rice. In the west of the district is the Kalantar, a low lying tract of black clay soil which stretches from the Murshidābād district through the gap in the north-western boundary between the Jalangi and Bhāgirathi, down into the Kāliganj and Tehata thanas. This tract bears only winter rice and is specially liable to famine when the monsoon fails: it is also liable to serious injury from inundations from the Bhāgirathi when the Lāltakuri embankment in the Murshidābād district gives way.

RIVER SYSTEM. At present all the Nadiā rivers may be described as off-shoots of the Padmā, or main channel of the Ganges, but it seems clear that at one time the Ganges found its way to the sea along the course of the Bhāgirathi, and in those days, before the Padmā broke its way to the eastward and intersected the drainage of the Darjeeling Himalayas, there must have been some earlier streams to carry that drainage to the sea, of which the Bhairab is said to have been one. Now-a-days, however, all the drainage of Northern Bengal is intercepted by the Padmā before it reaches Nadiā.

Padmā. The Padmā impinges on the district at its most northerly corner, at the point where it throws off the Jalangi, and flows along the northern border in a direction slightly south of east, until it leaves the district some miles to the east of Kushtiā. It carries an immense volume of water and is very wide at places. Except where it is confined by high banks, the main channel is constantly shifting, whereby many disputes are caused as to the possession of the *chars* and islands which are thrown up.

Jalangi. The Jalangi leaves the Padmā at the extreme north of the district, and after forming the greater part of the north-western boundary, passes within the district at a point some miles north of Tehata. Thence it pursues a tortuous course in a southerly direction until it reaches Krishnagar, from which point it proceeds due west until it falls into the Bhāgirathi opposite the town of Nabadwip.

Bhairab. The Bhairab, which is by some thought to be of older origin than the Jalangi, its generally reputed parent, takes off from that river at a point a few miles north of Karimpur, and after a most tortuous course across the district, the general trend of which is to the south, loses itself in the Mātābhāngā not far from Kapāsdāngā. During the greater part of the last century there was very little current in this river, owing to its intake from the Jalangi having silted up; in 1874 a high flood cleared away the obstruction and widened the channel, but, for many years past, it has been practically dead, and the unhealthiness of Meherpur, which lies upon its banks, is in great measure attributed to the stagnancy of its waters.

The Bhāgirathi impinges upon the district near Plassey, and for some distance, forms its western boundary. It takes the name of the Hooghly from its junction with the Jalangi opposite Nabadwip town. In its upper reaches it is at present a comparatively insignificant stream, but the surrounding country gives evidence of the vast size which it attained, when it formed the main bed of the Ganges, the name of which is still applied to it by the villagers along its banks. Bhagirathi.

The Mātābhāngā or Hāuli leaves the Padmā about ten miles below the point where the Jalangi diverges from it. It flows first in a south-easterly direction as far as Hāt Boālia, where it bifurcates, and one branch, which is thereafter known as the Kumār or Pangāsi, proceeds, in the same direction, past Alamdāngā up to the boundary of the district which it forms for a few miles until it passes into Jessore, while the other branch pursues a very tortuous course, the general trend of which is to the south, until, after passing Chuādāngā, it reaches Kissengunge, east of Krishnagar, where a second bifurcation takes place, the two resulting streams being known as the Churni and Ichhāmati, and the name of the parent river being lost. Mātā-bhāngā.

The Churni passes in a direction slightly west of south, past Hānskhāli and Rānāghāt and falls into the Hooghly between Sāntipur and Chākdaha. Churni.

The Ichhāmati flows in a south-easterly direction and after forming the boundary of the district for a few miles passes into the Bangāon Subdivision of the Jessore district. Ichhāmati.

The Kabadak takes off from the left bank of the Mātābhāngā a few miles below its junction with the Bhairab, and takes an almost straight south-easterly course to the boundary of the district where it passes into Jessore. Its offtake is silted up, and, within this district, it is now nothing but a *khal*. Kabadak.

The Garai takes off from the Ganges not far from Kushtiā, and after flowing in a south-easterly direction past Kumārkhāli and Khoksā, passes over the border into the Goalunda Subdivision of the Faridpur district. It throws out two unimportant distributaries from its right bank, named the Kāliganga and Garai.

Daoko. The Garai is gradually silting up, and is now navigable only during the rainy season.

The whole district is a net work of moribund rivers and streams, but the Bhāgirathi, the Jalangi and the Mātābhāngā are the three which have been for more than a century, and still are distinctively known as the "Nadia Rivers." Until the advent of the railways, these watercourses afforded the regular means of communication between the upper valley of the Ganges and the seaboard. Ever since the British occupation of the country much difficulty has been experienced in keeping them open for navigation throughout the year. They have, when left to themselves, a very sluggish current which fails to carry off the large quantities of silt which they receive from the Ganges. In 1781 Major Rennel recorded that they were not usually navigable in the dry season. Captain Colebrook, in a memoir on the course of the Ganges (1797), writes thus:—"The Bhāgirathi and Jalangi are not navigable throughout during the dry season. There have been instances of all these rivers continuing open in their turn during the dry season. The Jalangi used formerly to be navigable during the whole or greater part of the year. The Bhāgirathi was navigable in the dry season of 1796. The Mātābhāngā, when surveyed in 1795, was navigable throughout in the dry season for boats of a moderate burden. This year (1797), however, I was informed that the passage was no longer practicable for boats proceeding to Calcutta. Experience has shown that none of these rivers are to be depended on." Early in the nineteenth century the Mātābhāngā appears to have been more easily navigable than either the Jalangi or the Bhāgirathi, and it is said to have continued open every year from 1809 to 1818. In 1813 measures were taken towards improving its channel, and a toll was established to defray the expense of the work. Very little good, however, appears to have resulted from the effort then made, for in 1818 "the obstructions had become so many and dangerous, as to cause the wreck of innumerable boats, and to entail heavy losses on account of demurrage paid for detention of ships waiting expected cargoes. The merchants of Calcutta in that year urgently petitioned Government that steps should be taken for remedying an evil from which the commercial interest suffered too severely."

In order to allow the ordinary large traffic-boat of 250 to 300 maunds to pass by this route, there must be a minimum depth of not less than 2½ or 3 feet. This amount of water can of course always be obtained during the rains from the middle of June to

October. But during the other seven months of the year, obstructions and shoals form, which render navigation always uncertain,
and often impossible, by the beginning of February. In 1819-20,
Mr. C. K. Robison was appointed Superintendent and Collector
of the Mátábhángá, and he succeeded in clearing the mouth of
the river, where it leaves the Ganges in the north of the district,
from the sand banks which had formed over sunken boats
and timber. The channel was also narrowed by means of
bandhals described below, and the river rendered navigable from
its head to the point where the Kumár branches off to the east.
This river carried away five-sixths of the supply of water from
the Mátábhángá, and an attempt to divert a portion of its current
into the Mátábhángá proved unsuccessful. Shortly afterwards,
Mr. Robison was succeeded in his office by Mr. May, who conducted the duties over twenty years, and first directed his attention to the damage caused by the numerous trees which were
allowed to grow on the river side, and which fell into the stream
wherever the waters cut into the banks. Many wrecks took
place every year from boats running against these fallen trees, and
Captain Lang states that in 1820 the number of sunken sál
timber logs was incredible. In a single year timber rafts to the
value of a lakh of rupees are said to have been lost. During 1820
and the following year, three hundred sunken timbers and many
boats and trees were removed from the bed of the river, some of
them being buried to a depth of twelve feet in the sand. During
1820-21, the upper channel of the Mátábhángá was deepened by
means of bandhals, constructed as follows:—At the shoals, to be
operated on, a line of bamboo stakes is run out from each bank
of the river. These stakes gradually converge so as to force and
concentrate the current into a narrow channel. They are well
driven into the bed of the river, supported by struts, and fastened
at the top by longitudinal ties. Large mat screens (jhámps) are
then let down as far as possible, and well secured to the bamboo
frame-work. The first result from the bandhal is a great velocity
within the channel it is intended to create, and a diminished
current on both sides. Owing to the increased pressure below, the
mat screems (jhámps) can never be sunk quite to the bottom of
the river, and through the space left there the water rushes with
immense force in a circular direction, cutting away the sand, and
carrying it under the matting and behind the line of bamboos,
where the stream being sluggish, constant deposit takes place.
The force of the current in the centre of the channel is at the
same time gradually cutting and bearing down stream the sand
in its course, so that by these two actions the depth is increased

in the channel enclosed by the *bandhal*, while on each side of it towards the bank, large collections of sand take place, materially narrowing and deepening the stream. The depth of the channel within the *bandhal* scarcely varies more than an inch or two, which is remarkable: and although the rivers may fall two or three feet after the *bandhals* are constructed, and shoal proportionately at other points, the uniform depth, be it three, four or five feet, is generally maintained within their channels till the next rainy season. All that is necessary is to drive the bamboo piling further down as the water cuts away the sand, and to sink the *jhāmps* from time to time to suit the fall of the river. It sometimes happens that the weight of gravel and sand swept away by the current within the *bandhal* sinks immediately on getting beyond it, thus forming another shoal which requires the construction of another *bandhal* to remove it.

These works, carried on in the upper channel of the Mātābhāngā during the dry season of 1820-21, rendered the river navigable till the end of March, from its mouth to the entrance of the Kumār, at which point further measures were undertaken to divert a portion of its current into the Mātābhāngā. A cut, 1,540 yards in length, was made to shorten one of the bends of the latter river, and to increase the fall; a caisson was also sunk, together with a number of old boats, across the mouth of the Kumār. These operations involved an expenditure of Rs. 14,000. When the river fell again to its usual dry season level, it was ascertained that the works had not been without effect, that the entrance of the Kumār had shoaled considerably, and that the depth of the Mātābhāngā had increased in proportion. Throughout 1821-22, a depth of three feet of water was always to be found at the worst shoals, and boats of three hundred maunds burden passed without difficulty. In the beginning of 1823, a dredging machine worked by oxen was supplied at a cost of Rs 10,400. In the meantime, however, the condition of the river had altogether changed, and although the dredge only drew 2 feet 4 inches of water, it was conveyed up the river with difficulty, and the entrance was found so shallow from the masses of sand which had been thrown up across the mouth by the Ganges, that the machine could not be used. Having found the Mātābhāngā so obstructed, and seeing no prospect of improving it, Mr. May proceeded in 1823, by order of Government, to inspect the Bhāgirathi and Jalangi. The channel of the former was discovered to be greatly obstructed by trees which had fallen into its bed during the two preceding inundations. At the Jalangi head, a little to the west of the Mātābhāngā entrance, sufficient water was found for boats of three hundred maunds burden, there being a depth of ten feet at the entrance, and only one shoal of three feet in its course. Here a *bandhal* was erected, and a depth of four feet secured. The Bhāgirathi head, which turns off from the Ganges in Murshidābād district, had shifted about half a mile to the east of its former position before the rains, and in the month of December was even more favourable than the Jalangi; for, although there was less water at the entrance, yet it lay so well open to the stream of the Ganges, with no detached sand-banks near, that there was every prospect of its being kept open for large boats throughout the season. The dredging boat was therefore despatched to this river. During 1824, Mr. May was appointed to the additional charge of the Bhāgirathi and Jalangi, and a regular establishment was sanctioned for the three rivers. A great change, however, took place soon afterwards in the Bhāgirathi. At the end of the year it was found that the entrance of the river had shifted five miles forther westward. Its new head lay quite open to the direct current down the Ganges which forced itself with such violence down it, that its breadth rapidly enlarged from two hundred and fifty feet to half a mile. Across this entrance there was a depth in January 1825 of twenty-two feet, the shoals down the river were easily removed by means of *bandhals*, and a depth of three feet was maintained throughout the dry season from the Ganges to Nadiā.

The favourable condition of the Bhāgirathi head did not last long. In 1825 the Ganges altered its course, and the entrance to the Bhāgirathi shifted eight miles to the south-east. The river became wholly unnavigable as early as November, and it was found that it would be a useless expenditure to attempt to improve it. In spite of a second dredging boat, which was supplied at a cost of Rs. 15,000, all the rivers became closed at the beginning of March 1826.

During the following five years, 1826-27—1830-31, all the rivers, with the exception of the Jalangi, continued in an un-satisfactory state as regards navigation, although the usual operations were vigorously carried on. In 1826-27, the sand-bank at the mouth of the Bhāgirathi was found to have in-creased in breadth and length. After the rains of 1826 it extended far below the entrance, and the river became impassable, except by small boats, before the end of December. During the inundations of 1829, however, another change took place at the head of the Bhāgirathi, by which the entrance was removed three and a half miles from its position of the previous year, and the old channel of 1823 re-opened; but its course for

some miles being through a loose sandy soil, shoals soon began
to appear, and before January 1830 it again became impassable.

The Jalangi, however, was in a much more favourable state.
In 1826-27 it was closed for a portion of the year. In 1827-28
it continued navigable for boats of two feet draught during the
greater part of the dry season, and in the two following years,
by constant attention to the usual works for removing obstacles, it
remained navigable for small boats throughout the dry season. In
1830-31 the river continued navigable for large boats to the end of
December, and for boats drawing two feet throughout the year.

The Mátábhángá continued in a bad state throughout the
five years 1825–30. In 1828-29 a steam dredger received from
England was sent to work on this river, but the machinery did
not answer well, and the draught of the boat, six feet, rendered
her very ill adapted for the river.

During the next few years, very little improvement appears to
have been effected, and, in the case of the Jalangi, greater
difficulties were experienced in navigation than during the previous five years. In the early part of 1831-32 an unusual flood
occurred in the Bhágirathi, caused by heavy rain in the
Rájmahál Hills swelling the tributary streams. The force of
the current cleared away the shoals below Berhampore, and re-
opened the communication for small boats, which had been
entirely closed since January. During the inundation of 1832
an unfavourable change took place at the entrance of the Jalangi,
the head having shifted five miles to the north.

In 1835 doubts seem to have arisen whether the benefits that
accrued from the works were commensurate with the expense
incurred. Orders were given in February to stop operations and
the establishment was discharged. Mr. May's report on the work
done during the previous three years showed that 359 *bandhals*
had been constructed on the different rivers, 118 sunken boats
raised, 219 sunken trees and timbers removed, 12 masonry buildings pulled down, and 1,731 trees cut down on the banks to prevent them falling into the stream. He explained that the
extraordinary deviations annually occurring in the course of the
Ganges, affecting as they did all the streams that flowed from it,
rendered it impossible to lay down any fixed rule of guidance
or plan of operations by which the navigation of the Nadiá
rivers could be permanently maintained. An experience of
thirteen years had convinced him that the changes which took
place in the great river during one inundation afforded no data to
determine what the next would bring forth, and therefore there
was no assurance that the measures adopted for mitigating or

repairing the evils of one season would be of the least avail in the ensuing one. Dredging machinery could only be usefully employed where the stream was rapid. Its use was to stir up the sand, so that the current might carry it away, rather than to lift the sand itself out of the bed. In sluggish water, where a bucketful was raised it was instantly replaced by the falling in of the surrounding mass.

During two years (1835-37) the operations were stopped, but in February 1837, Mr. May proceeded, by order of the Government, to again inspect and report upon the state of the rivers. He found that obstacles to navigation had much increased since the suspension of the works, and in June 1837, he was reappointed Superintendent. For the next three years the Bhāgirathi was the most favourable of the three rivers for navigation.

In August 1840, Mr. May resigned his office, and was succeeded in November of the same year by Captain Smyth. The operations carried on by this officer during the next seven years were the same as those previously adopted by Mr. May. The rivers continued in much the same state as before, the Bhāgirathi being the most favourable for navigation. In 1840-41 this stream was kept open for large boats throughout the dry season, and in 1841-42 for boats of 2½ feet draught. In 1842-43, however, it was found to be in a worse state than at any time during the previous five years, and many complaints came up of the obstructions to navigation. Strenuous efforts were made to clear it of its shoals, and with much difficulty a passage was maintained throughout the season for boats of from 250 to 350 maunds burden. In 1845-46 the river was kept navigable throughout the dry season for boats drawing two feet, but in the following year, 1846-47, it shoaled at the entrance to such an extent as to close altogether in February 1847. A fresh opening was made from the Ganges to the Bhāgirathi, and in May, when the rains set in, this cut rapidly enlarged itself, and gave a depth of from five to ten feet of water, whereas at the old entrance there was only a depth of one foot. The cost of the excavation was soon repaid by the increase of the toll collections.

The Jalangi remained in a very bad state throughout the whole seven years (1840–47), and the Mātābhāngā was never navigable in the dry season below the point where the Pangāsi branches off from it.

In December 1847, Captain Lang was appointed Officiating Superintendent of the Nadiā rivers, and, in support of further remedial operations, he brought to the notice of Government that, during the eight previous years, the total toll collections on the rivers had yielded an average annual surplus of Rs. 1,65,090 over the amount expended in keeping open the navigation, includ-ing the cost of collecting the tolls, and of all establishments. During the year 1847-48 the amount of tolls realised from each of the rivers was as follows:—Bhāgirathi, Rs. 1,51,482; Jalangi, Rs. 63,222; Mātābhānga, Rs. 24,028; total toll collections, Rs. 2,38,733. On the expenditure side the charges for facilitat-ing the navigation were Rs. 36,122; for collection of tolls, Rs. 22,360; total expenditure, Rs. 58,482. Surplus of receipts over expenditure, Rs. 1,80,250.

The same system of operations without much variation was carried on in the succeeding years. In 1859 a further attempt was made to improve the current down the Mātābhānga, at the expense of the Kumār, by cutting channels across a few of the bends in the former. The following year some experiments were made by towing a rake or harrow over the entrance shoals by a steamer when the Ganges began to fall in the autumn, but no success was obtained.

In 1881, Mr. Vertannes, Superintending Engineer, submitted a memorandum on the state of the rivers. At that period the Mātābhānga had the best entrance. It was said, however, that this was the first year for nearly 20 years that that river had been navigable for large boats. Alluding to the cuts on the Mātā-bhānga made in 1859, Mr. Vertannes said:—"Of the five cuts-off made in the river by the late Mr. J. W. Armstrong, four have already deepened out, and are only a little narrower than the normal width of the river. These cuts, now that they have been worked out, seem to have benefited the river, as far as navigation is concerned, but I fear that they must have tended to raise considerably the flood level of the river lower down, and the damages recently caused to the Eastern Bengal State Railway, are, I think, more due to this than to any breaching of the embankments above Murshidābād."

In 1888, the revenue administration of the Nadiā Rivers, which had up till then been controlled by the Board of Revenue, was transferred to the Public Works Department, and a separate division, called the "Nadiā Rivers Division," was constituted, and placed in charge of an Executive Engineer. Since that year an average sum of about 1¼ lakhs of rupees has been spent annually, chiefly on training works, to increase the depth in the dry season over the many shoals which form every year as soon as the rivers begin to fall. From December 1906 to March 1907 two small dredgers were hired and worked on the head shoal of the Jalangi river. The experiment cost nearly Rs. 38,000; it was temporarily successful, but no permanent improvement was effected. Two dredgers were again employed, at a cost of Rs. 12,000, during the following cold weather, in dredging 6¼ miles of the Jalangi river. The result was—in two miles, less depth than before dredging; in two miles, depth slightly increased; and in 2¼ miles, maintenance of full depth dredged.

The possibility of maintaining a navigable entrance to the Bhāgirathi was discussed in 1906, 1907 and 1909. In 1909 the Steamer Companies submitted a representation strongly urging that the river be made fit for steamer traffic throughout the year, as the water-route from Calcutta to up-country would thereby be shortened by 425 miles. In September 1906 the Chief Engineer estimated that the initial cost of the plant necessary for dredging the off-take of the river from the Ganges would be 126 lakhs of rupees, and that, if the scheme were undertaken, the yearly recurring charge for maintenance would be very heavy, and such as could not possibly be met by any tollage which the steamer companies could afford to pay : he also pointed out the necessity of caution in the execution of any works in these rivers, as it was possible that any channels which might be made might become larger and deeper, and that this might eventually lead the main Ganges into the Hooghly and thereby ruin the port and city of Calcutta. A further point to be remembered was that any increase in the volume of water passed down these rivers must mean a decrease in the volume passing down the Ganges below their off-takes, and that such decrease would produce a deterioration in the present navigable channels of the Ganges.

According to the figures given in Hunter's Statistical Account of Nadia and Jessore, the net revenue from the Nadiā rivers in the year 1847-48 was Rs. 1,80,250, and during the ten years ending with 1870-71, Rs. 1,04,538, the average annual expenditure during this same decade being Rs. 1,45,094. The following table shows the average income, expenditure and financial result since then : —

PERIOD.	Average annual income.	Average annual expenditure.	Average annual net surplus or deficit.
	Rs.	Rs.	Rs.
1871-72 to 1880-81	2,32,938	87,019	+ 1,45,918
1881-82 to 1890-91	1,95,632	1,18,136	+ 77,495
1891-92 to 1900-01	1,27,479	1,25,864	+ 1,615
1901-02 to 1907-08	76,629	1,23,689	− 47,060

Since 1871, there has been a steady decline in the average income, while the average expenditure has maintained an almost steady increase : from 1895-96, there has been a deficit every year ranging from Rs. 2,657 in 1899-1900 to Rs. 1,07,804 in 1906-07. In 1907-08 the total receipts amounted to only Rs. 35,229. The falling off in the receipts is, of course, mainly due to the extension of the railway systems, which now carry off a very large portion of the traffic, which used to find its way down the rivers, but a further cause is to be found in the reduction of the tolls which was introduced in 1906. The last two revised schedules of tolls, sanctioned in 1879 and 1906, are reproduced below :—

Schedule of tolls to be levied on the Nadia Rivers under Act V of 1864, whatever the distance travelled.

No.	Notification No. 175, dated 30th July 1879—*vide Calcutta Gazette* of 30th July 1879, Part I, page 789.	Rs.	A.
1	Pinnaces of 10 oars and under that number, each	3	12
	Ditto exceeding 10 oars	6	0
2.	Budgerows of 10 oars and under that number ...	2	4
	Ditto exceeding 10 oars	4	8
3.	Bholeahs and boats for personal accommodation, cutters not being of the description specially defined, and bulwars, pansways and baggage boats, per oar ...	0	4
4.	Empty boats and boats laden with bricks, tiles or other earthen substances, baked or otherwise, per 100 maunds tonnage	0	2
5.	Boats laden with quick-lime, chunam, straw, firewood, gurran-sticks, thatching grass or such like, per 100 maunds tonnage	0	8
6.	Boats laden with grain, pulse, seed or vegetables of whatever description and indigo seed, per 100 maunds tonnage	0	12
7.	Boats of burthen freighted with timbers and bamboos or with any article not included in the above enumeration, per 100 maunds tonnage	1	0
8.	Timbers with chowkars and dowkars, if floated on rafts or otherwise, not being boats, each timber ...	0	6
9.	Unwrought timbers called ghole or floated as above, each	0	3
	Rafts floating 200 bamboos or less, each raft ...	0	3
	Rafts floating more than 200 but not more than 400 ...	0	6
	Rafts floating more than 400 but not more than 1,000 ...	0	12
	Rafts floating more than 1,000, each raft ...	1	8

Schedule of tolls to be levied on the Nadia Rivers under Act V of 1884, whatever the distance travelled.

No.	Calcutta Gazette, Notification No. 6, dated 31st July 1906.	Rs.	A.
1.	Passenger boats, accommodation boats, bholeahs, budgerows, pinnaces, bulwares, pansways and baggage boats, per oar	0	4
2.	Empty vessels, except steamers, per 100 maunds of measured tonnage	0	4
3.	Vessels laden with cargo of any description per 100 maunds of measured tonnage	1	0
4.	Cargo carried in flats or steamers and charged on the manifest per 100 maunds of cargo	1	0
5.	Steamers that have been surveyed under Act VI of 1884, whose tonnage is determined by measurement, whether laden or empty, per 100 maunds of measured tonnage	1	0
6.	Floats or rafts of roughly squared timbers, each timber	0	6
7.	Floats or rafts of unwrought timbers, each timber ...	0	3
8.	Rafts of bamboos, each 100 bamboos	0	2
9.	Reeds, for each hundred bundles of reeds	0	4
10.	All boats the tollage of which does not exceed 4 annas will be allowed to pass *free.*		

N.B.—During the flood season (June to October, both inclusive) half the above schedule rates will be charged.

This account of the Nadia Rivers may fitly be closed with two extracts from an article by Sir William Hunter entitled 'A River of Ruined Capitals,' which appeared in the Nineteenth Century of January 1888 :—

"The Hugli is the most westerly of the net-work of channels by which the Ganges pours into the sea. Its length under its distinctive name is less than 150 miles, a length altogether insignificant compared with the great waterways of India. But even its short course exhibits in full work the twofold task of the Bengal rivers as creators and destroyers. The delta through which it flows was built up in times primæval a thousand miles off. Their inundations still add a yearly coating of slime to vast low-lying tracts, and we can stand by each autumn and see the ancient secrets of land making laid bare. Each autumn, too, the network of currents rend away square miles from their banks, and deposit their plunder as new alluvial formations further down. Or a broad river writhes like a monster snake across the country, leaving dry its old bed and covering with deep water what was lately solid land.

"Most of the channels do their work in solitude, in drowned wastes where the rhinoceros and crocodile wallow in the slush, and whither the wood-cutter only comes in the dry months, after the rivers have spent their fury for the year. But the Hugli carries on its ancient task in a thickly-peopled country, destroying and reproducing with an equal balance amid the homesteads and cities of men. Since the dawn of history it has formed the great high road from Bengal to the sea. One Indian race after another built their capitals, one European nation after another founded their settlements on its banks. Buddhists, Hindus, Musalmans, Portuguese, Dutch, Danes, French, Germans and English have lined with ports and fortresses that magnificient waterway.

" The insatiable river has dealt impartially with all. Some it has left high and dry, others it has buried under mud, one it has cleft in twain and covered with its waters : but all it has attacked, or deserted, or destroyed. With a single exception, whatever it has touched it has defaced. One city only has completely resisted its assaults. Calcutta alone has escaped unharmed to tell of that appalling series of catastrophes. The others lie entombed in the silt, or moulder like wrecks on the bank. The river flows on relentless and majestic as of old, ceaselessly preaching with its still small ripple, the ripple that has sapped the palaces of kings and brought low the temples of the gods, that here we have no abiding city. It is a vision of the world's vanities such as the world has not seen since Spenser mourned the 'Ruins of Rome' :—

> Ne ought save Tyber hastning to his fall
> Remains of all : O world's inconstancie !
> That which is firme doth flit and fall away,
> And that is flitting doth abide and stay."

" Of all the cities and capitals that man has built upon the Hugli only one can now be reached by sea-going ships. The sole survival is Calcutta. The long story of ruins compels us to ask whether the same fate hangs over the capital of British India. Above Calcutta, the head-quarters of the Hugli still silt up and are essentially decaying rivers. Below Calcutta, the present channel of the Damodar enters the Hugli, and at so acute an angle, that it has thrown up the James and Mary sands, the most dangerous river-shoal known to navigation. The combined discharges of the Damodar and Rupnarayan rivers join the Hugli, close to each other from the same bank. Their intrusive mass of water arrests the flow of the Hugli current, and so causes it to deposit its silt, thus forming the James and Mary. In 1854 a committee of experts reported by a majority that, while modern ships required a greater depth of water, the Hugli channels had deteriorated, and that their deterioration would under existing conditions go on. The capital of British India was brought face to face with the question whether it would succumb, as every previous capital on the river had succumbed, to the forces of nature, or whether it would fight them. In 1793 a similar question had arisen in regard to a project for re-opening the old mouth of the Damodar above Calcutta. In the last century the Government decided, and, with its then meagre resources of engineering, wisely decided, not to fight nature. In the present century the Government has decided, and, with the enlarged resources of modern engineering, has wisely decided, to take up the gage of battle.

"It is one of the most marvellous struggles between science and nature which the world has ever seen. In this article I have had to exhibit man as beaten at every point; on another opportunity I may perhaps present the new aspects of the conflict. On the one side nature is the stronger, on the other side science is more intelligent. It is a war between brute force and human strategy, carried on not by mere isolated fights, but by perennial campaigns spread over wide territories. Science finds that although she cannot control nature, yet that she can outwit and circumvent her. As regards the head waters above Calcutta, it is not possible to coerce the spill-streams of the Ganges, but it is possible to coax and train them along the desired channels. As regards the Hugli below Calcutta, all that can be effected by vigilance in watching the shoals and by skill in evading them is accomplished. The deterioration of the channels seems for the time to be arrested. But Calcutta has deliberately faced the fact that the forces of tropical nature may any year overwhelm and wreck the delicate contrivances of man. She has, therefore, thrown out two advanced works in the form of railways towards the coast. One of these railways taps the Hugli where it expands into an estuary below the perilous James and Mary shoal. The other runs south-east to a deep river, the Matla. Calcutta now sits calmly, although with no false sense of security, in her state of seige, fighting for her ancient waterway to the last, but provided with alternative routes from the sea, even if the Hugli should perish. *Sedet aeternumque sedebit.*"

The Embankment Act is not, and never has been, in force in EMBANK-the Nadiá district, and there are no embankments which are MENTS. maintained from Government or public funds. In 1868 the Collector urged the necessity of action by Government in the way of repairing existing, and constructing new, bunds, as the zemindars could not be relied on to do anything, and the

C

cultivators had no ability for combination. An enquiry was made by the Executive Engineer, and estimates amounting to Rs. 3,494 were sanctioned by Government for repairs to embankments on the Jalangi and Mātābhāngā rivers. It was, however, made clear that this was a concession to meet an emergency, and was not to be regarded as a precedent. In 1880 a report was submitted by the District Engineer detailing the embankments which existed on the various rivers by which the district is bounded or intersected. There are many isolated embankments which were apparently nearly all submerged by the flood of 1879. In the case of a few of the embankments it was said that they were repaired by the Public Works Department ; for the rest, they were repaired to a small extent by the zemindars or cultivators. The only continuous line of embankment was that on the left bank of the Jalangi, and the District Engineer estimated that it would cost Rs. 18,000 to put it into efficient condition. The Commissioner recommended some grants in aid for repairing some of the more important of the embankments, but it does not appear that the proposal received the approval of Government. Two years later the Superintending Engineer reported that in his opinion it was not advisable to retain the Jalangi embankments generally, though portions might be kept up to prevent inundation water from needlessly damaging the crops at every rise of the river. In 1895 the Superintending Engineer was directed to have the embankments which had been scheduled in 1882 inspected, and to ascertain whether they had been added to or altered. A list with notes of the state of repair of each, was accordingly submitted, but no further action was taken. The flood water is, however, not greatly affected by such private works as are still in existence.

LAKES AND MARSHES. The names of the chief lakes and marshes in the district are given in the following list :—

Sadar Subdivision.—Abhāngi, Adityapur, Arangsarisā, Aundhāri, Bāchāmāri, Bairāmpur, Bakshi, Bāliādaha, Bara Chāprā, Barbhāngā, Bhajanghāt, Bhālukā, Chāprā, Chārātolā, Chingrimāri, Chinichorā, Digri, Dubli, Dumri, Chidaha, Goārādaha Gurguriā Hānsādaha, Hānsādāngā, Haridaha, Jhorā, Jhori, Jiddha, Kaichuni, Kālātolā, Kālidaha, Kālinagar, Kālingā, Kalmā, Kāniādaha, Keturi, Khairā, Khānā, Nelor, Nutan, Padma, Pāglā, Pānighātā, Poāldaha, Sājānipur, Sāt-tālā, Sonājuli, Sukni, Tengrā, Tungi, Usidpur.

Rānāghāt Subdivision.—Amdā, Bāli, Bara Kachuā, Bāyeswar, Bhomrā, Chāmptā, Chāprā, Chinili, Dāmrāil, Dhoktādaha, Dohār, Gangāprasādbāor, Gopāyā, Haripur, Jhākri, Kachuā,

Kulia, Kátáganj, Mogrā, Mondourā, Morāil, Nāstā, Nrisingha-pur, Pánikhāli, Pochā, Sagunā, Sāt Sholāki, Shejdiār, Ukundi.

Chuādāngā Subdivision.—Bārādi, Begampur, Bharbhariā, Buichitolā, Chākli, Chāndmāri, Dalkā, Dhānkholābāor, Dukmāri, Ektārpurbāor, Hārdā, Kāmlādaha, Khayerhudā, Kobikhāli, Kulbilā, Kumridāngā, Loknāthpur, Medinipurbāor, Mrigamāri, Nalbilā, Nalgāri, Padmabilā, Pākār, Pākhi, Purapārā, Raipurbāor, Rāisā, Sankarohandra, Sankhariā, Solmāri, Tentuliā.

Meherpur Subdivision.—Alālgāri dāmosh, Asrafpur, Bāghā-dobā, Bātkemāri, Chāklā, Chāmu Khāndaha, Dubukholā, Elangi, Fatehpur dāmosh, Gobri, Ichāmatidaha, Jālangā, Kishorpur, Kol Kulbilā, Mohishkholā, Mohishmāri, Nishchintāpurbāor, Nonā, Padma, Pāngasi, Pātābukā, Roākul, Ruimāri, Sonādaha, Tengrāmāri, Terāghariā, Toplā.

Kushtiā Subdivision.—Amlā, Bārādi, Boāliā, Chāpālgāohi, Choroikhol, Gholdaha, Kachudaha, Mohishkundi dāmosh, Sāgar-khāli, Tālberiā.

The following remarks are taken from the Gazetteer volume of the Khulna district, as they are equally applicable to Nadia:—

"Many (bils) are of small size, but others are practically inland lakes. Some are mere accumulations of water upon low-lying ground, while others are natural drainage basins, the level of which does not admit of drainage. Their formation is due to the configuration of the district, which is divided by the interlacing of the rivers, into what are practically islands. Each of these is bounded by rivers, and the highest level is along their banks, so that the fall from all directions is towards the centre, which again is drained by a creek or *khāl* communicating with one of the surrounding rivers. In some places the basin thus formed is on a fairly high level, and the central depression, being suffi-ciently high to be above water at least during some months of the year, is used for growing crops. Other such depressions are water-logged, but can still be used for growing rice, while others again are inland lakes always under water and cannot be used for cultivation."

The soil of the district is composed of recent alluvium, and GEOLOGY. the surface consists of sandy clay and sand along the course of the rivers, and fine silt consolidating into clay in the flatter portions of the plain, such as the tract known as the Kalantar.

The stretches of low-lying land under rice cultivation afford BOTANY. a foothold for many marsh species, while the numerous ponds and ditches are filled with submerged and floating water plants. Remarkable among these for its rarity, and interesting on account of its distribution to Europe on the one hand, and to Australia

c 2

on the other, is the floating *Drocera*. The edges of sluggish
creeks are lined with large sedges and bulrushes, and the banks
of rivers frequently have a hedge-like shrub jungle. The sides
of embankments and village sites, where not occupied by human
habitations, are densely covered with large growths of semi-
spontaneous vegetation, often interspersed with clumps of
planted bamboos, and groves of *Areca, Moringa, Mangifera*,
and *Anona*. Waysides and waste places are filled with grasses
and weeds, usually of little intrinsic · interest, but sometimes
striking because of their distribution. A large proportion of the
species of this class to be met with in the district have been
inadvertently introduced by human agency, and besides weeds
that are indigenous in other parts of India, European, African
and American species are sometimes found, which can not · only
hold their own with, but actually spread more plentifully than,
similar weeds of truly Indian origin. In many places the soil
does not seem to suit mango, jack and other indigenous fruit trees,
and consequently the poorer classes are, in times of scarcity and
famine, deprived of one resource which they can fall back upon
in more favoured districts.

FAUNA.   At the beginning of the nineteenth century tigers were common in the more sparsely inhabited portions of the district near
the Bhāgirathi. A reference has been made to their depredations
in the Gazetteer article on Chākdaha in the last chapter of this
volume. It is, however, many years since the last of these animals
disappeared, and none are now to be found nearer than in the
Sundarbans. Leopards, however, are still fairly common, especially in the Meherpur and Kushtiā subdivisions : they do a good
deal of damage to goats and young cattle, and are reported to
kill two or three human beings yearly. Wild hogs are common,
especially where protected for the purpose of pig-sticking : the
record bag of boar for the whole of India was made recently on
the *chars* of the Padmā in the north of the district.

Among lesser fauna are foxes, hares and porcupines. Monkeys
(the black-faced Hanumān or langur) are numerous and destructive in the towns, especially Krishnagar, where they cause much
damage in gardens, and to the mango crop when it is ripening.
Jackals are credited with carrying off about 100 infants yearly,
and many cases of hydrophobia are caused by their bites.
Crocodiles are fairly common, especially in the Garai and other
rivers in the north of the district, and they occasionally kill
human beings.

Of game-birds, the florican used to breed on the field of
Plassey, but appears to have deserted the district during recent

years. Snipe are very common in the south of the district during the latter part of the rains and the beginning of the cold weather. Various kinds of wild duck and other aquatic birds are found in large numbers in the east and north of the district during the cold weather, and wild geese are common in the Padmā. A few partridge and quail are occasionally met with. Snakes are common, and account for some 400 deaths annually.

Fish abound in most of the rivers and *bils*, and very large catches of hilsa are made in the Padmā during the rainy season, and are exported freely by rail from Damukdia, or Sara, on the opposite bank of the river.

The seasons in Nadiā are substantially the same as in other CLIMATE. parts of Lower Bengal. The cold weather may be said to commence in the latter part of November (the first part of this month is frequently very warm), and to last until the middle of February. During these months the prevailing winds are from the north and north-west, and there is a very heavy dew at night. During March and April the weather becomes increasingly hot during the day, though the nights remain fairly cool; the daily range of temperature is frequently very high during these months. The temperature in May is often tempered by severe " nor'-westers", which generally come on in the evening, and last about an hour, during which the rainfall is very heavy, and the thunder and lightning practically incessant. The monsoon as a rule sets in about the middle of June, and causes some diminution in the maximum temperatures The rains abate in September, when the heat again becomes very trying, and remains so until the cold weather gradually sets in. The mean temperature for the year is 79°, and it ranges between 69° and 89°. The mean minimum varies from 52° in January to 79° in June, and the mean maximum from 77° in December to 97° in May. The average humidity is 79 per cent. of saturation, varying from 71 per cent. in March to 87 per cent. in August.

The rainy season begins about the middle of June and lasts RAINFALL. till October. The average annual rainfall for the district is 57 inches, of which 6·5 inches fall in May, 9·7 in June, 10·5 in July, 11·3 in August, 8·1 in September, and 4·1 in October. Kushtiā receives rather more rain than the other rain-registering stations in the district, but, with this exception, the variations from the district average are very slight.

CHAPTER II.

HISTORY.

EARLY HISTORY.

THERE can be little doubt that the delta through which the Ganges flows was built up from the sea in prehistoric times by the silt which the various distributaries of that river brought down from the plains and mountains far inland. As Sir William Hunter has remarked, the "inundations still add a yearly coating of slime to vast low-lying tracts, and we can stand by each autumn and see the ancient secrets of landmaking laid bare." Ptolemy's map of the second century shows the southern portion of the Gangetic delta as cut up to such an extent by rivers and waterways as to consist practically of a succession of islands. This marked the first stage in the reclamation of the land from the sea, and Nadiā in those days appears to have been a fen country intersected with rivers and morasses, and probably inhabited by a few scattered settlements of fishermen and boatmen. In course of time each successive distributary of the Ganges deposited silt along its banks, and raised the level of the country until it no longer afforded sufficient fall for the escape of the drainage of the hinterland into the sea, when it broke a fresh channel for itself to the east, to repeat the same process further on.

According to the references in the Mahābhārata, the Raghubansa and some of the Purānas, the delta lay on the boundary between two powerful kingdoms, namely, Suhmā, corresponding to Western Bengal, and Vanga, or Eastern Bengal, and it is probable that the Nadiā district was under the control of the kingdom of Vanga in the time of the Raghubansa, *i.e.*, about the fifth century A.D. When the Chinese traveller Hiuen Tsiang visited Bengal in the seventh century, he found two large kingdoms in the lower delta, namely, Samatata and Tāmralipti. From the general description which he gives of the former, it seems clear that it must have included what is now known as the Nadiā district. Samatata appears to be another.

name for Vanga, given to it on account of its flat and level aspect.

In the tenth aud eleventh centuries the northern delta seems to have formed part of the empire of the Pāl kings, and it is certain that it was included in the kingdom of the Sen Rājās, who were masters of both Vanga and Rādhā. The town of Nabadwip is said to have been founded by Lakshman Sen, son of Ballāl Sen, and it is probable that Ballāl Sen himself used to visit the locality, as his name is still connected with a mound and a tank in the villáge of Bāmanpukur which is close by Nabadwip.

The Sen dynasty is said to have been founded towards the close of the tenth century by an adventurer named Samanta Sen, who is believed to have come from the Carnatic and established a kingdom on the banks of the Bhāgirathi. Samanta had a son by name Hemanta, about whom very little is known, and it is doubtful whether he ever actually ascended the throne : he appears, however, to have been a man of valour, for in one of the *slokas* it is said of him that his enemies withered at sight of him. Hemanta's son Bijay ruled for a time, and was succeeded by his son, the famous Ballāl Sen, who drove the Pāl Rājās out of Bengal and conquered Bihar. Ballāl Sen was succeeded by his son Lakshman Sen, towards the close of whose lengthy reign the incursion of the Muhammadans under Muhammad Bakhtiār Khilji took place. It seems that Lakshman on being driven out of Nabadwip, retreated to Subarnapur, near Dacca, and it is said that from there he and his successors continued to govern eastern and southern Bengal until the middle of the fourteenth century. There has been some controversy as to the caste of the Sen kings. The name Sen is now generally borne by Baidyas, but in ancient times it appears to have been borne exclusively by Rajputs. The Baidya caste is found nowhere in India except in Lower Bengal, and there can be no doubt that the Sens referred to in the Māhābhārata (*e.g.* Bir Sen) were Rajputs and not Baidyas. In the work Dān Sāgar, the authorship of which has been imputed to Ballāl Sen himself, it is expressly stated that the Sen Rājās were Kshattrias. On a stone tablet found by Mr. Metcalf at a place near Rāmpur Boāliā, there is an inscription to the effect that Samanta Sen was a descendant of the Lunar Dynasty ; his forefathers were reigning kings in the Deccan, and his grandson Bijay Sen conquered Kamrup, Gaur and Kalinga. Two copperplates of Lakshman Sen have been found, one in Dinājpur, and the other in the Sundarbans; both of these trace the descent of the Sen family from the

The Sen Dynasty.

Moon, *i.e.*, proclaim them to be of the Lunar Dynasty, feuds between the two branches of which caused the celebrated war of the Māhābhārata. Again a copperplate of Kesav Sen, son of Lakshman Sen, was found in Bakarganj, in which the same claim as to the descent of the family is set out, and the genealogy is carried down from Samanta to Kesav Sen. In this latter plate Lakshman is said to have constructed triumphal pillars in Guzerat, Benares and Tribeni. All these copper plates purport to make grants of land, etc.; they are of different generations, and were found in different places, but they all unite in saying that the Sens were the descendants of Kshattrias of the Lunar Dynasty, and in each is an invocation to the moon. There can thus be little doubt that the Sens were not Baidyas. The copper plate of Kesav Sen, in which he is described as an independent king, is of further interest as showing that the Muhammadans had not forced their way into Eastern Bengal during the first half of the thirteenth century at any rate.

Lakhsman, the last of the Sen dynasty, who exercised any sway west of the Bhāgirathi, was driven from Nabadwip by Muhammad Bakhtiār Khilji, when he captured and sacked the town in 1203 A.D. The latter was an Afghan by birth, but he took service at Delhi, and soon became well known for his activity, courage and abilities. About the year 1199 A.D. he was placed in command of an army destined to conquer Bihar. He carried out his orders with complete success and firmly established himself at Gaur, from which base he made preparation for an incursion into Bengal. It is said that the Brahmans and astrologers of Nabadwip warned Rājā Lakhsman that the long appointed time for the subjugation of Bengal by the Turks was at hand, and begged him to remove his family, property and the seat of government from Nabadwip to a more secure and distant part of the country, where they would be safe from any sudden incursion from the enemy. The Rājā, however, being very advanced in years and also attached to his capital, declined to listen to the advice, and took no steps to avoid the impending danger. In 1203 Muhammad Bakhtiār secretly assembled his army, and marched from Bihar with such expedition that he was at the gates of Nabadwip before the king had any warning of his near approach. The surprise was complete, and the Rājā only escaped with his life. After sacking the town Bakhtiār retired to Lakhnauti, and firmly established Muhammadan sway in the neighbourhood. It is doubtful whether the whole of Bengal immediately fell into the power of the Muhammadans, as has frequently been stated. It seems that from

Bakhtiār onwards there was for over 100 years a regular succession of Muhammadan Governors at Gaur or Lakhnauti, but the probabilities are that the part of Bengal in which Nadia lies did not entirely acknowledge the Mussulman Government until many years later. This point has been dealt with in an article by Manmohan Chakravarti, entitled "Disputed or Doubtful Events in the History of Bengal," published in the Journal of the Asiatic Society of Bengal, April 1898. The following extract is taken from the article:—"The nature of Muhammad-i-Bakhtiār's conquest appears to have been much exaggerated; the expedition to Nadiā is only an inroad, a dash for securing booty natural to these Turkish tribes. The troopers looted the city with the palace and went away. They did not take possession of that part, and if they had tried, they would have most likely failed, as their base in Behar was too far off and too recent to be of much avail. On removing the seat of Government to Lakhnauti, there was an attempt to secure permanent possession of some part of Bengal. On the north Diwkot, where he (Khilji) died on his return from the disastrous inroad to Tibet, was evidently in possession of {Mussalmans. On the south Lakhnor was outside their jurisdiction, because Muhammad-i-Sheran had been deputed with a force towards it at that time. Diwkot is identified with Damdamma about 70 miles north-east of Gaur, Lakhanor is identified with Nagor by Stewart and with Lacarcondah by Blochmann, but neither identification is satisfactory, both being far away from the river Bhagirathi. Even if either of these identifications be accepted, it would not be more than 90 miles from Gaur. The tract between the two is thus hardly large, and forms an insignificant part of the Bengal Province. Tabakat-i itself carefully speaks of Lakhnauti only; it is only the later writers who dila'e on the vaunted conquests of Bengal. In fact if such plundering inroads be magnified into conquests, and the Hindus of Bengal blamed and vilified for allowing the so-called easy conquests, then Muhammad of Ghazni has better claims for being credited with the conquest of all Hindustan."

It seems probable that the hold of the Muhammadans upon the part of Bengal in which the Nadiā district lies was very slight for the two centuries which succeeded the sack of Nabadwip by Bakhtiār Khān. It apppears, however, that by the middle of the fifteenth century the independent Muhammadan kings of Bengal had established their authority, for there is in Bāgerhāt, in the Khulna district, a tomb bearing an inscription which shows it to contain the remains of one Khān Jahān Ali,

EARLY MUHAMMADAN RULE.

a Muhammadan governor who died in the year 1459 A.D. Very little beyond legend is known of this man. In the latter part of the sixteenth century the northern half of the Nadiā district was probably under the rule of Pratāpādityā, who exercised sway over the greater part of the Jessore and Khulna districts. Pratāpādityā was the grandson of one Rām Chandra, a Kayasth of Eastern Bengal, who obtained favour at the court of Sulaimān Kararāni, one of the last of the independent Muhammadan kings of Bengal. It is said that Pratāpādityā went to the court of the Emperor at Delhi, and was granted a sanad making him a Rājā, and that he thereupon returned and ousted his father. Before long he declared himself independent of the Emperor, and he succeeded in defeating several Mughal generals who were sent to bring him to subjection. Finally Mān Singh, governor of Bengal, with the assistance of Bhabānand Majmuādār, one of the Rājās of Nadiā, surprised his capital, and captured him; he was sent off in custody towards Delhi, but he put an end to his life on the way, preferring death to the fate which he expected was in store for him.

MUGHAL RULE.
In order to keep some hold upon the greater *zamindārs*, and to endeavour to secure as far as possible the regular and prompt payment of the revenue by them, the country was parcelled out into districts, each under a military governor, called the *Faujdār*, with a small force of soldiers under his command. The *Faujdārs* were responsible to the Nawābs for the maintenance of order and the realization of the revenue. The Nadiā district fell within the Jessore *Faujdāri*. In 1696 Subhā Singh, a zemindar of Bardwān, rose in revolt, and, having induced Rahim Khān, the leader of the Afghāns in Orissa, to join him, advanced on Bardwān, seized it, and killed the Rājā. The latter's son escaped to Dacca, and laid his complaint before the Nawāb, who directed Nurullah Khān, the *Faujdār* of Jessore, to punish the insurgents. "But that officer," says Stewart, in his History of Bengal published in 1813, "who, instead of attending to his own business, had long employed himself in commerce and in amassing wealth, and possessed nothing of the military character but the name, having with much loss of time, collected a few of the 3,000 horse of which he was the commandant, marched from Jessore and crossed the river; but on the approach of the rebels, he shut himself up in the fort of Hooghly and implored assistance from the Governor of the Dutch settlement of Chinsura. The rebels convinced by this pusillanimous conduct that they had little to fear from the merchant soldier, advanced boldly, and laid siege to Hooghly; they carried on

their attacks with such vigour that the *Faujdār* became alarmed for his personal safety, and during the night, having crossed the river in a boat, made his escape to Jessore. The garrison finding that their commandant had fled, opened the gates, and the rebels got quiet possession of that opulent city without any loss." The rebels then proceeded to harry the districts of Nadiā and Murshidābād. In the meantime Subhā Singh was stabbed by the daughter of the Rājā of Bardwān, and Rahim Khān was unanimously elected as the leader of the rebel army. When tidings of these affairs reached the ears of the emperor Auiangzib, he appointed his grandson, Azim-us-Shān, as Governor of Bengal, Bihar and Orissa, and directed that Zabardast Khān, the son of the disgraced Nawāb, should at once take the field against the rebels, with the assistance of a number of troops from up-country. The operations, in the course of which Māhārājā Rām Krishna of Nadiā appears to have given material assistance, were finally successful (though the Nadiā district was in the meantime plundered for the second time), Rahim was killed, and the Afghān raiders were finally hunted down and destroyed.

Some fifteen years later, during the viceroyalty of Murshid REVOLT Kuli Khān, the north of the Nadiā district was again pillaged, OF SITĀRĀM during the revolt of Sitārām Rai, the following account of which RAI. is taken from the Riyāzu-s-Salātin:—"Sitārām, *zamindār* of pargana Mahmudābād, being sheltered by forests and rivers, had placed the hat of revolt on the head of vanity. Not submitting to the Viceroy, he declined to meet the imperial officers and closed against the latter all the avenues of access to his tract. He pillaged and raided the lands adjoining to his *zamindāri*, and also quarrelled with the imperial garrison and *Faujdārs*. Mir Abu Turab, *Faujdār* of the Chākla of Bhushna, who was the scion of a leading Syed clan, and was closely related to Prince Azim-us-Shān and the Timuride Emperors, and who amongst his contemporaries and peers was renowned for his learning and ability, looked down upon Nawab Jafar Khān. Mir Abu Turab tried to capture Sitārām, but was not successful. At length he detailed his general, Pir Khān, with 200 cavalry to chastise Sitārām. On being apprised of this, Sitārām, concentrating his forces, lay in ambush to attack the aforesaid general. One day Mir Abu Turab with a number of friends and followers went out for hunting, and, in the heat of the chase, alighted on Sitārām's frontiers. Pir Khān was not in Abu Turab's company. The *zamindār* (Sitārām) on hearing of this, fancying Mir Abu Turab to be Pir Khān, suddenly issued out from the forest with his forces, and attacked Mir Abu Turab from the rear. Although the latter with a loud voice announced his name, Sitāram, not heeding it, inflicted wounds on Abu Turab with bamboo clubs, and felled him from his horse.

"When this news reached Nawāb Jafar Khān, his body trembled from fear of the Emperor's resentment. Appointing Hasan Ali Khān, who had married Jafar Khān's sister and was descended from a noble family, to be *Faujdār* of Bhushna, and supporting him with an efficient force, Nawāb Jafar Khān directed him to capture that troublesome villain (Sitāram). The Nawab issued mandates to the *zamindārs* of the environs insisting on their not suffering Sitāram to escape across their frontiers, and also threatening that should the latter effect his escape across the frontiers of any one, not only would he be ousted from his *zamindāri* but be punished. The *zamindārs* from all sides hemmed him in, when Hasan Ali Khān arrived and captured Sitāram together with his women, children, confederates and adherents, and sent them with chains round their necks and hands to Nawāb Jafar Khān. The Nawab, enclosing Sitāram's face in cowhide, had him drawn to the gallows in the eastern suburbs of Murshidābād on the highway leading to Jahāngirnagar and Mahmudābād, and imprisoned for life Sitāram's women and children and companions. Bestowing his *zamindāri* on Rāmjiban, the Nawab confiscated to the State Sitāram's treasures and effects, and extirpating his family root and branch, he sent an account of the affair to the Emperor."

Subse-
quent
History. The execution of Sitāram Rai took place in 1712. Māhārājā Krishna Chandra of Nadiā came to the *gadi* in 1728. During his administration the district was constantly oppressed by Marhatta raids, and he was forced for a time to transfer his residence to Sibnibās in the Kissengunge thana. In 1757 Clive defeated the Mughals at Plassey, and in 1765 the East India Company obtained the *diwāni* of Bengal, Bihar and Orissa. An account of the early British administration of the district will be found in the chapter in this volume dealing with Land Revenue Administration.

First
Collector
of Nadia. In March 1787 the President of the Board of Revenue Mr. John Shore, submitted proposals to the Board for the "abolition of the present division of the country into thirty-six different establishments for the collection of the revenues, eight of which have been created since my departure from Bengal in February 1785," and for the establishment in place of them of twenty-three Collectorships. In the proposed rearrangement it was suggested to annex "the greatest part of the **Hughly**

Collectorship to the district of Kishenagur", the President added
that "to this disposition some objections may be made, but I
know not any other that is preferable." The proposals were
approved by the Board of Revenue and submitted to the
Governor-General in Council on 13th March ¹787' and accepted
in their entirety at a meeting of the Council held on the 21st of
the same month. In accordance with these orders Mr. F. Redfearn
was appointed as the first Collector of Nadiā, with Mr. G. Cherry
as his assistant. It was resolved at the same time by the Supreme
Council that a commission upon the nett collections, at a rate to
be subsequently fixed, should be paid to the Collectors, as "at
present it is well known that their allowances are in few places
equal only to their unavoidable disbursements, and, in general,
inferior to them."

In the year 1808 the crime of gang-robbery or dacoity was
very prevalent in the district. Mr. Lumsden, in a minute recorded
on 13th June of that year, stated " that the existing system of
police has entirely failed in its object, and that the detestable
crimes of gang-robbery and murder are now equally prevalent in
every part of Bengal (the Division of Dacca, perhaps, excepted)
as at any former period, are truths of too much notoriety to admit
of dispute. The details of the enormities which are still committed with impunity in the immediate neighbourhood of the capital
of British India, as described in the report, are not too highly
coloured." In the course of a report upon the police submitted
by Mr. Secretary Dowdeswell in 1809, abstracts are given of three
Nadiā cases which had recently come before the Calcutta Court
of Circuit. A short account of one of these cases may be given, as
it is concerned with the last exploit of a famous outlaw, by name
Bishwanāth Sardār, who had for years terrorized the district.
Bishwanāth and eight companions were charged with being concerned with others in a robbery which was committed at the residence and factory of Mr. Faddy, an indigo planter in the district.
on which occasion Mr. Faddy's servant was murdered, and Mr.
Faddy himself, and a Mr. Lediard, who was staying with him,
were wounded, and property to a considerable amount carried off.
Three of the prisoners under trial were convicted criminals, who
had been sent to the Dinājpur Jail, but had succeeded in making
their escape and returning to the scene of their former depredations, where they had formed a numerous and powerful gang,
which committed the most daring robberies and cruelties, and
reduced the whole country side to a state of terror. Mr. Faddy
had been most active in communicating to the Magistrate such
information as he could procure for the detection and arrest of

Lawless-
ness in
beginning
of
eighteenth
century.

the leaders of the gang, and had succeeded through his head *paik* in compassing the capture of one of the principals. The gang then determined to wreak their vengeance upon him, and, between 3 and 4. A.M. on 27th September 1808, they attacked Mr. Faddy's house. He and Mr. Lediard were awakened by the report of a gun, and, on rising, found the house surrounded by dacoits, who, in spite of all resistance (in the course of which one of the gang was shot dead), forced their way into the bungalow from all sides, and four of them seized Mr. Faddy after a considerable struggle in which he was nearly strangled. Mr. Lediard's gun having repeatedly missed fire, he received a severe spear wound in his breast, and was disabled from further resistance. Bishwanath then called upon Mr. Faddy to deliver up his head *paik*, who appeared to be the immediate object of the vengeance of the gang, and to point out where his own money was. The dacoits repeatedly dragged Messrs. Faddy and Lediard to a short distance from the house, treating them with great insult and indignity, some proposing to put them to death, and others to cut off their ears and nose. At the approach of day the dacoits retired, carrying off with them all the arms in the house, about Rs. 700 in cash and other property to a considerable amount. On their way they set fire to the house of the head *paik* and murdered two of his relatives. The Court found them all guilty, and sentenced them to death.

In speaking of the atrocities committed by this and other gangs, Mr. Dowdeswell observed : "But robbery, rape and even murder itself are not the worst figures in this hideous and disgusting picture. An expedient of common occurrence with the dacoits merely to induce a confession of property supposed to be concealed is to burn the proprietor with straw or torches, until he discloses the property, or perishes in the flames, and when they are actuated by a spirit of revenge against individuals, worse cruelties (if worse can be) are perpetrated by those remorseless criminals. If the information obtained is not extremely erroneous, the offender hereafter noticed, who was apprehended through the agency of Mr. Blaquiere's *goyendas* at Patna, himself committed fifteen murders in nineteen days, and volumes might be filled with the recital of the atrocities of the dacoits, every line of which would make the blood run cold with horror."

Mr. Blaquiere, the Magistrate of Nadiā, dealt very vigorously with this state of affairs, and in the course of a year succeeded in almost freeing the district of these criminals. But those who had escaped arrest merely went over the borders and recommenced their depredations in the neighbouring districts. Mr. Blaquiere was then given jurisdiction over Jessore, Hooghly and Bakarganj, in addition to his own district, and he extended his system to those districts also with great success. In a letter of commendation which he received from Government it was said that "the Honourable the Vice-President in Council considers it only an act of justice to record on the public proceedings and to communicate to you, the high sense which he entertains of your services in the suppression of the heinous crime of gang robbery, and in the amelioration of the general state of police in those districts in which you were appointed to officiate as Magistrate, especially in the district of Nuddea, where that crime was most prevalent, and attended with the most fatal consequences." In token of the appreciation of Government Mr. Blaquiere was granted a bonus of Rs. 6,000, and an extra permanent allowance of Rs. 500 per mensem.

Up till the end of 1808 the police in each district had been a purely local force, with no departmental head with power to co-ordinate their efforts in the suppression of crime, but the success which attended the experiment of placing Mr. Blaquiere in charge of the police of four districts, led to the appointment of a Superintendent of Police (subsequently the Inspector-General), with powers over the whole police force throughout the Province.

One of the chief weapons used by Mr. Blaquiere was the employment of *goyendas* or spies. This practice led to a good deal of controversy at the time, and was strongly denounced by one or two of the Magistrates, and some of the judicial authorities, especially by the Judge of the Court of Circuit of the Murshidābād Division. It was, however, approved by the Government, and also accepted by the Nizāmat Adālat, from whose register the following extract, dealing with the manner in which *goyendas* should be employed, is taken :—" The established duty of *goyendas* is to discover the haunts of the dacoits, to watch their movements, to mix with them occasionally, with the view of obtaining accurate intelligence respecting their operations and designs for their employer, to communicate to him the result of their observations and enquiries, and, finally, to point out to *goyendas*, who are usually regular police officers, the persons of the individuals whom the Magistrate, in the discharge of his public functions, may order to be apprehended."

The Mutiny affected the district very slightly. In the article on Kapāsdānga in Chapter XVI of this volume an extract has been given from a letter written in 1857 by the Manager of one of the largest indigo concerns in the district. There was a certain amount of trouble in the sister district of Jessore, but practically

THE MUTINY.

none in Nadiā. In his minute on the Mutiny dated September 30th, 1858, the Lieutenant-Governor, Sir. F. J. Halliday, wrote: "In the Nadiā Division, Berhampore, garrisoned by native troops, both cavalry and infantry, was rescued from threatened danger, first by the rapid despatch of European troops by land and by steamer, and secondly by the prompt and well conceived measures for disarming the native garrison. An uneasy feeling meanwhile extended itself through Krishnagar, Jessore and the whole Division. * * * * The districts generally have been perfectly tranquil, and furnish little matter to remark upon."

INDIGO.　　During the first half of the nineteenth century the manufacture of indigo was the most important industry in the district. It sprang originally from very small native factories which were bought up by Europeans. The district became gradually dotted with indigo concerns, owned by English capitalists, or by proprietors backed by money advanced by agents in Calcutta. A great impetus was thus given to the cultivation and manufacture of indigo. Large factories rapidly sprang up, taking the place of the smaller native ones. Money was plentiful with the planters, and the ryots eagerly took advances to grow indigo. The cultivation increased, and the high rates which the dye then commanded yielded large profits. One of the greatest difficulties which presented itself in the earlier days of indigo cultivation was the contention which arose between neighbouring planters as to the right to sow in the different villages. This difficulty, however, gradually righted itself, and boundaries were laid down between the different indigo factories, beyond which neither party could extend except under a penalty. At first the ryots were not averse to the cultivation, and as the country was then lower than during later years, and more liable to fertilizing inundations from the rivers, the plant grew more luxuriantly, and the crop was less liable to failure from drought. The European planter soon gained for himself an important position in the district, although at first he held but little property. The large native landlords, and holders of sub-tenures, finding that their influence was interfered with by the planters, endeavoured to stir up a feeling against them, and to prevent the spread of indigo cultivation. This led to quarrels, and the planter, failing to get redress from or through the courts, had recourse to fighting the native landholder with bands of clubmen, according to the practice in Bengal at that time. The planter began also to buy real property (when it became legal for Europeans to hold land), even at fancy prices, in order to get rid of the annoyance and injury to which he was subjected by hostile native proprietors.

This, however, was but the commencement of still greater troubles for the European planter. He had got over his early disputes with neighbouring planters, and had surmounted the difficulty of inimical *zamindārs* by himself becoming a proprietor, or at any rate by buying a sub-tenure upon the lands which surrounded his factory. But the greatest difficulty still remained. This was the native agency which he had to employ in carrying on the cultivation. The district was now dotted with large concerns, whose managers and sub-managers could give but slight personal supervision to their work, and had to leave it to native servants. A great deal too much was thus committed to underlings who fleeced the cultivators, and as the planter often declined to hear complaints from the latter and redress their wrongs, a very bitter feeling was engendered against the factories. This was intensified by illegal practices committed in the badly managed factories to enforce the cultivation of the plant, and also by a very marked rise in the price of other agricultural produce, which brought home to the ryots the loss which they sustained by the cultivation of indigo. Moreover, the commencement of the Eastern Bengal State Railway through Nadiā at about that time led to a sudden rise in the price of labour, with which the planters failed to keep pace. Also the ryots were in a chronic state of indebtedness to the factories for advances, which went on in the books from father to son, and were the source of a hereditary irritation against the planters, whenever a bad season forced them to put pressure upon the ryots to pay up. The dislike to indigo, thus generated, grew apace, and on a rumour being started that the Bengal Government had declared itself against indigo-planting, the whole district got into a ferment, which culminated in the disturbances of 1860. At first all the planters suffered equally, the good with the bad, and for some time the district lay at the mercy of the cultivators, and those of them who had acted on their own judgment, and sown their lands with indigo in the terms of the contract which they had entered into with the factory, were seized and beaten by the mob. The Bengal Government endeavoured to arrest the devastation, and eventually passed Act XI of 1860 "to enforce the fulfilment of indigo contracts, and to provide for the appointment of a Commission of enquiry."

This Commission sat during the hot weather of 1860, and its report was submitted in August of the same year. The report gave an account of the various systems of indigo cultivation in Bengal and Bihar, and divided the subjects of the enquiry into three heads:—(1) the truth or falsehood of the charges made

D

against the system and the planters; (2) the changes required
to be made in the system, as between manufacturer and cultivator, such as could be made by the heads of the concerns themselves; and (3) the changes required in the laws or administration, such as could only originate with, and be carried
out by, the legislative and executive authorities.

The general conclusion at which the Commission arrived was
that the cause of the evils in the system of indigo cultivation as
then practised was to be found in the fact that the manufacturer
required the ryot to furnish the plant for a payment not nearly
equal to the cost of its production, and that it was to the system,
which was of very long standing, rather than to the planters
themselves, that blame attached. The only remedy recommended
by the Commission which it was in the power of Government to
apply was a good and effective administration of the law as it
stood. Accordingly new subdivisions were created, and various
other steps taken to improve the efficiency of the Civil Courts.

The moral effect of the temporary Act of 1860, and the public
assurance given to the complaining ryots that proved grievances
should be remedied for future seasons, was such that most of the
planters were able to complete their spring sowings, but, as
autumn came on, the state of affairs became very critical. Lord
Canning wrote: "I assure you that for about a week it caused
me more anxiety than I have had since the days of Delhi," and
"from that day I felt that a shot fired in anger or fear by one
foolish planter might put every factory in Lower Bengal in
flames." The intensity of feeling aroused among the ryots may
be gauged from a note recorded by the Lieutenant-Governor in
September 1860. Sir J. P. Grant wrote: "I have myself just
returned from an excursion to Sirájganj on the Jamuná river,
where I went by water for objects connected with the line of the
Dacca Railway, and wholly unconnected with indigo matters. I
had intended to go up the Mátábhángá and down the Ganges; but
finding, on arriving at the Kumár, that the shorter passage was
open, I proceeded along the Kumár and Káliganga, which rivers
run in Nadiá and Jessore, and through that part of the Pabná district which lies south of the Ganges [i.e., the north-eastern corner of
the Nadiá district, as now (1909) constituted]. Numerous crowds
of ryots appeared at various places, whose whole prayer was
for an order of Government that they should not cultivate indigo.
On my return a few days afterwards along the same two
rivers, from dawn to dusk, as I steamed along these two rivers
for some 60 or 70 miles, both banks were literally lined with
crowds of villagers, claiming justice in this matter. Even the

women of the villages on the banks were collected in groups by themselves; the males who stood at and between the riverside villages in little crowds must have collected from all the villages at a great distance on either side. I do not know that it ever fell to the lot of an Indian officer to steam for 14 hours through a continued double line of suppliants for justice; all were most respectful and orderly, but also were plainly in earnest. It would be folly to suppose that such a display on the part of tens of thousands of people, men, women and children, has no deep meaning. The organization and capacity for combined and simultaneous action in the cause, which this remarkable demon- stration over so large an extent of country proved, are subjects worthy of much consideration."

Towards the end of September the Government of India authorized the issue of a notification in the affected districts to disabuse the minds of the rural population of the erroneous impression said to have been conceived by them, that Government was opposed to the cultivation of indigo; to convey an assurance to the ryots that their position in regard to past arrangements would not be made worse than it was, and that, in future arrangements, their right to free action in regard to indigo, as in regard to all other crops, would be respected in practice; to warn all parties concerned against having recourse to violent or unlawful proceedings; and to announce the intention of Govern- ment not to re-enact the temporary law of 1860.

Reports that the ryots would oppose the October sowings led the Government to strengthen the military police in the indigo districts, and to send two gun-boats to the rivers of Nadiā and Jessore, and Native Infantry to the head-quarters stations of these two districts. Subsequently in the spring of 1861, the planters complained of the difficulty of realizing their rents, of being forcibly dispossessed of their *nijābād* lands, and of danger to their own lives and those of their servants. The difficulty as to rents being undeniable, extra officials were appointed where required, and Messrs. C. F. Montresor and G. G. Morris of the Indian Civil Service were appointed special Commissioners, the former for the Nadiā district, and the latter for Jessore, Pabnā and Faridpur to settle the rent difficulty. Further steps were taken to prevent disturbances during the ensuing sowing season. For a long time there was a complete overthrow of the industry in Nadiā and the adjoining districts, but by degrees, as the excitement cooled down, those factories which had been most carefully managed before the disturbances, recovered themselves, and eventually most of the concerns which were well backed by capital succeeded in weathering the storm, and were carried on until the invention of synthetic indigo reduced the price of the natural dye to so great an extent as practically to destroy the industry. Throughout the whole district there is only one concern in which the manufacture of indigo is now (1909) carried on, and the outturn of the dye during 1908-09 was only nominal.

Krish- nagar as Divisional Head- quarters.
Up till 1854 Nadiā was in the Jessore Division, but, when the office of Superintendent of Police for the Lower Provinces was abolished in that year, a rearrangement of the Commissioners' Divisions was made, under which the Nadiā Division was consti- tuted, with head-quarters at Krishnagar. For various reasons the Commissioner did not take up his residence at Krishnagar for more than a year. In February 1855 he applied for permission to remain at Alipore, but after correspondence with the Board of Revenue, the Lieutenant-Governor decided that the head-quarters of the Division must be at Krishnagar. In 1860, however, the Murshidābād district having in the meantime been included in the Rājshāhi Division, the head-quarters of the Nadia Division were retransferred to Alipore.

Nadia as a Li- terary Centre.
The district of Nadiā was, for centuries, famous as a centre of literature and learning. In the article upon Nabadwip in the Gazetteer chapter in this volume will be found a short account of the best known among the men of learning who have brought fame to the district. Below will be found some remarks, based chiefly upon Mr. R. C. Dutt's "Literature of Bengal," on the connection of Nadiā with the literature of the Province.

The earliest of all the Bengali poets was Jayadeb, who was one of the ornaments of the court of King Lakhsman Sen at Nabadwip, in the twelfth century. Many tales are told about him, but very little is definitely known of his life. He is chiefly famous as the composer of the Sanscrit poem *Gita Govinda*, which consists of a number of songs on the amours of Krishna and Rādhā. Mr. R. C. Dutt in his work referred to above speaks of "the exquisite music of the songs" and adds "and if the book is rich in its music, it is no less rich in its descriptions. The blue waves of the Jumna, the cool shade of the Tamal tree, the soft whispering of the Malaya breeze, the voluptuous music of Krishna's flute, the timid glances of the love-stricken milkmaids, the fond working of a lover's heart, the pangs of jealousy, the sorrows of separa- tion, the raptures of reunion—all these are clearly and vividly described in the song of the immortal bard of Birbhum."

The first Bengali poet to write in his own vernacular was Chandidās, who was born in the Birbhum district in the fourteenth century. In the fifteenth century came Krittibās, who was born

at Fulia near Sāntipur. His great work was a translation, or to
be more accurate, a rescript, in Bengali, of the great Sanscrit epic
Rāmāyana. Mr. Dutt writes, " It will thus appear that Krittibās'
is not a translation of the Sanscrit work. A class of reciters
called *Kathakas* have flourished in this country from olden times;
they recite legends before large audiences, they amuse and entertain
their hearers by their wit, or move them to tears by their
eloquence; and they thus teach the unlettered public in the
traditions of the past, and preserve from age to age the literary
heritage of the nation. The Rāmāyana is a fit subject for
Kathakas; and the recitation lasts for a month or more, the
speaker taking up the story every day from the point where he
left it on the preceding day. It is supposed with reason that
Krittibās learnt the story of the Rāmāyana from *Kathakas,* and
that, without attempting to translate the Sanscrit epic, he has
given his version of the story as he heard it. The poet has
himself told us in several places in his work that he has composed
it as he heard it recited." Mr. Dutt then proceeds to give an
interesting comparison between Krittibās' Rāmāyana and the
Māhābhārata of Kāsirām Dās, who also flourished in the fifteenth
century, and who was born at Katwa, on the opposite bank of the
Bhāgirathi to Nadiā. " But if Krittibās fails us as a translator,
as a poet and composer he rises in our estimation. His narration
is fluent and easy and often sparkles with the richest humour.
Kāsirām Dās is a pious and learned student, who has endeavoured
to give his countrymen a condensed translation of the Sanscrit
Māhābhārata; Krittibās is a sprightly story-teller who tells the
story of the Rāmāyana with his own native wit. Kāsirām Dās
is anxious to teach his countrymen in the sacred traditions, the
undying legends, and the didactic narrations which compose the
bulk of the Māhābhārata. Krittibās delights in depicting in vivid
colours the deeds of Hanumān, the fierce rage of the Rākshasas,
the marvellous prowess of the god-like Rāma. Kāsirām Dās
approaches his subject with reverence and writes in a chaste and
dignified though simple style; Krittibās delights in the somewhat
primitive battles between monkeys and giants, colours his description with his wit, and writes in the style of ordinary villagers.
Kāsirām Dās' work is the favourite study of pious Hindu ladies,
and of religious and elderly men of the upper classes; Krittibās
appeals more effectively to the million. The village *Mudi* (con-
fectioner) reads his Rāmāyana when waiting for his customers, and
the village *Kalu* (oil-manufacturer) chants the story of Rāma and
Sita as his bullock turns his primitive oil-mill with a slow creaking
sound. To the upper ten thousand Kāsirām Dās' work is the

repository of all the sacred traditions and moral lessons of the
Hindus; to the class of vendors, shopkeepers and the like, as well
as to the upper classes, Krittibâs' work is a joy which endureth for
work (? ever). For the millions of Bengal, the two works have
been a means of moral education, the value of which cannot be
over-estimated."

None of the writers of the sixteenth and seventeenth centuries
are particularly connected with the Nadiâ district, but in the
eighteenth century, when the famous Krishna Chandra Rai was
the Mâhârâjâ of Nadiâ, literature flourished at his court. The two
chief poets of this period were Râm Prasâd Sen and Bhârat
Chandra Rai. Râm Prasad Sen, who was a Baidya by caste, was
born in Kumârhatta in the Kushtiâ Subdivision. He commenced
life in a merchant's office in Calcutta, but having shown distinct
literary ability his employer allowed him to return to his native
village on a small allowance; here he devoted himself entirely to
writing poetry, and his fame spread until it reached the ears of
Mâhârâjâ Krishna Chandra, who sent for him to his court and
favoured him with his patronage. He excelled principally in short
poems. Mr. Dutt says of him, "One great charm of his poetry
consists in the simple homely similes, always drawn from familiar
objects of lowly village life. The cultivated rice-field, the ferry-
boat, the village market, the oil mill, such are the objects of his
similes, round which he entwines his feeling songs with the most
touching effect." Bhârat Chandra Rai was a man of good family
in the Bardwân district. Owing to various misfortunes he was
compelled to leave his home, and after many vicissitudes he came
to the notice of Mâhârâjâ Krishna Chandra, who took him to his
residence at Krishnagar, and appointed him as a pundit of the
court. Mr. Dutt has no great opinion of his abilities; he
describes him as a somewhat unsuccessful imitator of Mukunda
Râm, who flourished in the seventeenth century; at the same
time he says that he was a complete master of the art of versifica-
tion, "and his appropriate phrases and rich descriptions have
passed into bye-words. It would be difficult to over-estimate the
polish he has given to the Bengali language." After the death of
Mâhârâjâ Krishna Chandra, the connection of later writers with
the district became very slender, and descriptions of them and
their works would be outside the scope of this volume.

CHAPTER III.

THE PEOPLE.

WHEN the first census was taken in 1872, the population of VARIA- the district as now constituted was 1,500,397. During the TIONS IN POPULA- succeeding nine years, there was an increase of 10·8 per cent., TION. the figures for the 1881 census showing a population of 1,662,795. There has been very little variation since then, a slight decrease of 1·1 per cent. found at the census of 1891, having been rather more than made up by the increase of 1·4 per cent., which the census of 1901 showed. At this last census the population was returned at 1,667,491. At the censuses of 1872 and 1881, the district included the Subdivision of Bangāon, which was transferred to the Jessore district between 1881 and 1891, but the effect of this change upon the population of the district has been taken into account, and the figures have been adjusted accordingly. The net variation in the period from 1872 till 1901 was an increase in the population of 167,094 persons, which is equivalent to 11·1 per cent. This was considerably less than the percentage of increase in all other districts in the Presidency Division, with the exception of Murshidābād, which showed an increase of 9·8 per cent.

In the Bengal Census Report for the census of 1901 it is CENSUS OF 1901. remarked that, what with the terrible outbreak of epidemic fever between 1880 and 1885, and two destructive floods in 1885 and 1890, it was small wonder that at the census of 1891 a decrease of rather more than one per cent. should have been recorded. The report continues :—

.. "The decade which has just passed has witnessed no such widespread calamities as that which preceded it, but the conditions have not been favourable to the growth of the population· Fever has been very prevalent in the south of the district› especially in the Krishnagar town and in the old jungle-smothered villages of the Rānāghāt Subdivision. In the extreme north-east of the district also, obstructed drainage 1sfavoured the spread of a virulent form of malarial fever which has caused a very heavy mortality. Cholera also was very prevalent, especially in 1891, 1892 and 1896. The only two healthy years of the decade were 1897 and 1898. The seasons were, on the whole, unfavourable to the crops, especially those of 1895 and 1896, in which years the early rice crop was a little more than a half and a third, respectively, of the normal outturn. The winter rice suffered even more, yielding less than half of an average crop in 1895 and barely a seventh in 1896. Distress was severe throughout the district and deepened into famine in the tracts where late rice is the staple crop. The relief afforded by Government was eminently successful in preventing loss of life, and the deaths reported in the years 1896, 1897 and 1898 were less numerous by nearly 50 per cent. than those of the preceding triennium. The statistics were tested, but the results showed that the reporting was quite as accurate as usual, and the fact that during the same period the reported births exceeded by 7 per cent. those of the previous three years points to the same conclusion.

"The net result of the present census is an increase of 23,383 persons, or 1·4 per cent. The Rānāghāt Subdivision in the south of the district shows a loss of 5·6 per cent., or 1 per cent. more than that recorded ten years ago. The Krishnagar thana, in the head-quarters subdivision which joins this tract, has also lost ground, though not quite to the same extent as in the previous decade. The whole of this tract is, as has been already noted, malarious and unhealthy, and its continuous decline must be ascribed mainly to this cause. The decadent condition of the weaving industry of Sāntipur may also have contributed to the falling off in that direction. Calcutta and the mills in the neighbourhood attract immigrants from this neighbourhood, but the total number of Nadiā-born settlers in Calcutta and the 24-Parganas was less in 1901 than it had been ten years previously. The district has lost by migration during the decade to the extent probably of about 1 per cent.

"The two eastern thanas of the head-quarters subdivision, Hānskhāli and Kissengunge, show the greatest increase of any in the district. These thanas lie in the hollow across which the floods of the Bhāgirathi sweep whenever the great Lālitakuri embankment in the Murshidābād district gives way, and they suffered severely in the floods of 1885 and 1890. The population of Kissengunge was stationary in 1891, while that of Hānskhāli showed a great decrease. In the two thanas together the present figures represent a very slight improvement on the population recorded twenty years ago. The only other part of the district that shows a satisfactory rate of progress is the line of thanas stretching through the centre of the district from Kāliganj to Kushtiā, which corresponds very closely to the area in which famine relief operations were found necessary. This area, taken as a whole, is probably at the present time the healthiest part of the district. The decrease in Kumārkhāli, in the north-east, is due to malaria which, as will be seen further on, has caused an even greater loss of population in the adjoining parts of Jessore and Faridpur. The falling off in Karimpur to the north-west is less easy to explain."[*]

The following table shows the salient statistics of the census of 1901:—

Subdivision.	Area in square miles.	Number of		Population.	Population per square mile.	Percentage of variation in population between 1891 and 1901.
		Towns.	Villages.			
Krishnagar	701	2	740	361,333	515	+3 53
Rānāghāt	427	4	568	217,077	508	−5·63
Kushtiā	596	2	1,011	486,368	816	+0·71
Meherpur	632	1	607	348,124	551	+3·39
Chuādāngā	437	...	485	254,589	583	+3·74
District Total ...	2,793	9	3,411	1,667,491	597	+1·42

The Kushtiā Subdivision is by far the most populous portion of the district. Kumārkhāli is the most densely populated thana within the subdivision, notwithstanding that it lost 4·65 per cent. of its population during the ten years ending with 1901. It now supports 947 persons to the square mile, and this though it only contains one small town with a population of 5,330 only. The density of the population decreases towards the west, being 923 in Kushtiā, 813 in Naopārā and 588 only in Daulatpur, which is on the extreme west and borders upon the northern part of the Meherpur Subdivision. The subdivision which shows the least density is Rānēghāt, notwithstanding that it contains a larger

Density of Population.

_____

[*] The Drainage Committee of 1907 came to the conclusion that the falling off in Karimpur was due to malarious fever.

urban population than any other subdivision. Ránághát lost
4·6 per cent. of its population between 1881 and 1891, and 5·63
during the following ten years, and its density in 1901 was only
508 persons to the square mile. The falling off was most marked
in Sántipur and Chákdaha thanas. The low density is primarily
due to the continued unhealthiness of the tract, which in its turn
is caused mainly by lack of drainage to carry off surplus water.
In the Krishnagar Subdivision the density varies from 661
persons to the square mile in the Kissengunge thana, to 411 in
Hánskháli; in Meherpur, from 631 in the Gángni thana to 521 in
the Tebata thana ; and in Chuádángá, from 691 in the Alamdángá
thana to 477 in the Jibannagar thana. During the decade
ending with 1901 the greatest loss in density occurred in the
Sántipur thana, and the greatest gain in the Kissengunge thana.

Towns and Villages.
The district has nine towns, viz , Krishnagar, Sántipur, Ránághát, Chákdaha, Birnagar, Nabadwip, Meherpur, Kushtiá and
Kumárkháli. The average population of these towns is 10,595,
and their inhabitants represent 5 per cent. of the total population
of the district. This percentage is far greater than the corresponding percentage in the sister districts of Jessore and Khulná.
Fifty-four per cent. of the urban population is contained in towns
inhabited by 20,000 persons or over. The rural population is
contained in 3,411 villages, each of which, on an average,
has 461 inhabitants. The average population of the villages is
higher than that in any other district in the Presidency Division.

The following remarks on the towns of the district are taken
from Mr. Gait's report on the Census of Bengal, 1901 : --
"Nadiá has nine towns, but only one, Ránághát, can boast of an
increase. The apparent loss of population in Kushtiá and Kumárkháli is due to the exclusion of a considerable area from municipal
limits; Kushtiá at least, on its present area, has gained rather
than lost ground. Santipur was once the centre of a flourishing
weaving industry, and its muslins had a European reputation ;
but the modern machine-made article has driven them out of the
market; the weavers are no longer prosperous, and in many cases
they have been driven to supplement the earnings from their
looms by agricultural pursuits. There was also at one time a
considerable trade in date-sugar, but this too is becoming less
profitable. The earthquake of 1897 destroyed many of the largest
buildings, and these the impoverished owners have been unable to
replace. The result of these adverse conditions is a decline of 11½
per cent. Krishnagar, the district head-quarters, is also decadent,
chiefly on account of malarial fever which is very prevalent in
the older part of the town. The decline in Nabadwip is, to

a great extent, fictitious. It is celebrated amongst Vaishnavas as the birth-place of Chaitanya, and is a favourite place of pilgrimage. There happened to be very few pilgrims on the date of the present census, whereas in 1891 and 1881 a great number were present, especially in the former year, when the *Dhulut* ceremony was in progress at the time when the census was taken."

The total number of residents of other districts who were Immigra-found in Nadiā at the census of 1901 was 59,010, representing tion. 3·5 per cent. of the total population. The great majority of these, viz., 44,233, came from contiguous districts. In 1891 72,945 immigrants were found in the district. The excess over the number found in 1901 is probably due to the fact that the *Dhulut* ceremony was in progress in Nabadwip when the census was being taken in 1891, and was attended by 15,000 persons from neighbouring districts.

The total number of residents in Nadiā who were enumerated Emigra-in other districts at the census of 1901, was 123,737, which tion. represents 7·4 per cent. of the total population of the district. This is a far larger percentage of emigration than is shown by any other district in the Presidency Division. Mr. Gait remarks, "Nadiā loses population to all the districts that adjoin it, even to unhealthy Jessore." One reason which may account to some extent for the large excess of emigration over immigration is the fact that the demand for labour in Nadiā is slack during the cold weather when the census is taken; the main crop of the district is the *aus* or early rice crop, and when the reaping of that is finished, it is probable that a large number of agricultural labourers betake themselves to other districts where there is a demand for labour to cut the winter rice; many of these would no doubt remain away until the time for reaping the *rabi* crop, and later for preparing the land for the *bhadoi* crop, afforded them the prospect of regular employment in their native district. It is also not improbable that the continued unhealthiness of the district has a tendency to drive away to more congenial districts those who are not too much tied down to their own villages.

The language commonly used is the dialect of Bengali called Lan-"Central Bengali." It is the same dialect which is employed guage. in the districts of 24-Parganas, Murshidābād, Midnapore, Hooghly and Howrah, and, as spoken by the higher classes, is claimed to be the most pure form of Bengali. Ninety-nine per cent. of the people of the district use this language, and of the remainder, about three-quarters use Hindi, and the rest other languages. The number of persons speaking Hindi rose from 9,098 in 1881 to 12,319 in 1901.

RELI-
GIONS.

The population of the district is almost entirely made up of Hindus and Muhammadans; the former number 676,391, cr 40·56 per cent. of the total population, and the latter 982,987, or 58·95 per cent.; there are 8,091 Christians; but no other religion has even 20 adherents in the district. In 1872 Hindus formed 45·3 per cent. of the total population, and the Muhammadans 54·3; in 1881 the corresponding figures were 42·85 and 56·82; in 1891 they were 41·9 and 57·0. It will thus be seen that the proportion of Hindus to Muhammadans in the district has been steadily declining during the last 40 years. A similar and nearly equal decline has taken place in the Jessore district, while in Khulnā the reverse tendency is to be observed, though not to a marked degree. It is a curious circumstance that in these three adjoining districts the Muhammadans are overtaking the Hindus in the two most unhealthy districts, while in the comparatively healthy district of Khulnā, the Hindus are very slowly over-taking the Muhammadans. In the province, as a whole, Muhammadans are increasing more rapidly than Hindus, and at the 1901 census Mr. Gait made an enquiry as to why this should be so, and he came to the conclusion that in the province as a whole the main explanation of the relatively more rapid growth of the Muhammadan population must be its greater fecundity, one reason for which is that the Muhammadan widow remarries more readily than her Hindu sister, and another that the Muhammadan has a more nutritious dietary than the Hindu.

Hindus.

The most remarkable fact in connection with Hindus disclosed at the census of 1901 was that the decline in their numbers was almost entirely among females; the total loss was 12,833, and of these only 162 were males. This disparity is not to be observed in the sister districts of the Presidency Division. Hindus out-number Muhammadans in the Krishnagar and Rānāghāt Sub-divisions, but by only about 4 per cent. in the former and 16 per cent. in the latter; in the other three subdivisions Muhammadans largely predominate, Hindus forming considerably less than a third of the population in the Kushtiā Subdivision and only slightly over a third in the Meherpur Subdivision. One reason for the preponderance of the Hindus in the two southern sub-divisions is that in them are situated the large municipal towns, and it is a curious circumstance that although Muhammadans form the majority of the whole population, they are in a very considerable minority in the towns, where they form only 26·3 per cent. of the population. A further reason is that these two subdivisions lie along the most sacred part of the Bhāgirathi, and are therefore specially attractive to Hindus. A third reason may be that Krishnagar has for many years been the head-quarters of the Hindu Nadiā Rāj.

The Kaibarttas are the most numerously represented caste in the district; they were returned at nearly 111,000 at the 1901 census. There are seven other castes with more than 25,000 representatives each, namely, in numerical order, Ahirs or Goālās, Brāhmans, Bāgdis, Muchis, Namasudras (Chandāls), Kāyasthas and Mālos. Nadiā is, in this respect, differentiated from the sister districts of Jessore and Khulnā chiefly by the relative importance of the Kaibarttas and the unimportance of the Namasudras and Pods. *HINDU CASTES.*

The Kaibarttas are mainly agriculturists and occasionally fishermen. They have representatives in every thana in the district, but are most numerous in Tehata, Daulatpur and Dāmurhudā. In the Tehata thana they form about 20 per cent. of the population. They are nearly all classed as *Chāsi Kaibarttas.* At the time of the census they urged that they should be treated as entirely different from the *Jaliya Kaibarttas,* and many of them entered their caste as Mahishya, an ancient caste of much respectability which is said to be descended from a Kshatriya father and Vaisya mother. They were permitted to enter themselves as Mahishyas, as this is a name which is assumed by no modern caste, and it was not likely to lead to confusion; but in the course of tabulation all the so-called Mahishyas were classed as *Chāsi Kaibarttas.* There seems to be no room for doubt that the two sections of Kaibarttas are of common origin, and in remote tracts inter-marriage is still permitted between them; at the same time the process of differentiation has proceeded so far in the more advanced portions of the Province, that they constitute practically separate communities. *Kaibarttas.*

The census of 1901 showed 71,380 Ahirs and Goālās in the district. In Bihar the two terms are interchangeable; in Bengal the term Ahir is used only by persons of the Bihar caste, but doubtless many of these also showed themselves as Goālās; it was not therefore found practicable to differentiate them in the course of tabulation. *Ahir and Goālā.*

This community numbered 47,002 at the 1901 census. They are divided into two classes, Rārhi and Bārendra, so called according to the names of the different divisions of the country assigned to the Brāhmans by Ballāl Sen, King of Bengal, in the twelfth century. The Rārhi Brāhmans originally came from the districts west of the Bhāgirathi, and the Bārendra Brāhmans from the country north of the Padmā. The Brāhmans form, by themselves, the first group in caste precedence in Bengal proper. *Brāhmans.*

Bāgdis. The number of Bāgdis in the district is steadily increasing ; in 1872, with the Bāngaon Subdivision included, there were 35,576, whereas in 1901 there were 46,435. They are fishermen, cultivators, palanquin-bearers, etc., and, in caste precedence, they rank very low, being in the last group but one. Mr. Gait remarks of them, "This caste gave its name to, or received it from, the old division of Ballāl Seu's kingdom known as Bāgri, or South Bengal Mr. Oldham is of opinion that they are the section of the Mal who accepted life and civilization in the cultivated country as serfs and co-religionists of the Aryans." The distribution of the Bāgdis is very local, their habitat being practically confined to the Bardwān Division and two of the adjoining districts of the Presidency Division.

Muchis. Muchis numbered 40,113 at the 1901 census. This caste is on the decline in the district.

Namasu-dras.
Chandāls. The Namasudras were returned at 37,695 at the census of 1901.. The main habitat of this caste is in the more eastern districts, and Nadiā is the most westerly district in which they form an important item in the sum total of the population. It is only within comparatively recent years that they have assumed the name of Namasudra ; formerly they were known as Chandāls. The following story as to the origin of the Pods and Chandals is current in Khulnā :—A beautiful girl succumbed to the blandishments of a low caste lover and gave birth to a son. The intrigue and its result were kept secret, and in due course the girl was married to a man of her own rank in life. She had several other sons, who were brought up in comfort, while her first-born shifted for himself as best he could. When the legitimate children grew up they learnt the story of their mother's frailty, and persecuted their half-brother in all possible ways. Once when he was away from home they pulled up his paddy seedlings and planted them upside down. This was more than the bastard could bear, and he was about to commit suicide when the goddess Lakhsmi appeared and caused the plants to bear a crop of golden grain. The bastard is said to be the ancestor of the Pods, while the legitimate sons were the forebears of the Chandāls.

The Namasudras show considerable aptitude for organization, and it was at much pains that they succeeded in getting their present designation recognized, in place of the term Chandāl, to which they objected. They appear to have a genuine desire to raise themselves as a class, and in March 1908, they held a very largely attended meeting at which the following resolutions were passed :—" (1) That the Namasudra conference be made permanent by yearly meetings to be held in the different districts for the discussion of social matters and the spread of education; (2) that a village committee be formed in every Namasudra village, and unions of 15 such villages, and a district committee in every district; (3) that for acquiring funds for a Namasudra contribution fund, village communities, unions and district committees be authorised to collect subscriptions. A handful of rice should be set apart before meals in every family, and collected weekly by the village committee. Every member of village committee will pay a monthly subscription of one anna, of unions two annas, and district committees four annas. Three per cent. of the expenses incurred in *srāddha*, marriages and other occasions must be reserved for this fund; (4) that as some active measure should be adopted towards social reform, it is resolved that any Namasudra marrying his son under 20 or daughter under 10 will be excommunicated. The committees and unions must be specially careful about strict compliance with these resolutions."

There were 30,578 Kāyasthas in 1901. This caste appears to Kāyasthas. be somewhat on the decline. They are to be found all over the district, but are most numerous in the Kāliganj, Krishnagar, Nakāsipārā and Kumārkhāli thanas.

The Mālos numbered 26,049. They are of low caste and are Mālos. chiefly fishermen, boatmen and labourers.

There are only two Hindu sects which call for special remark; HINDU these are the Kartābhājās and Vaishnavas. SECTS. *Kartā- bhājās.*

The Kartābhājā sect was founded about the middle of the eight. eenth century, and took its origin at the village of Ghoshpārā, in the Chākdaha thana. The name of the founder was Rām Saran Pāl, who was by birth a Sādgop and by profession a cultivator. With him was associated a religious mendicant who was known as Fakir Thākur. A local legend relates how, while Rām Saran was tending his flock, Fakir Thākur suddenly appeared before him and asked for a cup of milk. While he was drink. ing it, a messenger came up and said that Rām Saran's wife had been taken seriously ill and was at the point of death. Fakir Thākur offered to go and cure her, and taking some mud from the nearest tank, he anointed the body of the dying woman with it and restored her instantly to full health and strength. He then said that he must himself be born of the woman whose life he had saved, and, miraculously disappearing, was in due time born as Rām Saran's son, and received the name of Rām Dulāl.

According to another account Rām Saran was born in Jagdis. pur near Chākdaha; he caused dissensions in his family owing to the fact that he gave himself up entirely to religious exercises and neglected temporal affairs; not caring to remain with his family under such circumstances, he left them and went to Ghoshpārā where he found favour with one of the leading residents, and was allowed to settle there and marry the daughter of one Gobinda Ghosh. Not long after his marriage he was visited by a strange Fakir, who informed him that he had just been beaten by some soldiers of the Nawāb of Bengal, and had had to make his escape by miraculous means; he had in his hand a small vessel, and he said that he had gathered the water of the Ganges in it, in order that he might pass over dry shod. Rām Saran comforted him, and before he took his departure persuaded him to leave behind the miraculous vessel, which is still preserved as a valuable relic in the family of Babu Gopāl Krishna Pāl. The Fakir settled in his own village in the Bangāon Subdivision of Jessore, and there established a band of Fakirs, who performed many miracles, and propagated many tenets of the new faith over all the districts of the Presidency Division.

Rām Saran Pāl is believed to have died in the year 1783, and his place as head of the sect was taken by his son Rām Dulāl, or Dulāl Chand. He appears to have been a man of marked personality and considerable power of proselytism. He impressed a number of leading men of his time with his teaching, and had added very largely to the numbers of sect by the time of his death, which took place in 1833. He was succeeded as Kartā (which was the name given to the head of the faith) by his son Iswar Chandra, but since the death of the latter, there has been no generally recognized Kartā; at present each of the four sur-viving members of the family of the founder heads a separate church, which is attended by his special adherents and admirers. Under these circumstances the popularity of the sect is naturally declining.

The census of 1901 furnishes no reliable indication as the number of the sect. The great majority entered their religion as Hindu or Muhammadan, as the case might be, and in compiling the returns it was not found possible to differentiate the sect.

The following account of the tenets of the sect is taken from a note furnished by Babu Gopāl Krishna Pāl: "The Kartabhaja sect, or as the members themselves call it, the "Satya Dharma," or the "Sabaj Dharma" (the true religion, or the easy religion) is, if I may be permitted to say so, a man-worshipping sect, and its object is to call forth and develop the latent divinity in man. This it seeks to accomplish, not by renouncing the world and its cares as something transitory and illusive, but by going through life's struggles manfully and heroically, sustained throughout with love for mankind and reverence for nature. Far from being atheists, as some writers have described us to be, we believe in the existence of a personal God, whom we can love and adore, but the *Mukti*, or salvation, we seek to attain is not one of annihilation, or of absorption, but one in which we shall live in subordinate co-operation with the supreme Godhead.

" We have no outward characteristic that would mark us out, no marks on the forehead or elsewhere, no special garb, no particular ornament or instrument. Neither have we any secret signs, nor any secret rites and ceremonies. Ours is not a guru-worshipping sect, as some have taken it to be. In fact as a safeguard against any possible misconception as to the rights and obligations of a religious preceptor, and the consequent misuse of his privileges, the terms 'guru' and 'sishya' are never employed among us; on the contrary the words used are "mahashay" and "varati". * * It will thus be seen that the "mahashay" is merely a teacher and has no right to exact any divine homage from his 'varatis'.

" The duties enjoined upon the members are, *inter alia*, the following :—

(1) Never to utter any untruth. *N.B.*—This injunction is so strictly observed by the majority of the members, that our sect has come to be called the ' Satya Dharma ' sect. * * *

(2) Every day to repeat the mantra in the prescribed manner for at least three times on each of these five occasions, early in the morning when rising from bed, then again after morning ablutions, in noon after bath and before dinner, in the evening, and lastly in the night when retiring to bed.

(3) Fridays to be held as sacred, and to be observed with fast and religious meditation and discourses, and, where practicable, to hold or attend in the evening religious meetings of the sect.

(4) Always to abstain from meat and intoxicating liquors. To the above may be added.

(5) To attend diligently the festivals held at Ghospara, and to pay or remit something to the *gadi* in recognition of the spiritual headship of the Kartā.

" One of the most important points to be noticed in connection with our sect is the complete separation that has been made both in theory and practice between social and spiritual matters. In respect of the former the members are at perfect liberty to follow

E

the customary rules and usages of their families and communities, and it is only in matters purely spiritual that they are amenable to the control of the sect. From the spiritual point of view all members stand upon the same footing, and no distinctions based on caste, wealth, etc., are recognized, so that a person of however low a social status he may be, provided that he has sufficiently advanced in spirituality and in the development of his physical powers, is unhesitatingly accepted as the spiritual guide by those who are socially his superiors.

"Thus persons who would otherwise have practically no status in the Hindu society, do find that by being admitted into our sect, vast opportunities open before them of being useful to others and thereby incidentally of distinguishing themselves. It is this highly liberal and democratic character of our sect, coupled with proofs positive of its utility in the shape, for instance, of a rapid development of psychical powers, which chiefly induces outsiders to join our ranks. And however much one may differ from the founder as regards his tenets and similar other matters, one certainly cannot deny that he who has laid the foundation of this all-comprehensive system of spiritual co-operation, in which degraded humanity finds a cordial welcome and ready recognition, is simply for this, if for nothing else, entitled to the everlasting respect and gratitude of the whole mankind."

The sect is, of course, anathema-maranatha to all the followers of pure and orthodox Brahminism, and this accounts, to a great extent, for the unfavourable comments upon it which have occasionally appeared in print, and also for the fact that it does not appear to bear a very high repute amongst Hindus generally.

Vaishna-vas.

The following extract is taken from Mr. Gait's report on the census of 1901 :—"Modern Vaishnavism, as preached by Chaitanya, represents a revulsion against the gross and debasing religion of the Tantras. Chaitanya was a Baidik Brahman and was born in Nabadwip in 1484. He preached mainly in Central Bengal and Orissa, and his doctrines found ready acceptance amongst large numbers of people especially among those who were still, or had only recently been, Buddhists. This was due mainly to the fact that he ignored caste and drew his followers from all sources, so much so that even Muhammadans followed him. He preached vehemently against the immolation of animals in sacrifice and the use of animal food and stimulants, and taught that the true road to salvation lay in Bhakti, or fervent devotion to God. He recommended Rādha worship, and taught that the love felt by her for Krishna was the best form of devotion. The acceptable offerings were flowers, money and the like, but the great form of worship was that of the Sankirtan, or procession of worshippers playing and singing. A peculiarity of Chaitanya's cult is that the post of spiritual guide or Gosain is not confined to Brahmans, and several of those best known belong to the Baidya caste. They are all of them descended from the leading men of Chaitanya's immediate entourage. The holy places of the cult are Nabadwip, Chaitanya's birthplace, and in a still greater degree Brindāban, the scene of Krishna's sport with the milk-maids, which Chaitanya and his disciples rescued from jungle, and where he personally identified the various sacred spots, on which great shrines have now been erected. At Nabadwip the most important shrines are in the keeping of Brahmans who are themselves staunch *Saktas*.

" In course of time the followers of Chaitanya split into two bodies, those who retained and those who rejected caste. The latter, who are also known as Jat Baishtams or Bairagi, consist of recruits from all castes, who profess to intermarry freely among themselves, and, except for the fact that outsiders are still admit-ted, they form a community very similar to the ordinary Hindu caste. Its reputation at the present day is tarnished by the fact that most of its new recruits have joined owing to love intrigues, or because they have been turned out of their own caste or for some other sordid motive. Those who have retained their caste and are merely Vaishnavs by sect are, of course, in no way connected with the Jat Baishtams just described, and their religion is, on the whole, a far purer one than that of the *Saktas*. The stricter Vaishnavs will have nothing to do with Saktism and are vegetarians, but amongst the Bagdis and other low classes many of the professed followers of the sect will freely eat animal food and follow in the Durga procession, though they will not on any account be present when the sacrifices are offered up."

The Muhammadan population of the district increased from 947,390 in 1891 to 982,987 in 1901. As noted above, the loss of the Hindu population was almost entirely among women; the same tendency is to be observed among the Muhammadans, though not to so marked an extent, for the increase in their numbers was made up mostly among males. The following remarks may be quoted from Hunter's Statistical account of Nadiā : "The existence of a large Musulman population in the district is accounted for by wholesale forcible conversions at a period anterior to the Mughal Emperors, during the Afghān supremacy, and also to the circumstance that Nadiā was the highway between the great Muhammadan settlements of Murshidābād and Dācca. The only form of sectarianism which Muhammadan religion has

MUHAM-
MADANS.

developed in the district is a rather powerful Faraizi community. They are not actively disloyal, but cultivate their fields like the rest of the peasantry. Forty-two years ago the case was very different, and the fanatic leader, Titu Miān, found in Nadiā a sufficient body of disaffected Faraizi husbandmen as to lead him to set up the standard of revolt and for a short time to defy the British Government." The Faraizi sect is not now of much importance.

The Kushtiā Subdivision contains the largest Muhammadan population, and next to it the Meherpur Subdivision. Generally speaking, Muhammadans predominate in the eastern portion of the district, away from the Bhāgirathi, sacred to the Hindus.

Muham-
madan
classes.
The vast majority of Muhammadans returned themselves as Shekhs at the 1901 census, this class showing a total of 895,724. The number of Jolāhas was 20,016, and of Atrafs 19,332. No other class returned even as many as 10,000. The higher classes were in a very small minority, only the Pathāns (8,794) and Saiads (7,093) numbering over 1,000. There is a good deal of ambiguity in the term Shekh, and it is certain that most of those who have been returned as such are not true Shekhs.

Chris-
tians.
The total number of Christians enumerated in 1901 was 8,091, being 794 more than were enumerated in 1891, and 1,669 more than were enumerated in 1881. All but 179 of these are natives of India. The Church of England has 5,836 followers; next to this is the Roman Catholic Church with 2,172 followers; there are very few followers of other Churches or sects. Nadiā has more Church of England converts than any other district in Bengal except Ranchi. For further information about the Christians in the district, a reference should be made to the chapter upon Christian Missions in this volume.

Social
charac-
teristics.
Food.
The ordinary food of the people consists of rice, fish, pulses (dāl), vegetables and milk. Well-to-do Muhammadans indulge in animal food, generally the flesh of fowls or goats. There is a tendency among the more advanced of the Hindu community also to partake more freely of meat. The lowest classes of the Hindus eat pork, and Bunās are fond of the flesh of the flying-fox. All classes are partial to feathered game when they can get it.

The cultivator generally starts the day with a meal of cold rice, (which has been kept over from the evening meal. About midday he usually partakes of a hot meal, which is brought out to him in the field by one of his household. The principal meal of the day is taken after sunset, generally at about 9 P.M. The consumption of tea and aërated waters is increasing among those who can afford these simple luxuries.

The Collector; reports that the condition of the people as Clothing.
regards dress and other comforts has improved greatly of recent
years. A well-to-do man dresses during the hot weather in a
dhuti, worn long and loose, and a shirt, worn outside the *dhuti*,
or a loose coat. He also wears a *chadar*, or shawl, of silk or light
cotton during the summer, and of wool or heavy material during
the winter. The richer people use coats made of serge or flannel,
and costly shawls. Some Muhammadans prefer their characteristic costume consisting of a long *chapkan* and *pyjamas*. The
pandits and Brahmans who perform priestly duties wear plain
borderless *dhutis*, and cover their bodies with a *chadar* of cotton or
broadcloth. They generally wear slippers of Indian pattern,
whereas the English pattern of shoe is preferred by all other
classes who can afford it. The ordinary cultivator wears a short
coarse *dhuti*, and carries a *gamcha* (towel) on his shoulders. In
the winter a woollen vest or jersey is frequently worn. By women
the *sari* is universally worn; this is a single cloth about five yards
long, half of which is worn below the waist, and the other half
over the head and body. A bodice is also commonly used under
the *sari*. Well-to-do ladies have rich silk *saris* worked with gold
thread, and fine silk bodices trimmed with lace. Gold and silver
ornaments are worn more or less by all women except widows.

As is the case in most of the Lower Bengal districts, the village Houses.
is generally a loose agglomeration of *baris*, or homesteads, rather
than a compact collection of houses. Except among the poorest
classes, the ordinary *bari* contains at least three huts or houses,
and is frequently surrounded by a fence made of grass or the dried
stalks of jute. The principal house serves as a bedroom, another
is used as a reception room and the third as a cow-shed. The dwelling house usually has a high plinth so that the floor may be well
above flood level in the rains. The walls of the houses are
generally made of mud; but in the Chuādāngā and Kushtiā
Subdivisions split bamboos, or bamboo mats plastered with mud are
frequently used. The doors and door-frames are as a rule made
of wood, with wooden bolts or chain fastenings; the poorer classes
use mat screens for doors. The roof is thatched with the long
coarse grasses of various kinds which grow in the district, and in
bazars corrugated iron sheets or flattened kerosine oil tins are
frequently placed on top of the thatch as a protection against fire.
In the old Hindu *baris* there is always to be found a *pujar dalān*
or a *chandi mandap*. The former is a large brick-built structure
with a certain amount of architectural decoration, in which the
presiding deity of the house is installed and worshipped. The
latter, which serves the same purpose, is a thatched house in the

bāri of humbler folk. These arrangements for worship are sometimes omitted in modern built *bàris*. Every husbandman of
means has in his *bāri* a circular hut built on a raised platform
with bamboos and the leaves of the date palm, which is used as a
granary. The thatch of the houses has to be repaired every
year, and ought to be renewed every other year. Two-storied
brick-built houses are gradually becoming more common, especially in the towns. For fuel the ordinary villager uses cakes
of dried cow-dung, the stalks of jute and other plants, and the
dried branches of trees.

The Collector reports that owing to the facilities of communication afforded by the railway, there is a marked tendency on the
part of ‚the rural population to settle in towns and seats of commerce. Many inhabitants of Sāntipur and Rānāghāt are daily
passengers to Calcutta, where they have their business. Some
residents of the district live in Calcutta during the week, and go
home for the week-end. Day labourers migrate in search of work
to towns and into the neighbouring districts, but they always
retain their connection with their native villages.

Amuse-
ments.
The principal amusements of the people consist of various
theatrical and musical entertainments. The performance of what
is called the *Mansār Bhāsan* is very popular. In this a description is given of the strife between Chānd Saudāgar, a rich
merchant, and Mansā, the snake goddess; the latter, having
destroyed six of the merchant's sons, causes a snake to bite the
seventh and last son on the day of his marriage. Behula, the
bride, by her chastity and devotion to her husband, at last succeeds
in arousing the compassion of the goddess, and she restores the
husband to life. The legend is sung in verse to the accompani-
ment of music and dancing, the performers generally being either
Muhammadans or Muchis.

Pirer gān is a popular entertainment among Muhammadans.
It consists of a musical recitation of the supernatural powers and
wonderful feats of a Muhammadan saint named Mānik Pir. This
saint is held in much esteem even by Hindus, especially those of
the Goālā caste.

The *kathākala* is a recital of the Rāmāyana or the Mahābhārata by a Brahman to an audience consisting chiefly of
illiterate females, who cannot read the sacred books. The recital
goes on night after night for about three hours at a stretch.

The *jātrā* is an entertainment of a higher class, consisting of
the performance of a mythological piece, generally selected from the
Rāmāyana or Mahābhārata. There are many *jātrā* parties in the
district, but the chief among them is that which was conducted

and managed by the late Moti Rai of Nabadwip, which is considered the best in Bengal. The usual charge for a single performance by this party is Rs. 150.

In the towns there are amateur dramatic societies which give public and private entertainments; in Rānāghāt alone there are four such societies, each of which has its own stage and appurtenances.

In every large village, or group of villages, there is a place called the *bārāyāritalā*, which is reserved for the worship of the village deity, and for the performance of *jātrās* and other entertainments. There is usually a committee for the collection of subscriptions to pay the expenses of the *bārāyāris*, and though Hindus are generally the organizers, Muhammadans also subscribe willingly. A portion of the subscriptions is used on the worship of the local godling, but the greater part goes in defraying the expenses of the entertainments. The two *bārāyāri melas* held in the Rānāghāt bazar are the most-popular in the district; people come in from all the country round to attend them, and a brisk trade is carried on by local and other shopkeepers and itinerant vendors.

Among the younger generation cricket, football, and even lawn tennis, are gradually replacing the indigenous games.

The chief indoor games which are indulged in are chess, draughts and card games.

In the statement below will be found a list of the chief festivals held in the district. Festivals.

Serial No.	Month in which held.	Name of festival.	Duration in days.	Number of shops.	Daily average attendance of people.	Name of village where held.	Name of subdivision.
1	Jan.	Mallikpur ..	3	20	700	Pātuli ...	Rānāghāt.
2	,,	Tehata ...	8	200	5,000	Tehata ...	Meherpur.
3	,,	Mian Sāhiber	1	15	300	Rāghabpur	Rānāghāt.
4	Feb.	Dhulat ...	15	80	1,000	Nabadwip...	Sadar.
5	,,	Dharmatola...	5	200	3,000	Chāprā ...	,,
6	,,	Murāgāchhā	7	100	1,500	Murāgāchhā	,,
7	,,	Raita ...	25	9	150	Raita ...	Kushtiā.
8	,,	Kāli Puja ...	7	200	4,000	Khoksā ...	,,
9	,,	Maghi Purnimā.	4	300	2,000	Chākdaha...	Rānāghāt.
10	,,	Baidyanāth-tolā.	15	60	500	Baidyanāth-tolā.	Meherpur.
11	,,	Saraswati Puja.	15	60	500	Bhowānipur	,,

Serial No.	Month in which held.	Name of Festival.	Duration in days.	Number of shops	Daily average attendance of people.	Name of village where held.	Name of subdivision.
12	Mar.	Mahismārdini	5	150	1,000	Bara Bazār, Rānāghāt.	Rānāghāt.
13	,,	Chāndghar ...	14	150	4,000	Chāndghar	Meherpur.
14	,,	Kāli Puja ...	30	7	100	Bara Gāngdi	Kushtiā.
15	,,	Ghoshpārā ...	3	250	10,000	Ghoshpārā	Rānāghāt.
16	,,	Dol Purnimā	3	50	2,000	Birahi ...	,,
17	,,	Rām Navami	30	10	300	Bhairāmārā	Kushtiā.
18	Apr.	Annapurna ...	30	15	200	Khalisākundi	.,
19	,,	Bara Dol ...	3	200	3,000	Krishnagar	Sadar.
20	May	Juzal Kishor	30	25	200	Araughātā	Rānāghāt.
21	,,	Ulai Chāndi	5	200	2,000	Birnagar ...	,,
22	June	Dashāhara ...	2	48	4,000	Nabadwip...	Sadar.
23	,,	Murutia ...	8	60	5,000	Murutia ...	Meherpur.
24	July	Rath Jātrā ...	1	5	100	Haludbāria	Kushtiā.
25	,,	Ambubāchi ...	5	100	4,000	Mātiari ...	Sadar.
26	,,	Gazir	1	15	200	Sankarpur	Rānāghāt.
27	Aug.	Brahmanitola	4	50	500	Nakāsipārā	Sadar.
28	Nov.	Rāsh ...	4	100	8,000	Nabadwip...	,,
29	,,	,, ...	3	300	10,000	Sāntipur ...	Rānāghāt.
30	,,	,, ...	20	25	2,000	Beldāngā ...	Meherpur.
31	,,	,, ...	10	30	300	Chandbillā	,,
32	,,	Dharma Thākur.	1	15	300	Kayetpārā	Rānāghāt.
33	Dec.	Gangā Puja...	4	10	100	Gotpārā ...	Sadar.
34	,,	Annapurna ...	5	100	1,000	Chotā Bāzār Rānāghāt.	Rānāghāt.
35	,,	Kuliā ..	2	200	10,000	Kuliā ...	,,

CHAPTER IV.

PUBLIC HEALTH.

THE Census report of the Nadia district for the year 1901 speaks of the district as " once famous as a health resort," but this reputation appears to be based mainly, if not solely, upon a few vague references to visits to it from more unhealthy spots, and it is extremely improbable that the district, as a whole, could ever have been anything but absolutely unhealthy. Certainly during the last fifty years or more it has been uniformly malarious to a high degree, and it has, in addition, suffered from two serious epidemics of fever. Recent enquiries have shown that there is little or no justification for the opinion, which has occasionally been expressed, that the present condition is of comparatively recent date, and has arisen from causes which should have been preventible. The first serious epidemic of fever, of which there is any complete record, occurred in the early sixties of the nineteenth century; it was investigated by a committee (usually referred to as the Epidemic Commission) under the presidency of Mr. Anderson in 1864, in which year it began to abate, though there was a subsequent slight recrudescence in the early seventies.

This first epidemic of fever is thus described in " Bengal under the Lieutenant-Governors " by C. E. Buckland : —

" A very fatal epidemic had of late years shown itself in some of the villages of the Presidency and Burdwan Divisions, but the steps taken to afford relief, viz., the appointment of native doctors and the gratuitous distribution of medicine, failed to check its progress. Towards the close of 1862 a special officer, Dr. J. Elliot, was deputed to visit the affected districts. He traced the progress of the disease, from the Jessore and Nadia districts to Hooghly, Barasat and Bardwan, and explained the various predisposing causes which enabled an ordinary epidemic fever to become a scourge, less virulent, but, in its effects, not less desolating than cholera. The disease was described as differing only in its intensity from the ordinary form of malarious fever,

'being of a more congestive character than the ordinary intermittent, but presenting all the grades of severity between the
remittent and intermittent types'; and its excessive virulence in
these districts was attributed solely to villages being undrained,
houses unventilated, tanks uncleaned and overgrown with noxious
weeds, and to the tangled growth of jungle and rank vegetation
with which the Bengali loves to surround and to obscure his
dwelling.

"The mortality from the epidemic fever arising from this
sanitary neglect had in some villages amounted to 60 per cent.
of the population, and, in the presence of this constantly recurring
visitation, the remnant who had escaped immediate death lingered
on in a state of apathy and despair, unable to help themselves, and
destined, unlesss vigorous external aid was afforded them, to fall
certain victims to the fever which had already nearly depopulated
the neighbourhood. Government at once proceeded to carry out
the remedial measures proposed by Dr. Elliot, namely, the
removal of superabundant and useless trees, shrubs, bamboo
clumps and plantain groves, from the immediate vicinity of houses,
the pruning and thinning of trees, the removal of trees and
bamboos from the sides of tanks, the uprooting and burning of
low bushy jungle, vegetation and rank grass, the deepening and
cleaning of the larger tanks, and the filling in of all useless tanks,
watercourses, and other excavations in the neighbourhood of
houses, the appropriation of particular tanks exclusively for the
supply of drinking water, the construction of a few drains and
paths in each village, and the proper ordering of burial-grounds
and burning-ghats. This is one of the first notices of the so-
called 'Burdwan' fever which recurred again several years after
this date, and will be mentioned in due course. It not only
carried off its victims in large numbers, but the health of the
whole population appeared to be deteriorated thereby. The
sanguine hopes that were entertained in 1862-63 of the measures
adopted were never realized. The fever was, generally
speaking, an unusual phase of the malarial fever from which
Lower Bengal is never free. The efforts of Government to
mitigate its ravages were to some extent successful : after a time
it appeared to die away of itself. But in 1863-64 this epidemic
fever again appeared. The sanitary measures ordered had,
wherever carried out with tolerable efficiency, greatly mitigated
the intensity of the scourge, but they failed generally through
the want of willing co-operation on the part of the people and
their zamindars, and this again was owing to their inability to
understand that a comparatively new visitation like the epidemic

could be in any way connected with the unwholesome state of
the villages, which was assuredly no new thing. A special
commission drew up a report on the subject, containing a full and
complete account of the nature, history and probable causes
of the disease, and offering some valuable suggestions for
dealing with it. The epidemic was described as a congestive
remittent fever, running its course to a fatal termination, usually
with great rapidity, and, where not at once fatal, leaving the
patient so shattered as to be generally unable to resist a recurrence
of the attack. So fatal was it that no less than 30 per cent. of
the whole population of the affected area were carried off by it.
The Commission came to the conclusion that the miasma, which
was the immediate cause of the disease, was the result of a great
dampness of the earth's surface, and that this damp had been
intensified to an unusual degree of late years, owing to the fact
that there had been a gradual filling up of the *bils* by the deposit
brought in from the rivers, and that this again had been supplemented by a gradual, but continuous, rising in the level of the
river-bed itself, thus causing a general derangement of levels so
as seriously to affect the natural drainage of the country. The
remedies proposed were an improved system of drainage
throughout the country, the burning of weeds, dried grass and
jungle in the villages, especially at night time, the filling up of
the small and filthy holes and clearing of the larger pools and
tanks in the villages, and the removal of low brushwood and the
thick accumulations of fallen leaves and branches. It was proposed that steps should be taken for a supply of pure drinking
water, by reserving certain tanks under the charge of the police
for drinking water only, and by erection, if possible, of public
filters. The Commission insisted very strongly on the necessity
of stringent measures being taken in all larger villages for the
proper disposal of dead bodies. They condemned the practices of
uneducated medicine vendors who went about the villages
making money out of the ignorance of the people by the sale of
drugs of the nature of which they equally were ignorant, and
suggested the registration of qualified practitioners. It is on
record that 'the epidemic fever disappeared entirely after the
cyclone of 1864, and there was no return of it in 1865 to attract
attention.' But it reappeared in 1866 and 1867."

There was another serious epidemic which lasted from 1880
to 1885, and was enquired into by the Nadiā Fever Commission
in 1881-82. The district was again extremely unhealthy in the
years 1902 and 1905, and was visited by the Drainage Committee
in the cold weather of 1906-07. The following extract is taken

from the report of that Committee, which was submitted to the
Government in April 1907 :—

"It is impossible to differentiate between the physical features
of the different portions of the Nadiā district. The whole area
consists of an alluvial plain, which still receives a fair share of
the Gangetic flood through the channels of the Jalangi, Mātābhāngā and Gorai, but is subject to general inundation in years
of high flood only. Backwaters, minor streams and swamps
intersect it in all directions. A low-lying tract of black clay
soil known as the Kālantar, stretches from the adjoining district
of Murshidābād through the Kāliganj and Tehata thanas on the
west, but these areas do not present any special features from the
point of view of health. A comparison from the different
thanas arranged according to the average (a) total and (b) fever
mortality during the five years 1901-05 does not disclose any
marked variation in the position of each. Sāntipur is comparatively rather less feverish, and Kushtiā rather more so, than its
position in the list according to total mortality would presume.
Taking the average annual district death rate from fever for
the same period, 33·3, it may be said that those thānās which
have a corresponding rate of 35 and over are specially unhealthy,
and those with a rate of 30 and under comparatively healthy,
looking to the general conditions of the district. On this basis
the most unhealthy thanas in Nadiā are those of Gāngni and
Karimpur adjoining one another on the north-west, and Jibannagar, Kumārkhāli and Nāopārā in the east. The more healthy
thanas comprise those of Krishnagar, Chāprā and Meherpur,
forming a little strip from north to south in the centre of the
district, and Chākdaha in the extreme south. It is difficult to
connect the figures showing the variations in population in the
three censuses of 1881, 1891 and 1901 with a theory of the pro-
gressive deterioration of health in thanas which now show the
highest rates of mortality from fever, but the outbreaks of
epidemic fever in the district between 1861 and 1864 and
again between 1880 and 1885 have complicated the conclusions
as to normal health which may be deduced from the various
fluctuations. In the census report of 1901 the thanas of
Rānāghāt, Sāntipur and Chākdaha (comprising the Rānāghāt
subdivision), Krishnagar and Kumārkhāli are mentioned as
being specially malarious, but only in the case of Kumārkhāli
is this borne out by the figures of mortality from fever between
1901 and 1905. As regards Karimpur, recently particularly
feverish, the census report notes the falling off in population
between 1891 and 1901 as difficult to explain. The tracts reported

to us by the District Magistrate 'after consulting the local officers, old residents and well known zamindars,' as specially unhealthy are Kumārkhāli, Jibannagar, Chākdaha, Gāngni, Alamdāngā, Daulatpur, and some villages in the Meherpur and Krishnagar thanas. Except as regards Kumārkhāli, Jibannagar and Gāngni, the figures of mortality quoted scarcely support the statement, while the further allegation that 'almost in every village in the Meherpur Subdivision and in some villages of the Kumārkhāli, Daulatpur and Alamdāngā police-stations malaria fever has increased considerably in recent times' requires further verification before it can be accepted. A comparison between the total number of births and deaths registered during the five years 1901-05 shows an increase of population in the thanas of Krishnagar, Chāprā, Kāliganj, Daulatpur, Meherpur and Alamdāngā only. The local enquiries of Captain Stewart and Lieutenant Proctor in Nadiā were too brief to permit of a comparison covering the whole district, but in the three thanas of Gāngni, Kumārkhāli and Jibannagar total spleen rates of 80, 47 and 67 were recorded, although the number of villages examined (43 in all) was small. The most interesting point elicited was the probable presence in the Gāngni thana of Leishman-Donovan infection in considerable amount, which renders nugatory the spleen test as evidence of the prevalence of malaria. In respect of malaria only it was surmised that the three thanas suffer about equally. The statement of the villagers in Gāngni that fever had been severe within the last two or six years is noticeable, and is consistent with the fact that between the censuses of 1891 and 1901 the thana showed an increase of 8·5 per cent., *i.e.*, was not particularly unhealthy. * * * Looking to the available evidence touching the medical history of the district we arrive at the following, conclusions:—

(a) the whole district is very unhealthy;
(b) similarly, the whole district is feverish;
(c) investigation upon a small scale has demonstrated the fact that some of the fever is probably due to Leishman-Donovan infection, but that the greater part is malarial;
(d) the most malarious thanas are those of Gāngni, Karimpur, Jibannagar, Kumārkhāli and Nāopārā;
(e) the least malarious areas are the Krishnagar, Chāprā, Chākdaha, and Meherpur thanas."

Drinking water-supply is still bad, though the District Board WATER-SUPPLY. has for some years been endeavouring to improve it by constructing masonry wells along the principal roads, and in many of the big villages. Kutcha ring wells are common, but are not often used for drinking purposes owing to religious scruples. Tanks are very common in the villages, and form the usual water supply when there is no river handy; they are generally very dirty and weed-grown, and are used for washing and other domestic purposes as well as for drinking. Where no tanks or wells exist, drinking water is got from any casual collection of water, however dirty and unwholesome it may be. When river water is drunk it is generally obtained at a spot which is also used as a bathing-ghāt, and it must be remembered that, for the greater part of the year, most of the rivers have very little current. The sides of the rivers and *khāls* are generally used as latrines.

In 1867 the general want of water and the decadence of the tanks in the district were brought to the notice of Government. An enquiry was held, and the Executive Engineer advocated the digging of tanks at the expense of Government. The Collector suggested that legislative interference was necessary in order to compel the landlords to provide their tenants with an adequate water supply, but no action was taken by the Government.

PRINCIPAL DISEASES. Fever. By far the greatest number of deaths are returned under the head of fever. It is probable that the total death rate as now recorded is reasonably accurate, but there can be no doubt that a very large proportion of the deaths attributed to fever are due to diseases other than malaria. The village chaukidar is able to detect cholera, small-pox and some other diseases with well defined symptoms, but most of the diseases which present any difficulty in diagnosis are classed as fever. The returns under this head are, therefore, less accurate than those under any other head. The Medical Officers who were deputed to assist the Drainage Committee of 1906-07 specially enquired into 195 deaths in the Nadiā district which had been reported as due to fever; they found that 40 per cent. of these cases were due to malaria, acute or chronic, and the remaining 60 per cent. to bronchitis, pneumonia, phthisis, dysentery, diarrhœa, typhoid, Leishman-Donovan infection and other causes. A similar enquiry was held in the Dinājpur district iu 1904, when it was found that less than one-third of the deaths classified as due to fever were actually caused by malaria. It seems probable that, ordinarily speaking, not more than one-third of the deaths imputed to fever are the direct result of malaria, though it must be remembered that malaria is probably the indirect cause of a much larger proportion, owing to the enfeeblement which repeated attacks of it cause. The conditions of registration being much the same in all districts, the returns, though incorrect absolutely, give a fairly accurate idea of the relative prevalence of malaria in different districts. During the five years ending with 1907, the death rate from fever averaged $34 \cdot 12$ per annum, which was the highest return from this cause of any district in the Province. During the five years ending with 1903, and during the previous five years, the corresponding figures were $28 \cdot 82$ and $27 \cdot 13$, the district taking the 7th and 13th place, respectively, in the Province.

The Drainage Committee of 1906-07 found that the local conditions which contributed to the spread of malaria were :—

(a) The insanitary state of the village sites due to,

(1) the thick jungle in which the houses lie imbedded (the spleen rate in villages in which jungle was thick was found to be $71 \cdot 7$, as against $44 \cdot 5$ in villages in which it was moderate or little).

(2) the large number of tanks, pits and collections of water scattered about them,

(3) the cultivation of rice in close proximity to the houses,

(4) the bad drinking supply, and

(5) promiscuous defœcation ;

(b) the water-logged state of the country.

The operation of these two factors is in two directions, namely, that of directly increasing the amount of malarial infection by facilitating the breeding of mosquitoes, and of predisposing the constitutions of the local residents to attacks of malaria by weakening them in other directions.

Next to fever the greatest mortality is caused by cholera, for Cholera. which disease the Nadiā district has an unenviable reputation. It has been said that cholera made its first appearance in India in the town of Nabadwip. The disease is endemic in the district and severe epidemics occur from time to time. It is generally at its worst during the cold weather months, and it gradually subsides as the year advances, and usually ceases during the rains. There was a very severe epidemic during the cold weather of 1895-96, the daily number of deaths at one period being as many as 300. During the five years ending with 1907 the death rate from cholera averaged $3 \cdot 83$, Nadiā taking the fourth place in this respect of all the districts in the Province. In the five years ending with 1903, and in the previous five years, the rates were $3 \cdot 95$ and $2 \cdot 32$, Nadiā being 3rd and 11th, respectively, in the Province.

Other diseases and infirmities. Other diseases are not important, and claim very few victims compared with fever and cholera. Diarrhœa and dysentery prevail at times, but not of a severe type, the deaths due to these diseases seldom exceeding ·12 per mille. Small-pox is even less prevalent and is responsible for very few deaths. Plague has never become epidemic. Leprosy is not common. Infirmities such as insanity, deaf-mutism, and blindness are comparatively rare; according to the census of 1901 there are only 26 insane persons and 38 deaf-mutes per 100,000 of the population, the figures in respect of the former comparing vary favourably with those of the other districts in the Presidency Division.

MEDICAL INSTITUTIONS. There are 12 dispensaries and hospitals in class III under Government supervision in the district; they are supported by local funds. There are also two dispensaries in class V. The most important of all these is the institution at Krishnagar, in which 16,420 out-patients and 412 in-patients were treated during the year 1907. Attached to this hospital is a separate building for the accommodation of female patients, which was erected in 1895 through the munificence of Bābu Nafar Chandra Pāl Chaudhuri. The next institution in respect of attendance is that at Rānāghāt, the headquarters of the Rānāghāt Subdivision; this was attended in 1907 by 10,004 out-patients and 102 in-patients. There are three other class III institutions in the Rānāghāt Subdivision, namely at Sāntipur (attended by 9,951 out-patients and 23 in-patients), at Ulā (attended by 6,276 out-patients), and at Chākdaha (attended by 5,978 out-patients). There is also a class V dispensary at Belgharia, supported by the trust fund created by Bābu Kailāsh Chandra Mukhopādhyāy. In the Sadar Subdivision, besides the hospital at Krishnagar, there is a hospital at Nabadwip called the Garrett Hospital, after a former Collector, and a dispensary at Debagrām; the former was in 1907 attended by 4,238 out-patients and 35 in-patients, and the latter by 6,110 out-patients. In the Chuādāngā Subdivision there is only one medical institution, namely a dispensary at Chuādāngā itself, in which 5,741 out-patients were treated in 1907. In the Meherpur Subdivision there is a hospital at Meherpur (attended by 8,120 out-patients and 59 in-patients), a dispensary at Shikārpur (attended by 5,644 out-patients) and a dispensary for women and children at Ratnapur, maintained by the Church of England Zenānā Mission Society, aided by the District Board. In the Kushtiā Subdivision lie the remaining two class III medical institutions, namely a hospital at Kushtiā and a dispensary at Kumārkhāli; during 1907, 7,088 out-patients and 66 in-patients were treated at the former and

2,854 out-patients at the latter. There is also in the Kushtiā Subdivision a class V dispensary at Amtā, maintained by the Shāha Bābus of that place.

The total income of these hospitals and dispensaries during the year 1907 was Rs. 28,100 and the expenditure Rs. 22,433. Out of the income nearly Rs. 16,000 was contributed from the funds of the District Board and Municipalities.

Out of the 89,370 cases treated during 1907 by far the largest number fell, as was to be expected, under the head of malarial fevers. The next most prevalent disease was "other diseases of the skin," which accounted for rather over 10,000 cases, as compared with 36,000 cases of malarial fever. It is noteworthy that skin diseases appear to be relatively much less prevalent in Nadiā than in Khulnā and Jessore, the two sister districts on the east of the Presidency Division. Diseases of the digestive system, diseases of the respiratory system, diseases of the eye, ulcers and worms account, in the order mentioned, for between three and four thousand cases each. The only other diseases calling for mention are leprosy and rheumatic affections, of which the district appears to be relatively free, as compared with other districts in the Presidency Division; and diseases of the spleen which are relatively far more common than in the other districts of the Division.

Besides the above institutions which are under Government supervision, there are nine private hospitals and dispensaries at which free medical aid is dispensed. The most important of these is the dispensary and hospital at Dayābāri, on the outskirts of Rānāghāt, instituted by the Rānāghāt Medical Mission but now maintained by the Church Missionary Society; at this institution 18,350 patients were treated in 1908. Next to this comes another institution maintained by the Church Missionary Society at Sāntirājpur, in the north of the Meherpur Subdivision; here 15,064 patients were treated in 1908. The other private institutions are at (1) Natuda in the Chuādāngā Subdivision, maintained by Bābu Nafar Chandra Pāl Chaudhuri; (2) Nakāsipārā in the Sadar Subdivision, maintained by Bābu Debendra Nāth Singh Rai; (3) Meherpur, maintained by the Mallik family; (4) Meherpur, maintained by the Church of England Zenana Mission Society, for women and children only; (5) Selaida, in the Kushtiā Subdivision, maintained by Bābu Rabindra Nāth Tagore; (6) Sutrāgarh, in the Rānāghāt Subdivision, maintained by Bābu Kārtik Chandra Dās; and (7) Krishnagar, maintained by the Church of England Zenana Mission Society, for women and children only.

F

Vaccination is compulsory within the limits of the nine Municipalities, where paid vaccinators are employed. In the rural
areas, where vaccination is voluntary, the operation is performed
by licensed vaccinators who charge two annas for each successful
case. It is reported that the people have no particular prejudice
against vaccination. During the year 1907-08 (the season for
vaccination is September to March) 54,493 persons were successfully vaccinated, giving a ratio per thousand of 34·66; this ratio
is higher than in any other district in the Presidency Division,
with the exception of the 24-Parganas.

CHAPTER V.

AGRICULTURE.

ACCORDING to the census of 1901, 56 per cent of the population of the district are employed, or directly interested, in agriculture. This percentage is remarkably low,* being less than that in any other district in the Province, except Hooghly and Howrah, which show 53·8 and 42·3 per cent., respectively, of their populations as engaged in agriculture. This is accounted for to a certain extent by the fact that Nadiā has a relatively high urban population, but the main reason is the infertility of the land. The soil varies but little all over the district; except for the tract known as the Kālantar, and some portions of the Kushtiā and Rānāghāt Subdivisions, it is almost universally a light sandy loam, possessing but little fertilising power, and incapable of retaining moisture. In earlier days, before the rivers had completed their work of land making, the district was far more liable than it is now to considerable inundations, which, although they might destroy the crop which was actually standing at the time of their visitations, brought with them a coating of silt, which ensured an excellent outturn for the following crop. This enrichment of the soil, however, no longer takes place as frequently as it is used to, and as the very light manuring which is applied is insufficient to compensate for the loss occasioned to the soil by cropping, there can be little doubt that the land is getting less and less capable of giving a good return.† This is particularly noticeable in the steady diminution which has been taking place of late in the net area cropped in the district, which means that it is becoming increasingly necessary to allow the land to lie

---

* The Collector states that he doubts the accuracy of these figures : he would put the percentage at about 80, as many day labourers are directly interested in agriculture, and rely on field work for a living : he thinks that 56 per cent, probably represents only those who actually hold lands on lease, *utbandi, jama* o otherwise.

† The abandonment of indigo cultivation has also reduced the fertility of the land; it is reported that bumper crops [of paddy were obtained when it was grown in rotation with indigo

fallow for longer periods between croppings. During the last five years for which statistics are available, the average area of culturable waste other than fallow was about 348,000 acres; of current fallows, about 400,000 acres; and of net cropped land, about 520,000 acres; in other words the net cropped area was only about 41 per cent. of the total culturable area. The corresponding percentages in the two sister districts of Khulná and Jessore for the same years were about 74 and 89, respectively. The only conclusion that can be drawn from these figures is that the soil in Nadiá is not sufficiently fertile to enable the same percentage of the population to depend upon agriculture as would be the case were the district more favourably circum-stanced in this respect than it is. Other reasons have been suggested, such as the precarious nature of the tenure under which a large proportion of the land is held, and loss of vitality and energy among the inhabitants owing to repeated attacks of malaria; but though these may be contributing causes, there seems little doubt that the main reason why the percentage of the population engaged upon agriculture is so comparatively low in Nadiá is that the land is, on account of its infertility, incapable of affording a livelihood to a large percentage.

The physical characteristics of the district are almost uniform throughout, and the agricultural conditions vary but little. The only tract of any size which presents any marked differences from the general average is that known as the Kálantar. This tract commences in the Murshidábád district, comes into Nadiá through the gap on the western boundary between the Bhágirathi and the Jalangi, and stretches through the district in a south-easterly direction. It is about 15 miles long and 8 miles broad. It is low-lying, and the surface soil has hardened into a comparatively stiff black clay, which, under favourable condi-tions, produces a good crop of *áman* rice, but is too water-logged for any autumn crop, and is unsuitable for regular winter crops. The inhabitants of this tract, being dependent upon the one crop, which is liable in some years to be swept away by violent floods, and in other years, when the monsoon fails, to die for want of moisture, are naturally more exposed to famine than those of the other parts of the district, where a second crop may afford some compensation for loss of the first.

No irrigation is practised in the district, the chief reason being that the surface is so uniformly level as to afford little or no scope for canals and distributaries.

PRIN-
CIPAL
CROPS.   As elsewhere in lower Bengal, the most important crop is rice, but Nadiá differs from all other districts in depending far

more upon the autumn variety than upon the winter variety. In this district the autumn rice crop occupies 69 per cent. of the normal net cropped area; this percentage is more than double that of any other district in the province, except Sambalpur, in which it is 47. Winter rice covers 23 per cent. of the normal net cropped area No summer rice is grown. *Rabi* crops, of which the most important are (1) gram and (2) other *rabi* cereals and pulses, occupy 56 per cent. of the normal net cropped area ; jute occupies 14 per cent.; while sugarcane is comparatively unimportant, occupying only 2 per cent. The reason why the total of these percentages exceeds 100 is that so large a proportion as three-fourths of the total cropped area is twice cropped. It is said that more than a thousand different varieties of rice are grown ; many considerable villages have a variety of their own, and old varieties are constantly being replaced by new ones. In a report issued by the Director of Agriculture it is remarked that "paddy is perhaps the best instance known of the variations which plants have undergone under cultivation. Originally an aquatic grass, the one characteristic which it has most persistently retained amidst all the changes brought about by differences in climate, soil and mode of cultivation, is the need of a large quantity of water for its proper growth * * * It is the belief of the raiyats that, give the paddy but this one thing needful, it will grow in any soil and under any climate. Indeed the facility with which it adapts itself to the different classes of soil from the stiffest clay to the lightest of sands, and from the peaty to the saline, is simply wonderful. Compared with the advantages of a proper supply of water, all other questions in its cultivation, namely the quality of the seed used, the nature of the soil on which it is grown, the manures applied, and the mode of cultivation adopted, are things of very minor importance."

The autumn rice or *aus*, is also known as *bhadoi* rice, after the name of the month in which it is harvested. As already stated it is by far the most important crop which is grown in the district. It requires less water than the other varieties of rice, and in fact it cannot be grown on land which is liable to be flooded during the rains to a depth of more than two feet, as it does not grow to a height of more than three or three and-a-half feet, and it does not possess the power of accommodating its growth to the depth of the water surrounding it, as do the long stemmed varieties. Cultivation of the land for it commences as soon as the early showers permit of ploughing and the seed is sown broadcast in April or May. As soon as the young plants have attained the height of 5 or 6 inches, the

Autumn rice or *Aus*.

field is harrowed with a view to somewhat thin out the crop, and also to prepare the way for the first weeding. During May and the first half of June it is most necessary to keep the fields clear of weeds, and it is the amount of labour required · in this operation which makes the *aus* a more troublesome crop even than the transplanted *áman*. Under favourable conditions the crop is ready for the sickle in August or September. The rice yielded is of coarse quality, and difficult to digest ; it is used by the lower classes only. The outturn is less in weight, and fetches a lower price than that afforded by the *áman* crop,' but it provides the raiyat with a food grain, and his cattle with fodder, at a time of the year when both are scarce. Moreover it is off the ground early enough to permit of the preparation of the land for the *rabi* or winter crop, which gives it another advantage over the *áman*, The normal outturn of *aus* rice in Nadiā is 12 maunds per acre, which compares favourably with the figures for other districts, notwithstanding the infertile nature of the soil; but this result is only obtained by allowing the soil far more frequent and prolonged periods of rest than are necessary elsewhere. *Aus* paddy is one of the best cleaning crops for lands which have become badly infested with weeds ; and it is occasionally grown for this purpose. It is specially useful for ridding from *ulu* grass land on which it is desired to plant out an orchard.

Winter rice or *áman*. The crop of next importance to the district is the winter rice or *áman*. It is in this class that the most varieties occur, and it furnishes all the finest qualities of rice. The preparation of the land for this crop begins early in the year, In April or May the seed is sown very thick in a nursery, and when the seedlings make their appearance another field is prepared into which to transplant them. For this purpose it is necessary to repair the embankments round the field so that it shall retain all the rain which it receives. It is then repeatedly ploughed up until the surface is reduced to thick mud. The seedlings are then taken out of the nursery and transplanted into rows about nine inches apart, where they are left to mature, the only subsequent operation being one or two weedings in the latter part of August. The crop is harvested in November or December. The most critical period for this crop is when it begins to blossom in the latter part of October. If there is not sufficient moisture at this time, no grain will form in the ear. The soil most suited to the *áman* crop is one that contains a large admixture of clay. In Nadiā *áman* rice is nearly the sole crop in the Kalantar, and it is also grown fairly extensively in the Kushtiā

Subdivision. The normal yield is about 13½ maunds of rice per acre, which is less than what is obtained in the other districts of the Presidency Division.

The cultivation of jute has been steadily increasing of late Jute. years, and this crop now occupies 14 per cent. of the normal net cropped area. Generally speaking, it does well on lands which are suitable for *aus* rice. The preparation of the land for this crop begins as soon as sufficient rain to moisten it has fallen. It is first ploughed twice or thrice and then allowed to rest for a time, while the cultivator manures it with cow-dung and any other fertilizing agent upon which he can lay his hands. It is ploughed again in May, and the surface rendered as fine as possible, after which the seed is sown. When the seedlings are five or six inches in height, a harrow is passed over the field with a view to thinning out the plants where they are too thick, and also to assist|in the absorption of moisture by breaking up the surface of the ground. The first weeding does not take place until the plants are about a foot high; every effort is then made to entirely eliminate the weeds, and if the work is well done no further weeding is required. The crop matures in August or September, and it is then cut and tied up in bundles about 15 inches in diameter, which are steeped in the nearest stagnant water for about a fortnight until the stalks have become sufficiently decomposed to admit of the extraction of the fibre from them. In performing this operation the stem is broken near the root, and the broken portion drawn off; the protruding end of the fibre is then grasped, and, by gradual pulling and shaking, the rest of the fibre is extracted from the stalk. It is then well rinsed in water, and hung up on bamboos in the sun to dry. Jute is an exhausting crop to the land, and cannot be grown on the same plot for two years in succession. Some of the loss to the land is made up by scattering on the surface the leaves of the plant which are stripped from the stalks before they are steeped.

The quality of the jute grown in the Nadiá district is inferior to that grown in the districts north of the Ganges. One reason for this is that in the latter districts the best lands are devoted to the crop, whereas in Nadiá and other districts in the Presidency Division less care is taken in this respect; a further explanation as regards Nadiá itself lies in the inherent infertility of the soil. The best jute has its fibres in long thick clusters, soft and fine, yet strong, of a white glistening colour and free from particles of bark or wood. The inferior qualities have a coarse red fibre. The length or shortness of the stem is said not to affect the price; only its fineness, cleanness and silkiness are looked to.

Rabi *Rabi* crops generally are sown in October and early November,
crops. and reaped in March. The most important of these are gram,
the normal acreage of which is 80,000, representing 14 per cent.
of the normal net cropped area ; and those which fall under the
head of "other *rabi* cereals and pulses," such as peas and *masuri*:
these latter occupy 10 per cent. of the normal net cropped area.
Wheat has declined in importance, and its normal acreage is now
only 23,100. Barley is only grown on 7,500 acres. The normal
outturn of the *rabi* crops in Nadiá is rather under the average
outturn in the other districts of the Presidency Division.

Other   Crops producing oilseeds occupy, between the different
crops.   varieties, about 22 per cent. of the normal net cropped area. In
some parts, especially in the Chuádángá Subdivision, the cultivation of chillies (*capsicum frutescens*) and turmeric forms an
important feature of the rural industry, and the peasant relies
upon it to pay his rent. Indigo, the manufacture of which was
once the most important industry in the district, now occupies
only about 1,000 acres About 20,000 acres are devoted to
orchards and market-gardens. Generally speaking, the quality
of the mangoes is not good, and in some parts of the district,
especially in the Kálantar, even the common mango does not do
well.* The cultivation of potatoes is extending especially in the
south of the district near the railway line, in which parts other
garden produce is freely grown (where the conditions of the soil
permit) and exported to Calcutta.

Cultiva-   So long ago as in 1872 the Collector reported that the
tion gene- proportion of spare land capable of being brought under cultivation
rally.   was small, and probably as scarce as in other district in Lower
Bengal. The proportion of such land is still smaller now, and
consequently there is room for very little extension of cultivation.
Moreover, little or no improvement in the methods of agriculture
is observable, and but little progress in the way of the introduction of new or better varieties of crops.

RAINFALL.   The character of a harvest depends, within certain wide limits,
more on the seasonable distribution of the rainfall than on its
absolute quantity. Although a well marked deficiency in the
rainfall will certainly entail a deficient crop yield, yet the
magnitude of the deficiency will depend on the distribution of the
rain which fell. In the month of Baisákh (April-May) there
should be light showers to facilitate the preparation of the land
and supply moisture for the sowing of the *aus*. During the
month of Jaistha (May-June) rain is not required, but in Asárh

---

* The cultivation of good mangoes from grafts is increasing, and many of the
amindars now have good mango orchards.

(June-July) there should be heavy falls to give plenty of moisture for the young *aus* crop, and to permit of the sowing of the *áman* seed in the nurseries. Heavy rain with intervals of fine weather for transplantation of the *aman* seedlings and for weeding is required during the month of Srában (July-August). During Bhadra (August-September) longer intervals of fine weather are required to facilitate the reaping and threshing of the *aus* crop. Showers at intervals of about a week are required in Aswin (September-October), and lighter and less frequent showers in Kártik (October-November). There should be no rain in Agrahayan (November-December), but showers in Mágh (December-January) are useful; a proverb which is frequently quoted in the district runs "*jadi barsha mágher sheshdhanya rájá punya desh*," if it rains at the end of Mágh, rich will be the king and blessed the country. No rain is required in the last two months, Phálgun and Chaitra.

The local cattle are very inferior; the pasturage available for CATTLE. them is deficient both in quantity and quality, and no care is taken to improve the breeds by selection or otherwise. The prices are low, averaging about Rs. 25 for a cow and Rs. 30 for a bullock. The practice of employing buffaloes in agricultural operations has become in recent years much more common than it used to be, as one pair of them can do the work of two pairs of the miserable local bullocks. The price of a buffalo is about Rs. 40.

The local breed of ponies is wretched; the average price is Other about Rs. 37. Goats are fairly common, but are not as a rule domestic kept as a means of making a livelihood. Sheep are occasionally animals. imported, but are rarely bred in the district. Pigs are kept by Bunás, and some of the lowest castes of Hindus.

The District Board expends about Rs. 1,000 per annum on its VETERI. Veterinary establishment. NARY WORK.

CHAPTER VI.

NATURAL CALAMITIES.

FLOODS. BEFORE the Ganges broke its way to the east, the district must have been liable to terrible floods, but there have not been many occasions during the last hundred years on which inundations sufficiently serious to affect the general prosperity of the people have] occurred. In 1801 a very destructive inundation took place necessitating Government aid for the sufferers, and a sum of Rs. 3,171 was expended on relief. The next serious inundation took place in 1823, but no definite information is now forthcoming as to its extent. Such also is the case with the floods of 1838, 1857, 1859 and 1867, but a full account of the inundation of 1871 is on record. Rain fell at short intervals throughout the hot weather of that year until the ordinary monsoon set in, but though it was unseasonable, the prospects of both the early and late rice crops were excellent until the beginning of August, when the rivers began to rise. By the middle of that month it had become evident that a serious inundation was to be expected. The portions of the head-quarters subdivision lying in the Bhágirathi and the Meherpur Subdivision were the first to suffer ; the north-east and central parts of the district were next affected, and, lastly, the eastern part of the Chuádángá Subdivision. The Bhágirathi rose and fell three times, and the other rivers twice, on each occasion the Bhágirathi being some days in advance. Rather more than half the rice crop was lost, and it is estimated that 200,000 head of cattle perished either from starvation or disease. The people suffered severe hardships for two and a half months, but there was very little loss of life, as the water rose slowly. It was hoped that with the subsidence of the floods the cold weather crops would give a good outturn, but this did not prove to be the case, as the sowing season was much retarded and many valuable crops were not put down at all. However, the poorer classes benefited by the increase in the demand for labour occasioned by the loss of so many cattle, and only a small amount was expended from public funds for the relief of pressing necessities.

In 1885, which was a year of a very high flood, the embankment breached at Laltakuri on 23rd August, and water passed
through it until the end of September. For three weeks the
discharge through the breach was at the enormous rate of 50,000
cubic feet per second. The inundation came down into the
district through the Kalantar, and by 1st September it had
reached the Bagula railway station ; eight days later it topped,
and then breached, the railway embankment, and it then passed
along into the Ichhamati and finally breached the Central Bengal
Railway.

The Bhagirathi went into very high flood again in the year
1889, but much less damage was done in the district than in
1885, as the Jalangi and Matabhanga did not simultaneously go
into flood.

In September 1900, owing to torrential rain over the whole of
south-west Bengal, the district was again visited by floods.
Considerable damage was done in some of the large municipalities,
and in the rural tracts nearly 3,000 kutcha and 1,000 pucka
houses collapsed, and seven lives were lost. The damage to crops
and cattle was not, however, very serious, and no distress requir-
ing Government relief came to notice.

There is no record to show the extent to which the district FAMINES.
suffered in the famine of 1769-70. The famine of 1866 was
severely felt. Great damage had been done in the district by a
cyclone which swept across it in 1864, and a severe drought Famine of
occurred in the following year. At the end of October 1865 the 1866.
Collector reported that the outturn of the rice crop was expected
to be less than half that produced in ordinary years, and that the
prospects of the winter crops were very bad. By the beginning
of 1866 prices had risen to double the ordinary rates and distress
had commenced.

In March the missionaries of the Church Missionary Society
addressed the Lieutenant-Governor on the subject. One of these,
the Rev. T. G. Lincke, stated that " a certain measure of rice,
which some years ago cost three or four pice, now sells at thirteen
or fourteen pice, which alone is sufficient to account for the
present distress of the poor. Were I to tell the instances of how
long many must go without food, and what sort of materials they
contrive to convert into food, you could not believe it, for it
is really incredible and yet it is true nevertheless." Another
missionary, the Rev. F. Schurr, of Kapasdanga, declared that
" respectable farmers are so much reduced in circumstances that
they cannot employ nearly so many day-labourers as they used
to do in former times, and consequently the labouring classes are

reduced to the point of starvation. They are now able to glean
a little wheat, gram, etc., but after a month all the crops will
have been gathered in, when nothing can be obtained by gleaning
in the fields. They are now thrown upon roots, berries, etc., for
their chief support, and when that supply is exhausted, they will
be forced to eat the rind of trees, grass, etc. I never witnessed
such misery in my life."

This appeal of the missionaries resulted in official reports being
called for. A thorough inquiry was made, from which it
appeared that the distress was severest in the central portions of
the district, while in those parts in which much of the land is
devoted to date trees, chillies, tobacco, and other of the more
lucrative crops, the distress was least felt. On the 30th April
1866, it was reported that the suffering was much less in the
neighbourhood of Kushtiā, Chuādāngā and Meherpur than in
other parts. " Regarding the rest of the district," the Collector
stated, " all accounts agree that there is great distress. There is
no famine, for grain is to be had, but there is very little money
to buy it at the prevailing prices. For some months the poor
(and in this word I include all the working classes) have not had
more than one meal a day, and it is to be feared that many have
not had even that."

On receipt of this information, Government sanctioned the
expenditure of Rs. 20,000 on road-making and other relief-
works. In May public meetings were held at Krishnagar,
Rānāghāt and Chuādāngā, and subscriptions were raised for the
relief of the sufferers. Before the end of the month relief works
had been started at different places where most needed, and a sum
of Rs. 5,000 was assigned to the district by the Government from
the unexpended balance of the North-West Provinces Famine
Fund. In June the distress became severe, and it was calculated
that about 2,500 persons were employed on the special relief works,
and on public works of all kinds about 4,000. In August a
further sum of Rs. 30,000 was granted for relief works. Kitchens
were established at different places for the distribution of cooked
food, and in some few instances allowances were made to a limited
number of people at their own homes. The general distress
began to diminish in August, when the early rice crop, which is
extensively grown in the district, began to come into the market.
In the beginning of September steps were taken to gradually
contract the relief operations, and in October only three or four
centres remained open in the part of the district which had
suffered most. Relief works were suspended on 10th October,
but it was found necessary to resume them for a time in November,

as the cold weather crop did not afford so much employment as was expected. In the western part of the district the distress caused by the famine was aggravated by floods from the Bhāgirathi, which almost totally destroyed about 18,000 acres of rice. The aggregate daily number of persons who received gratuitous relief throughout the operations was returned at 601,123, and the aggregate daily number employed on relief works was 337,059 including those employed up to February 1867, in order to finish some works of great public importance. The average daily number employed during the last week of May was 550; during the last week of June, 4,415; during the last week of July, 12,059; during the last week of September, 460. The total expenditure on gratuitous relief was Rs. 35,488, of which Rs. 24,500 was provided by Government and the balance raised by private subscriptions. The expenditure on relief works was Rs. 48,000. As regards the method of payment to persons attending relief works the Collector reported that no wholesale contractors were employed; "the work-people were paid direct, generally by daily wages, which varied according to sex and age from three pice to ten pice, but sometimes by task work. Payment in food was attempted once or twice, but it was found that charitable relief gave quite enough in that respect, and money payments prevailed everywhere."

The district suffered again from famine in 1874. Great distress had been caused by floods in 1871. The following year was on the whole prosperous, though there were not wanting periods of unpropitious weather or circumstances of partial failure in some of the crops; it was not however, a bumper season, nor such as to make good all the losses which had been incurred in the preceding year. The rainfall in 1873 was both deficient in quantity, and unseasonably distributed, the most marked feature being the failure in September and October, in which months only five inches fell. The effects on the harvest varied remarkably in different localities; in some the early rice crop was excellent, in others it was much below the average; but the winter rice on high lands completely failed, though a fair outturn was obtained in marshy lands. Taking the whole district, the early rice probably gave an average outturn, while the outturn of the winter rice did not exceed one-third of what it usually yielded. The area affected covered 528 square miles and comprised the whole of thanas Kāliganj and Nākāsipārā, three-fourths of Tehata and Chāprā, and one-fourth of Kotwāli, the last-named being the tract adjoining the Nākāsipārā thāna severe distress was, in fact, practically confined to that portion

Famine of 1874.

of the district, which is known as the Kālantar. Relief works were opened in February 1874, and were maintained until September. The average daily number of persons who attended them varied from 1,662 in February to 5,006 in July. The amount expended on relief works was Rs. 1,39,712, and in gratuitous relief Rs. 54,000. In addition, 264 tons of food-grains were distributed in charitable relief works and 115 tons advanced on loan, also the sum of Rs. 1,30,662 was expended in cash loans.

Famine of 1897.   The famine of 1896-97 affected the district much more severely. As usual the Kālantar, in which nothing but *āman* rice is grown, suffered the most. The average outturn of the *āman* crop in the district during the preceding nine years was only 8 annas, nearly 3 annas worse than in any other district in Bengal: in the years 1894 and 1895 it was 12½ and 7½ annas respectively: in 1896 it was not more than 2 annas, as owing to the failure of the monsoon and the absence of the usual inundations, there was no moisture to swell the grain. The average outturn of the *aus* rice during the preceding nine years was under 10 annas, and in 1895 it was 9 annas; in 1896 the outturn was only 6 annas. The portion of the district which was first affected was the Kālantar, in which a test work was opened as early as 15th November. During January relief works had to be opened in thanas Karimpur and Daulatpur. Four more thanas, viz., Chāprā, Gāngni, Meherpur and Nāopārā, were affected during the following months, and, finally, between June and September it was found necessary to provide work, though not gratuitous relief, in thanas Ālamdāngā and Dāmurhudā. The total area affected covered 1,182 square miles, with a population of 625,840. The distress was intense over 503 square miles with a population of 266,777. Relief works were open from the middle of November 1896 till the middle of September 1897: they were attended in all by close on three million workers, who excavated 105 million cubic feet of earth at a cost of 3⅓ lakhs of rupees: this large amount of earthwork cost only 6 per cent. more than it would have at ordinary rates, which compares very favourably with the result obtained in the 1866 famine, when it was estimated that the earthwork cost double the ordinary rates. The average daily attendance on the relief works ranged from 573 in the last week of November 1896 to 29,545 in the third week in June 1897. Five major works were taken up by the Public Works Department, and 48 minor works under Civil Agency. Among the former the most important was the excavation of a channel to connect the Bhairab with the Mātābhāngā near Shikārpur; this was finished in time to carry the flood waters of the Mātābhāngā into the Bhairab, which greatly improved for a time the water-supply of a large part of the Meherpur Subdivision : the canal, however, has since then silted up to a great extent, and the Bhairab has lapsed into its old condition of stagnancy.

Gratuitous relief was afforded from January till September. The aggregate number of persons so relieved was rather over six millions. The daily average relieved ranged from 1,675 in the third week in January to 77,233 in the third week in June. No gratuitous relief was found necessary in the affected portion of the Chuādāngā Subdivision. The only form which gratuitous relief from Government funds took was the grant of doles of cleaned rice at the rate of half and quarter of a seer per diem for adults and children respectively. In return for the doles, those who were fit for light work were required to either twist $3\frac{1}{2}$ seers of jute into string, or spin one seer of cotton into thread, per week. Some of the string and cotton thus obtained was issued to a few weavers who were in distress, and the matting and cloths woven by them were sold. From 1st August kitchens for the issue of cooked food to the dependents of workers were opened. Poor-houses were very sparingly used. The following paragraph is taken from the chapter dealing with gratuitous relief in the final report on the famine submitted by the Collector.

"Very few general remarks would appear necessary. It was found in this district that the exaction of a task in return for doles made little or no difference to the number of applicants for relief, though it caused Government very considerable extra expense. If circle officers do their duty properly there should be no need to impose a task unless some task could be devised by which Government at any rate would not be a loser. These remarks do not of course apply to artizans. The system of sub-circle officers has worked well. Before it was introduced, circle officers had to spend so much of their time in the purely mechanical duty of superintending the issue of doles, that they were unable to give sufficient attention to the extremely important work of careful house-to-house visitation. The system of relieving dependents of relief workers upon the works does not appear satisfactory ; it is liable to abuse and is also rather hard upon the dependents themselves, in that they have to undergo a considerable amount of exposure to the weather. It is desirable that gratuitous relief and relief to workers should be kept entirely separate, and consequently it is, in my opinion, better that dependents of relief workers should be relieved in their own homes."

The total expenditure on relief was about $8\frac{1}{4}$ lakhs of rupees, of which $3\frac{1}{4}$ lakhs were expended on the wages of workers, and $3\frac{1}{2}$ lakhs on gratuitous relief; the expenditure works out to an average of a trifle over one anna per diem per person relieved.

In the chapter on general remarks and recommendations in the Collector's final report, the following passage occurs :—

"The famine of 1896-97 was far more severe in this district than was that of 1873-74. Notwithstanding this, it was found possible in the present famine to close Government relief a month to six weeks earlier than was possible in 1873-74. As stated, however, under chapter VII, I believe that it was mainly because by somewhat liberal administration during the time of cultivation of the *aus* crop, the people were enabled to obtain a better outturn than would otherwise have been possible, that it was not necessary to continue Government relief for a month or six weeks more. There are in my opinion no indications that the people have shown in the present famine increased resources and more resisting power than in previous famines. The people of the Kālantar are all wretchedly poor and hopelessly in debt; the great majority of them hold lands under the *utbandi* system, and being practically tenants-at-will, are entirely in the hands of zamindārs. In fact, under present circumstances, there is no reason for supposing that their power of resisting famine has in any single way increased during the last 20 years."

Distress of 1908.
Famine conditions prevailed again in the district in the year 1908, though it was not found necessary to formally declare famine under the Code. The rainfall in 1907 was very similar to that in 1896, the most prominent feature being the almost complete failure of the monsoon in the months of September and October, whereby the outturn of the *āman* rice was reduced to only 13 per cent. of a normal crop. The distress affected an area of about 800 square miles, with a population of 435,000 ; as usual, the Kālantar was the tract to suffer the most. A few relief works were opened in January, but they did not attract many labourers, and it was not until March that the pinch became sufficiently severe to cause the people to come in at all freely. In April about 3,400 persons attended the relief works daily, and this number rose to 5,677 in June, after which the attendance gradually fell off until September, by the end of which month it was found unnecessary to keep the relief works open any longer. A total sum of Rs. 9,859 was expended on gratuitous relief, but there was some confusion in the accounts which renders it impossible to state the total number of persons so relieved. No kitchens or poor-houses were opened. A total sum of Rs. 6,69,535

was distributed in loans under the Land Improvement and Agriculturists' Loans Acts, principally during the months of April and May, and the Collector remarks that this "put heart into the people, prevented demoralization, and stimulated agricultural operations."

The total amount expended on relief works was Rs. 1,59,414, and the total amount of earth-work executed was $63\frac{1}{4}$ million cubic feet; this gives the remarkably low rate of Rs. 2-5-6 per thousand cubic feet. The piece-work system was adopted, and the average daily wage earned amounted to 3 annas 2 pies owing to the adoption of this system, the expenditure on gratuitous relief was much less than it would otherwise have been.

There was far less actual lack of food than was the case in 1896-97, and no steps were necessary to bring grain into the affected area. The tendency which has been observed in other districts towards a considerable increase in the power of the people to resist famine conditions was clearly indicated in Nadiā in 1908; for though the failure of crops in 1907 was very similar to that in 1896, and the prices of food grains were considerably higher in 1908 than they were in 1897, yet the distress appears to have been far deeper in the earlier than in the latter of these two years.

CHAPTER VII.

RENTS, WAGES AND PRICES.

RENTS.

Rents of 1786.

BETWEEN the years 1786 and 1795 A.D. lists of rates of rent were filed by the landholders, and the following figures, which have been compiled from those lists, show the rates which then prevailed in twenty parganas of the district for the varying descriptions of lands which bear the most important crops. They are of interest in that they were the basis upon which the permanent settlement of 1793 was made. In considering them it should be remembered that the local bigha is equivalent to one-third of an acre. The figures noted against each crop represent the rate of rent in Indian currency per bigha of the land upon which that crop is grown.

	Aus rice.		Aman rice.		Home-stead.			Tobacco.			Jute.		Sugar-cane.			Pán.		
	A.	P.	A.	P.	Rs.	A.	P.	Rs.	A.	P.	A.	P.	Rs.	A.	P.	Rs.	A.	P.
Ashrafābād	9	7	7	3	1	3	6	...			...		1	7	7	...		
Bagwān ...	8	3	9	9	0	14	9	0	14	9	8	5	.	...		3	4	C
Faizullāpur	10	0	5	0	1	6	0	...			. .		...			...		
Hāvilishahr	9	9	9	9	1	10	0	...			...		1	6	9	...		
Jaipur ...	6	6	6	6	0	9	9	0	13	0	...		1	10	0	2	7	0
Khosālpur	4	0	5	0	2	4	0	...			...		1	8	0	3	0	0
Kusdaha ...	8	3	6	0	0	14	9	1	0	3	11	6	1	13	3	1	10	0
Krishnagar	9	9	8	3	0	14	9	0	14	9	...		1	13	3	3	4	0
Kubāzpur...	8	3	4	3	1	3	6	...			...		...			...		
Mahatpur...	9	9	7	3	0	14	9	0	14	9	..		1	13	3	..		
Mamjuāni	9	9	9	2	0	14	9	0	14	9	9	9	1	13	3	4	8	0
Matiāri ...	6	6	5	0	0	9	9	0	13	0	...		...			...		
Nabadwip	9	9	13	0	1	3	6	0	13	0	...		...			7	4	0
Pājnaur ...	9	9	7	3	1	3	6	1	10	0	...		1	13	3	4	1	0
Pāt Mahal	14	0	8	0	1	0	0	...			...		...			...		
Plassey ...	11	9	...		1	2	0	0	9	9	...		0	11	6	3	10	8
Rājpur ...	10	0	5	0	1	8	0	...			...		...			...		
Sāntipur ...	9	9	7	3	0	14	9	0	14	9	...		1	3	6	3	4	0
Srinagar ...	9	9	8	3	0	14	9	1	2	0	...		1	13	3	...		
Ukhrā ...	9	9	7	3	1	3	6	...			...		...			...		

No records exist to show the rates which prevailed in the other parganas.

In July 1872 the Government of Bengal called for a return
showing the prevailing rates of rent then paid by the cultivators
for the ordinary descriptions of land on which the common crops
are grown, and the following information is condensed from the
report which was submitted by the Collector of Nadiā. For
ordinary land producing rice or miscellaneous crops, the *utbandi*,
or year by year, rates are given; and as these rates were only
charged according to the quantity of land actually under
cultivation, they are higher than by the *jama*, or leasehold
system, under which land is taken for a term of years at an
annual rate, which has to be paid whether the land be cultivated
or not. The Collector stated that, as a general rule throughout
the district, the rate for *jama* lands was about half that for
utbandi. Garden or orchard lands, however, were never leased
on the *utbandi* system, and for such the *jama* or leasehold rates
have been given. This explanation must be borne in mind in
perusing the following list of rents for the several subdivisions of
the district:—

(1) Head-quarters subdivision, in which lie the following
parganas:—

1. Bagwān.	14. Nadiā.
2. Belgāon.	15. Palāshi.
3. Faizullāpur.	16. Pātmahal.
4. Islāmpur.	17. Rājpur.
5. Jehāngirābād.	18. Raipur.
6. Khosālpur.	19. Sāntipur.
7. Kubāzpur.	20. Taraf Munsifpur.
8. Mahatpur.	21. Umarpur.
9. Mahmudālipur.	22. Umarpur, taraf Digam-
10. Mamjuāni.	barpur.
11. Matiāri.	23. Umarpur Digambarpur.
12. Manoharshāhi.	24. Ukhrā, Chakla Krish-
13. Munsifpur.	nagar.

Ordinary high lands, producing *āman* rice only, or *aus*
rice, with a second crop of pulses, oilseeds, etc., or if sown
in jute, 12 annas to Re. 1-4 per bigha; the same land, if cultivated with pepper or indigo, from Re. 1 to Re. 1-4 per bigha;
the same land if under sugarcane, Re. 1-4 to Rs. 2 per bigha;
very deep marshy land in which the latest winter rice is sown
on the chance of its not being entirely submerged, from 6 annas
to 12 annas per bigha; exceptionally high lands, near homesteads, frequently formed by elevations made for houses, and
sides of tanks, and artificial mounds on which tobacco, betel-leaf,

cotton, mulberry, garden produce, etc., are grown, from Rs. 2-4 to Rs. 2-12 per bigha; the same land when used for plantain gardens from Re. 1 to Rs. 2 per bigha; *jama* rates for orchards of mango, jack, or bamboos, Rs. 2-8 to Rs. 5 per bigha.

(2) Chuádángá Subdivision, in which lie the following parganas :—

1.	Ashrafábád.	10.	Matiári.
2.	Bagwán.	11.	Nandalálpur.
3.	Burapárá.	12.	Nagarbánká.
4.	Husainujiál.	13.	Obania
5.	Hunkhani.	14.	Rájpur.
6.	Kasimnagar.	15.	Sháhujiál.
7.	Kasimpur.	16.	Taraf Munsifpur.
8.	Mahmudsháhi.	17.	Ukhrá, Chakla Krishna-
9.	Makimpur.		gar.
	18. Umarpur.		

High lands growing *áman* rice only, or *aus* rice with a second crop of pulses, oilseeds, etc., or for jute only, from 12 annas to Re. 1-4 per bigha; the same land, if cultivated with pepper or indigo, from Re. 1 to Re. 1-4 per bigha; the same kind of land, growing sugarcane, from Re. 1-8 to Rs. 2-4 per bigha; very deep marshy lands, in which late winter rice is sown, none in cultivation; exceptionally high lands near homesteads, on which tobacco, betel-leaf, cotton, turmeric and garden produce is grown, from Re. 1-8 to Rs. 2-12 per bigha; plantain gardens Rs. 2 per bigha; *jama* rates for jack, mango and tamarind orchards, Rs. 5 per bigha.

(3) Ranághát Subdivision, in which lie the following parganas :—

1.	Arsá.	12.	Pájnaur.
2.	Faizullápur.	13.	Pájnaur Srinagar.
3.	Hálikánda Pájnaur.	14.	Pátmahal.
4.	Hávilishahar.	15.	Ránihati.
5.	Hávilishahar and	16.	Raipur.
	Arsá.	17.	Selampur.
6.	Jaipur.	18.	Srinagar.
7.	Jaipur Atali.	19.	Taraf Sántipur.
8.	Kaugáchi.	20.	Ukhrá.
9.	Khosálpur.	21.	Ukhrá, Chakla Krishna-
10.	Krishnagar.		gar.
11.	Mamjuáni.	22.	Ukhrá and Pájnaur.

High lands, growing *áman* rice only, or *aus* rice, with a second crop of pulses, oilseeds, etc., or jute only, from 8 annas to Re. 1-1 per bigha; same description of land, if cultivated with pepper or indigo, 10 annas to Re. 1-1 per bigha ; same land under sugar-cane from Re. 1 to Re. 1-11 per bigha ; exceptionally high land near homesteads, on which tobacco, betel-leaf, cotton, turmeric, garden produce and plantains are grown, from Re. 1-4 to Rs. 2-8 per bigha; the same land on which betel-leaf alone is grown from Rs. 2-2 to Rs. 3-6 per bigha.   Potatoes were grown in this subdivision only. *Jama* rates for mango, jack and tamarind plantations, from Re. 1-11 to Rs. 2-4 per bigha.

(4) Kushtiā Subdivision, in which lie the following parganas :—

1.	Anupampur.	23.	Jhaudiā.
2.	Aurangābād.	24.	Kāntanagar.
3.	Begamābād.	25.	Kāsimnagar.
4.	Bhāndārdaha.	26.	Kururia.
5.	Baradi.	27.	Kāsimpur.
6.	Bāriā.	28.	Laduāni.
7.	Bāmankarna.	29.	Laskarpur.
8.	Bara Fatehjangpur.	30.	Makimpur.
9.	Brāhmapur.	31.	Mahmudshāhi.
10.	Birāhimpur.	32.	Nagarpotā.
11.	Brajamula.	33.	Nagarbānkā.
12.	Bajuras Mahābatpur.	34.	Nāzir Ināyetpur.
13.	Bhabānanda Diar.	35.	Rājpur.
14.	Bhaturia.	36.	Rukunpur.
15.	Fazilpur.	37.	Sankardih.
16.	Gajnābhipur.	38.	Shāhujiāl.
17.	Hapania.	39.	Shāh Jahānnagar.
18.	Husainujiāl.	40.	Sherpur Beriā.
19.	Hunkhani.	41.	Sadaki.
20.	Islāmpur.	42.	Tappa Chapila, pargana Bhaturia.
21.	Jahāngirābād.		
22.	Jiārakha.	43.	Tārāujiāl.
		44.	Tārāgunia.

High land, growing *aman* rice only or *aus* rice with a second crop of pulses or oilseeds, etc., or jute only, from 12 annas to Re. 1 per bigha; the same land growing indigo, the same rates; pepper or chillies were hardly ever grown in this subdivision; sugarcane land, Re. 1-13 per bigha ; very low marshy land on which late winter rice is grown, of which there was a good deal in the Kushtiā Subdivision, from 3 to 4 annas per bigha; exceptionally high land near homesteads on which tobacco, betel-leaf, cotton, turmeric, garden produce and plantains are grown, from Re. 1-7 to Rs. 2-3 per bigha ; *jama* rate for mango, jack and date orchards, Rs. 3-8 per bigha.

(5) Meherpur Subdivision, in which lie the following *par-ganas* :—

1.	Ashrafâbad.	14.	Kâjipur.
2.	Bagwân.	15.	Mânikdihi.
3.	Belgâon.	16.	Nandalâlpur.
4.	Betâi.	17.	Nagarpotâ,
5.	Bhândârdaha.	18.	Patkâbâriâ.
6.	Dogâchi.	19.	Palâshi.
7.	Fatehjangpur.	20.	Pipulbariâ.
8.	Goâs.	21.	Râjpur.
9.	Gurar Hât.	22.	Shâhujiâl.
10.	Husainujiâl.	23.	Shâhbâzpur.
11.	Hunkhani.	24.	Taraf Bati.
12.	Hauspur.	25.	Taraf Munsifpur.
13.	Kâsimnagar.	26.	Târâguniâ.

27. Ukhrâ, Chakla Krishnagar.

High lands, growing *aman* rice only, or *aus* rice with a second crop of pulses, oilseeds, etc., or jute only, from 6 annas to Re. 1-4 per bigha; for land growing pepper or indigo, the rates were about the same; sugarcane from Re. 1 to Rs. 2 per bigha; exceptionally high land near homesteads, growing miscellaneous crops as noted above, from Re. 1 to Rs. 2-8 per bigha; *jama* rates for mango, jack, tamarind and bamboos, from Rs. 5 to Rs. 6-4 per bigha.

During the eighty years separating the periods when these two sets of rates prevailed, rent generally rose at least 30 per cent., and in some instances as much as 100 per cent.

Current rents.

The *utbandi* system appears to be gradually giving way to the leasehold system, but it still covers about 65 per cent. of the cultivated land. This tenure is not peculiar to the Nadiâ district, but is specially common in it. Under it the tenant pays rent only for the land which he cultivates each year, and he cannot acquire occupancy rights unless he tills the same land for twelve years consecutively, which, in fact, he rarely does. Meanwhile the landlord can raise the rent at his pleasure, and if the tenant refuses to pay, he can be ejected. This tenure deprives the tenant of any incentive to improve the land, and at the same time encourages rack-renting. The land generally being sandy and of poor quality, it has frequently to be left fallow to recover some degree of fertility; during these periods, of course, the landlord receives no rent where the *utbandi* tenure is in force. This being so, the rate of rent for land under the latter tenure is naturally higher than for leasehold land, for which the ryot has to pay his rent every year, whether or not he has been able

to put it under crops. In 1872, as has been stated above, the
rate of rent for *utbandi* lands was about twice as high as that for
leasehold lands. Since then the disparity has increased, and it is
reported that as much as Rs. 4 to Rs. 8 per bigha is now paid for
utbandi lands, as compared with 5 annas to 14 annas for similar
lands held on long or permanent leases. The ordinary rate during
recent years paid by occupancy ryots for rice land varies from 7
annas to Re. 1-8 per bigha, and it is thus clear that the increase
in the rate observed up to 1872 has been more than maintained.

About the year 1850 the wages of ordinary labourers Wages.
were from 1½ to 2½ annas per diem; of agricultural labourers
from 2 to 3 annas; and of ordinary masons, about 2½ annas. In
1870 coolies were earning from 3 to 4 annas; agricultural labourers about the same; masons 4 to 5 annas; and blacksmiths and
carpenters about 4 annas. In 1890 agricultural labourers were
earning about 6 annas per diem, and masons, carpenters and
blacksmiths from 10 annas to Re. 1-4. At present (1909) day
labourers receive from 4 annas to 8 annas per diem, and, in times
of great demand, as much as 10 annas; masons, carpenters and
blacksmiths receive from 12 annas to Re. 1. There has thus
been an almost continuous rise in the wages of labour, both
skilled and unskilled, during the last sixty years. According to
the census of 1901 the percentage of the population engaged
upon general labour is as high as 17.

Agricultural labourers are frequently paid in kind when
employed on reaping, and arrangements are occasionally made
under which the labourers employed in cutting a field of paddy
receive, in lieu of wages, a proportion of the crop varying with
the state of the labour market. Women seldom engage in
agricultural labour, but children are regularly employed on
looking after cattle.

The following statement shows the number of seers per rupee Prices.
at which the three principal food-crops grown in the district sold
during each quinquennium from 1861 onwards :—

			Common rice.	Gram.	Wheat.
1861-65	...	...	22	28	19
1866-70	...	...	19	17	16
1871-75	...	...	17	23	16
1876-80	...	...	14	19	15
1881-85	...	...	17	23	16
1886-90	...	...	16	22	15
1891-95	...	...	13	18	15
1896-00	...	...	12	17	13
1901-05	...	...	12	18	15

During this period the average annual price of rice was cheaper than 20 seers for the rupee in three years only, namely in 1869, when it was 24 seers for the rupee, and in 1881 and 1882, when it was 21 seers. The average annual price was dearer than 12 seers for the rupee in ten years; namely, 1874 (11·46 seers), 1879 (11 seers), 1892 (10 65 seers), 1893 (11·64 seers), 1897 (8·87 seers), 1900 to 1903 inclusive (11·30 to 11·90 seers), and 1906 (8·93 seers). The high prices of 1874 and 1897 were, of course, due to the famines which visited the district in those years; those in 1879 were probably due to the famine of 1877-78 over a large part of India; those of 1892 and 1893 were probably due to the famine of 1891-92 in Bihar and other parts. There appears to be no special reason to account for the high prices in the other years mentioned, except the fact that the crop was not a good one in Nadiā and the neighbouring districts, and the general tendency to rise in prices.

MATERIAL CONDI- TION OF THE PEOPLE. The following extract is taken from Hunter's Statistical Account of Nadiā, as showing the material condition of the people in the early seventies of the nineteenth century :—

" The condition of the people, as regards dress and other com- forts, has of late years steadily improved. A well-to-do shop- keeper dresses during the warm weather in a waist-cloth (*dhuti*) and a loose sheet (*chadar*), both of thin cotton, costing together about 4s., and a pair of shoes costing about 2s. During the winter a stout cotton *chadar*, a woollen wrapper, or a coarse shawl takes the place of the thin muslin *chadar*. Generally speaking, he lives in a brick-built house, having four or five rooms, contain- ing as furniture two or three plank bedsteads (*takhtposh*), with one or two wooden chests for keeping clothes, and some brass plates, drinking vessels, etc. The female members of his house- hold wear a single cotton cloth, five yards long, with a broad stripe near the margin (*sāri*), throughout the whole year, with gold and silver ornaments to the value of £20 or £30. The widows, of whom one or two are generally to be found in a household, have, of course, no ornaments.

" The ordinary food of his household consists of rice, split peas (*dāl*), fish, vegetables and milk. The Collector estimates the following to be the monthly expenses in a middling-size household of a well-to-do trader:—Rice, two and a half hundredweights (three and a half maunds), value 18s.; split peas, 40 lbs. (half a maund), value 4s.; fish 5s.; vegetables, 4s.; oil, 5s.; clarified butter (*ghi*), 2s.; fuel, 4s.; fodder for cows, of which two or three are usually kept, 4s.; salt, 1s. 3d.; spices, including *pān*, 4s.; clothes, 8s.; sweetmeats, 4s.; a servant to look after the cows, 4s.; contingencies and other expenses, 8s.; total, £3 15s. 3d. This is the scale for a fairly prosperous shopkeeper or village merchant.

"An average husbandman dresses in a coarser *dhuti* and carries a bathing towel (*gāmchā*) over his shoulders in lieu of a *chadar*. Occasionally he wears a coarse muslin sheet or shawl and wraps it round his waist. In the winter he adds to his dress a thick Madras cloth *chadar*. He lives in a *bāri* or inclosed homestead, containing a hut which serves as a bed room, a cattle shed, and an outside shed for the master of the house to sit and receive his friends. The walls of the huts are built of mud or split bamboos, or bamboo mats plastered over with mud; the roofs are made of a bamboo framework covered with thatch-grass. The furniture of the house consists of one or two plank bed-steads (*takhtposh*) and a wooden chest. The ordinary food of a husbandman's household consists of coarse rice, split peas (*dāl*), vegetables and milk. Generally speaking, he obtains the rice, peas and vegetables from the land he cultivates, but has to buy fish, oil, salt, spices and clothes. As for fuel, the dung of his cattle, and the stalks of certain plants, such as *arhar*, which he cultivates, supply his wants in this respect. The Collector estimates the monthly expenses of such a household (not includ-ing the value of the rice, pulses or vegetables, which the head of the family grows himself) to be as under—Fish, 2s.; extra vege-tables, 1s.; oil, 3s.; salt, 1s.; spices, including *pān*, 3s.; fodder for cattle, over and above grazing, 3s.; clothes, 4s.; rent, 6s.; contin-gencies and other expenses, 4s.; total £1 7s. Such a scale would show a total outlay of about £2, if we add the home-grown rice and split peas. This, however, is the scale of living of a prosperous farmer. The majority of cultivators do not spend anything like that amount on the maintenance of their house-holds. A husbandman with five acres, which is a fair-sized holding, and as much as a man with a single pair of oxen can till, spends under £1 a month including everything."

Though there has been some improvement in the material condition of the people of this district, especially in their power of resistance to famine conditions, there can be no doubt that they are not as well off as the inhabitants of the neighbouring districts. This fact is probably due in the main to three causes—first, the unhealthy climate which must re-act unfavourably upon both the physical and moral qualities of the people; secondly, the compara-tively unfertile nature of the soil, and thirdly, the precarious tenure upon which so large a proportion of the land is held. There seems but little immediate chance of a marked improvement in any of these respects, and it is probable that for many years to come the material condition of the people of the Nadia district must compare unfavourably with that of the inhabitants of the other districts in the Presidency Division. The class who have suffered most during the recent years are the upper middle class, or *bhadralok*, especially those with small fixed incomes, who find it very difficult to keep up appearances and maintain their traditional style of living in these days of high prices. Landless labourers, of whom there are many in the district, also suffer, notwithstanding the marked rise in the wages which they receive. On the whole there has perhaps been some improvement in the standard of living, and simple luxuries are more commonly used than they were, but the vast majority lead but a hand-to-mouth existence.

CHAPTER VIII.

OCCUPATIONS, MANUFACTURES AND TRADES.

ACCORDING to the statistics obtained at the census of 1901, the number of persons in the district supported by agriculture is 934,451, which represents 56 per cent. of the total population. Of this number 33 per cent. are actual workers, and the remaining 67 per cent. dependents. Among the workers the largest groups are (1) rent-payers, who number 271,000, exclusive of 15,000 who are partially non-agriculturists ; (2) agricultural labourers, who number 25,000, and (3) rent-receivers, who number 12,000. The next most numerous class consists of those who are supported by the various industries; these number 264,290 or 15·8 per cent. of the total population. Forty per cent. of this class of the population are actual workers and amongst them the largest groups are (1) fishermen and fish-dealers 22,500, (2) milkmen and dairy farmers, 9,500, (3) cotton-weavers, 8,300, (4) oil-pressers and sellers 8,000, (5) rice-pounders and huskers 8,000, and (6) grain and pulse-dealers 7,000. The professional classes number 38,420, which represents 2·3 per cent. of the total population. Of these 41 per cent. are actual workers and 59 per cent. dependents. In this class are included 4,400 priests and 2,000 persons engaged in the practice of medicine. Commerce has only 16,173 followers, of whom 34 per cent. are actual workers; the commercial classes form 1 per cent. of the total population. Among those engaged in other occupations are 90,000 general labourers, many of whom, however, probably are mainly agricultural labourers, and 5,000 boatmen.

There is a great disinclination among the inhabitants of Nadiā to allow their women to work in the fields ; this is particularly noticeable among the Muhammadans, who form the majority of the population, and some trouble was caused in the 1897 famine owing to the difficulty of getting able-bodied women of the lower orders to attend the relief works. Only 800 female

appear among the 25,000 actual workers employed on agricultural labour. The occupations on which females are engaged
may be grouped into three classes; those which are followed by
women independently without reference to the work of their male
relatives, such as midwifery, domestic service, rice-pounding, etc.;
those which are supplementary to their husbands' occupation,
such as cotton-spinning carried on by the wives of weavers, and
the selling of fruit, vegetables, milk and fish by the wives of
fruit and vegetables growers, cow-keepers and fishermen;] and,
lastly, those in which both sexes work together, such as basket-
weaving, and, to a smaller extent, general labour. The occupations which females follow, either independently or as a supplement to some kindred employment of their male relatives, are
generally distinguished by two characteristics—their simplicity,
and the small amount of physical labour which they involve.
The only largely followed occupations in the Nadiā district in
which the females exceed the males are domestic service, grain and
pulsedealing, rice-pounding and religious mendicancy.

MANU-
FACTURES.
Cotton
weaving.
At the end of the eighteenth and beginning of the nineteenth
century, Sāntipur was the centre of a great and prosperous
weaving industry. It was of sufficient importance to be the
head-quarters of a Resident under the East India Company, and
during the first few years of the nineteenth century the Company
purchased here £150,000 worth of cotton cloths annually. By
1813 the industry had begun to decline, being unable to face the
competition of cheaper piece-goods from Manchester, and in 1825
it received a severe shock from the introduction of British thread,
which has since been used almost to the entire extinction of
country yarn. Another great industry which flourished during
the first-half of the nineteenth century, but has since been extin-
guished, was the manufacture of indigo. A full account of the
rise and fall of this industry has been given in the chapter on
History in this volume, and a reference may be made to that for
further information on the subject. There are now, in the
twentieth century, no large organized industries in the district,
which therefore possesses no commercial importance. Generally
speaking, the local artizans supply only the necessaries of life,
e.g., food and drink of the commonest description, coarse cloth,
roughly constructed boats, brass utensils, etc.

In 1898 the District Officer reported that "in almost all villages
in this district there are a few families of Tantis and Jolāhas.
They turn out coarse cloth for the use of cultivators, but their
number is gradually decreasing, and the profession is deteriorat-
ing on account of English-manufactured cloth which is cheaper.

In several villages which had a reputation for doing business in weaving, this industry is altogether abolished, such as Chākdaha, Tehata, Dāmurhudā and Dagalbi, though in some of these places the profession is still lingering." The main centres of the industry in the district are Sāntipur, Kushtiā, Kumārkhāli, Harinarāyanpur, Meherpur and Krishnagar. The only place in which fine muslin is manufactured is Sāntipur; the particular speciality of this place is known as Sāntipur cloth, and it is specially admired for its thin texture, and embroidered and flowered work. Mr. Banerjie, in his monograph on the cotton fabrics of Bengal, published in 1898, says that the outturn of the cotton cloths in Sāntipur was then worth about $3\frac{1}{4}$ lakhs of rupees per annum; if those figures are correct, there has been a very great decline during the last ten years, for the value of the present (1909) outturn is not nearly so much.

The only places in which the brassware industry is carried on to any extent are Nabadwip and Meherpur, and even in these two places no really fine work is attempted; practically nothing but utensils for ordinary household purposes, and for use in religious ceremonies, is turned out. Brassware.

Sugar-refining by European methods has been tried in the district, but it proved unsuccessful. There are, however, some refineries in native hands at Sāntipur and Alamdāngā. Sugar manufacture.

The sugar dealt with is almost entirely that derived from the juice of the date-palm. The following account of the manufacture of this class of sugar is taken from Mr. O'Malley's Gazetteer Volume on the Khulnā District :—" The first process consists of tapping the tree, which begins when the tree is ripe and continues each year thereafter. When the rainy season is over and there is no more fear of rain, the cultivator cuts off the leaves growing out of the trunk for one-half of its circumference, and thus leaves bare a surface measuring about 10 or 12 inches each way. This surface is at first a brilliant white, but becomes by exposure quite brown, and has the appearance of coarse matting. The leaves are cut off by a man who climbs up the tree supporting himself by a strong rope, which he passes round the tree and his own loins. He slides the rope up and down with his hands, setting his feet firmly against the tree, and throwing the weight of his body on the rope. In this manner his hands are free, and he cuts the tree with a sharp knife like a bill-hook.

" After the tree has remained exposed for a few days, the tapping is performed by making a cut into the exposed surface in the shape of a broad V, and then cutting down the surface inside the angle thus formed. The sap exudes from this triangular surface, and runs down to the angle where a thin bamboo is inserted, in order to catch the dropping sap and carry it out as by a spout. Below the end of the bamboo an earthenware pot is hung at sunset, and the juice of the tree runs down into it. In the morning before sunrise the pots are taken down, and are generally full. The juice is extracted three days in succession, and then the tree is 'allowed to rest six days, when the juice is again extracted for three days more.

"The next process consists of boiling the juice, and this every ryot does for himself, usually within the limits of the palm grove. Without boiling, the juice speedily ferments and becomes useless, but when once boiled down, it may be kept for long periods. The juice is therefore boiled at once in large pots placed on a perforated dome beneath which a strong fire is kept burning, the pared leaves of the trees being used with other fuel. The juice which was at first brilliant and limpid, become now a dark brown, half-viscid, half-solid mass called *gur*, which is easily poured when it is still warm, from the boiling pan into the *gharas* or earthenware pots in which it is ordinarily kept. It is then sold to refiners, and manufactured into sugar."

Minor manufactures. There is a factory at Kushtiá, under European management, in which are manufactured machines for pressing sugarcane on the well-known Bihia pattern. The ryots have taken readily to these machines, which are a vast improvement upon the primitive methods which were formerly adopted for extracting the juice from the cane. The machines are generally let out on hire, as the price of them is beyond the means of most cultivators. At Ghurni, a suburb of Krishnagar, clay figures of remarkable excellence are manufactured; they find a ready sale wherever offered, and have received medals at European exhibitions. Little or no manufactures are carried on in Nadiá in working up fibres or reeds into mats or baskets.

Fisheries. A not inconsiderable proportion of the population depend upon fishing for a livelihood :—The following description of the methods of capture employed is taken from Mr. O'Malley's book on Khulná:—"The methods employed for catching fish are both numerous and ingenious. One favourite engine consists of a large bag net suspended on two long bamboos stuck out at one side of the boat ; sometimes the boat with the net thus expanded under water is driven slowly against the current. Sometimes otters are tied by a rope to the boat, and trained to plunge about by the side of the net, so as to frighten fish into it.*

* Otters are rarely, if ever, used in Nadia.

The fisherman then raises the net quickly by standing on the inside ends of the bamboos, and thus gets all the fish that may be in it. Another common method (rather applicable to marshes than to rivers) is as follows. On the surface of the swamps, large patches of weed called *dhap* are formed, which on the subsidence of the water, sometimes float out of the marshes and so down streams. These patches the fishermen fix by placing stakes round their circumference, and then leave them for a day or two. The fish congregate beneath them, and the fishermen by drawing a net round the place and removing the weeds catch them in large quantities. On the borders of shallow rivers branches of trees are also placed in the water for the same purpose, viz., to attract fish to one place.   *   *   *

"The fishermen in the marshes often carry in their boats an instrument like a long broom, with spear heads in place of bristles. When they pass a big fish they dart this collection of prongs at it, and usually succeed in bringing it up impaled on one of its points. This, however, is not a regular, but only supplemental, mode of fishing, for men do not go out to fish armed solely with this weapon. On narrow shelving banks a round net is sometimes used. The fisherman goes along the bank, watching till he sees a place where some fish are lying. He then throws his net in such a manner that before touching the water it has spread out into a large circle. The edges of the net are heavily weighted with lead and falling on all sides of the fish imprison them. Cage-fishing by means of fixed cages of wicker work is also common. Every little streamlet, and even the surface drainage on the fields and ditches, show arrays of these traps placed so as to capture fish. The same method is used, but on a larger scale, in shallow and sluggish rivers, where, in many cases, lines of wicker traps may be seen stretched across the river from bank to bank. Another plan for capturing fish is by attracting them at night by a bright light and trapping them.

"The methods described above are used by single fishermen, or by a few men together. The fish, however, have sometimes to stand more formidable battues, when a party go out with nets or cages, and laying a large trap, drive into it many hundred fish at a time."

The exports from Nadiā consist mainly of its surplus crops, and TRADE. among these jute takes the foremost place. During the last two years the average export of jute has been close on one million maunds per annum, in addition to which some twenty thousand maunds of gunny bags were exported. About three-quarters of this large export is carried away by railway and the rest by water. Next to jute come gram and pulses, of which from one-quarter to one-half a million maunds are exported annually, the actual quantity varying with the outturn of the *rabi* crops. Un-refined sugar and *gur* between them form an important item in the list of exports ; in 1908-09 over 140,000 maunds of these items were exported. A considerable amount of linseed is grown in the district, and in good years the export of this article is not far short of 200,000 maunds. Other oilseeds are of little importance. The export of Indian made cotton goods is steadily decreasing, and in 1908-09 they only reached the inconsiderable total of 1,983 maunds.

Among imports the most important during the past two years have been rice and paddy, which between them have averaged nearly one and a quarter million maunds per annum. Other important articles of import are coal from Bardwān and Mān-bhum, and salt, kerosene oil and piece-goods from Calcutta. There has been of late years some increase in the use of small articles of luxury, such as umbrellas, shirts, coats, cigarettes and enamelled iron goods, and the import of these shows a corre-sponding rise.

Trading classes.

The principal castes engaged in commerce are Kāyasths, Telis, Bārnis, Sāhas, Mālos, Namasudras and Muhammadans.

Trade centres.

The chief railway trade centres are Chuādānga, Bagula, Rānā-ghāt, Dāmukdiā and Poradah : there are also less important centres at Darsana, Sibnibās, Kumārkhāli, Krishnagar, Debagram, Kushtiā and Chākdaha. Those of river traffic are Nabadwip, Kāliganj and Matiāri on the Bhāgirathi ; Karimpur, Tehata Andulia, Krishnagar and Swarupganj on the Jalangi ; Hānskhāli and Rānāghāt on the Churni ; Hāt Boāliā, Chuādāngā, Subalpur, Rāmnagar, Munshiganj, Dāmurhudā and Kissengunge on the Mātābhāngā ; Nonāganj on the Ichhāmati ; Alamdāngā on the Pangāsi ; and Kushtiā, Kumārkhāli and Khoksā on the Garai. Opportunity for trading purposes is freely taken of the numerous fairs and religious festivals which are held in the district. The best attended of these are the festivals held at Nabadwip in February and November ; at Sāntipur in November ; at Kuliā in January ; and at Ghoshpārā in March.

Trade routes.

The external trade of the district is carried on by the Eastern Bengal State Railway and its branches, and steamers and country boats on the rivers. A large amount of rice and paddy is also imported into the district by carts from Jessore and Khulnā. The internal trade is carried on by country boats and carts. The greater part of the trade, both import and export, is with Calcutta.

CHAPTER IX.

MEANS OF COMMUNICATION.

OF the five subdivisions in the district, all but Meherpur are traversed by at least one branch of the Eastern Bengal State Railway. The Meherpur subdivision is cut off from the railway and is unfortunate in its water communications as well; this subdivision is bounded on the north-east by the Mātābhāngā, and on the north-west by the Jalangi, which also cuts through a portion on the west, but the only river which traverses it is the Bhairab, and that is now so hopelessly silted up as to be useless as a means of communication except during the height of the rains. However, it is fairly well off in the way of roads, though it has only one road of the first class. The Rānāghāt subdivision is well served in every respect. Rānāghāt itself is an important junction on the Eastern Bengal State Railway; from this place the new branch leading to Murshidābād, and the central branch (formerly known as the Central Bengal Railway) both take off from the main line, the former roughly to the north-west and the latter in a direction slightly south of east. There is also the light railway which takes off from the east bank of the Churni, not far from Rānāghāt, and leads to Krishnagar *viâ* Sāntipur. As regards waterways there is the Hooghly which forms the eastern boundary of the subdivision, and throughout this part of its course is navigable by steamers throughout the year; there is also the Churni, which traverses the northern part of the subdivision and joins the Hooghly not far from Chākdaha. There are two first class roads, one from Rānāghāt leading to Sāntipur and the other from Chākdaha to the eastern boundary of the district. The Krishnagar subdivision is also very well served. It is traversed throughout its greater length by the Murshidābād branch of the Eastern Bengal State Railway; and, through the eastern portion, by part of the main line. It also has connection with Sāntipur by a light railway. As regards waterways it is bisected roughly from north to south by the Jalangi; its western boundary is the Bhāgirathi;

and towards the east it is traversed by the Churni. It has three first class roads, connecting the head-quarters station with Bagula on the east, the eastern bank of the Bhāgirathi opposite Nabadwip on the west and Sāntipur on the south; there are also good second class roads leading to the north and north-west. The Chuādāngā Subdivision is bisected by the main line of the Eastern Bengal State Railway, and is also served by the river Mātābhāngā from north to south, and by the river Kumār or Pangāsi on the north-eastern boundary. It is also traversed from north-east to south-west by a first class road, leading from Meherpur over the eastern boundary of the district into Jessore. The Kushtiā Subdivision is served by the main line of the Eastern Bengal State Railway from near Alamdāngā on the south to Dāmukdiā on the north, and by the Goālundo branch from the junction at Poradah to the eastern boundary of the district at Khoksā. It is almost completely surrounded by rivers, except for portions of the eastern boundary; the Padmā runs along the north and the Mātābhāngā along the west and south; the Kumārkhāli thana, which forms the north-eastern corner of the subdivision, is traversed by the Garai. As regards roads it is perhaps the least well served of the subdivisions.

Water communications. A full history of the river system of the district has been given in chapter I of this volume. Now that the railways have reached their present stage, the importance of maintaining a through connection by water between Calcutta and North-West India is no longer as paramount as it was. But the Nadiā rivers still have a good deal of local importance, and Government goes to a considerable expense to keep them open for navigation for as many months in the year as is possible. Several regular services of steamers are maintained. Messrs. Hoare Miller and Company run a daily service between Calcutta and Kalna in Bardwān, calling at Sāntipur. The same Company run another service between Kalna and Murshidābād, calling at Nabadwip on every alternate day during the rainy season, and, during the dry season, from Kalna to Nabadwip twice a week. These services are on the Hooghly or Bhāgirathi. Until Krishnagar was connected up by rail with the main line of the Eastern Bengal State Railway, and a bridge built over the Jalangi, steamers used occasionally to come up the Jalangi to Krishnagar, and even beyond that town, when there was sufficient water in the river for them. A steamer of the India General Steam Navigation and Railway Company plies twice a day (except on Sundays) between Kushtiā and Pabnā. Other steamers belonging to the same Company, and to the River Steam Navigation Company ply daily between Dāmukdiā and Godāgāri on the Padmā.. Other through steamers between Patna and Dacca call at Dāmukdiā at irregular intervals. Country boats on their way from up-country to Calcutta come down either the Bhāgirathi or the Jalangi, whichever at the time offers the better facilities for navigation. The annual report of the district for the year 1908-09 shows that the imports into, and the exports from, the district by the rivers were, in that year, 388,049 and 33,105 maunds 'of ' goods, respectively. The chief items among the imports were paddy 300,695 maunds; rice 69,268 maunds; and coke and coal 14,723 maunds. The only other article of which 1,000 maunds or over was imported by river was unmanufactured tobacco, the import of which was 1,343 maunds. Among exports by river the chief items were raw jute 12,751 maunds; gram and pulses 7,330 maunds; and *gur* (molasses) 2,781 maunds. Kerosene oil amounting to 6,302 maunds, also appears among the exports, but is not, of course, a true export of the district.

The Executive Engineer, Nadiā Rivers Division, has furnished a statement of the various classes of boats which are ordinarily used upon the rivers in the district, and it is reproduced below—

Name of boat.	Used by *manjhis* of—	DESCRIPTION OF IMPORTANT CARGO CARRIED.		Capacity in maunds.	REMARKS.
		Down	Up.		
Mālini ...	Up-country ...	Grain ...		500 to 2,500	⎫ Ply only during the
Patli ...	Ditto ...	Do. ...		Ditto ...	⎪ rains, *via* Bhāgirathi.
Bhar ...	Ditto ...	Do. ...		Ditto ...	⎬
Katra ...	Ditto ...	Stoneware		Ditto ...	⎭
Sārong ...	Ditto ...	Grain ...	Salt, hardware and miscellaneous.	200 to 1,000	⎫ All the year round if the
Sangri ...	Murshidābād and Māldā districts.	General cargo.		Ditto ...	⎬ river is navigable, *via* Bhāgirathi.
Pānsway ...	Nadiā and Bardwān.	Ditto ...		100 to 1,000	⎫ Throughout the year for
Khajnaghātta	Ditto ...	Ditto ...		Ditto ...	⎬ intermediate traffic, *via* Jalangi and Mātābhāngā.
Jang ...	Rājshāhi ...	Rice ...		200 to 500	⎫ Only during the rains,
Ulak ...	Faridpur ...	Jute ...		500 to 1,500	⎬ *via* Mātābhāngā.
Kosa ...	Purniā ...	Jute and unmanufactured tobacco.		100 to 500	All the year round, *via* Bhairab-Jalangi, a few *via* Bhāgirathi.
Phukni ...	Howrah ...	Rice and grain.		500 to 1,000	Throughout the year *via* Hooghly and lower reaches of Jalangi, Bhāgirathi and Mātābhāngā.

The *Mālini* is described as being round both in the stem and the stern, with stern somewhat higher than the bow ; it is wider and of greater draft than most other boats used on these rivers; the oars are worked from the roof.

The *Patli* is a flat-bottomed, clinker-built 'boat, of less width and draft than the *Mālini*; the oars are worked from the roof.

The *Bhar* is a strong, heavily built boat, capable of carrying stone, coal and similar articles; it is of equal width for nearly the whole of its length, and has very blunt stem and stern.

The *Katra* is a flat-bottomed, clinker-built boat, of very light draft for its size; when loaded it is generally towed; when empty it is driven by oars worked from inside the roof. This particular type of boat seems to suit the exigencies of traffic on the Nadiā rivers, and the proportion of them to be seen is yearly increasing.

The *Sārong* is a much smaller boat, with rounded bow, and flat stern; it is comparatively narrow, and has a deep draft for its size.

The *Sangri* is a peculiar shaped boat, with a bottom bulging down below the keel on each side; it has a very low free-board, and is in consequence liable to be swamped when the rivers are in flood.

The *Ulak* is a long, well-shaped boat, covered with a roof throughout its length.

The *Phukni* is a biggish boat, open with the exception of a small portion in the stem, which is roofed over.

Railways.
The district is now (1909) very well served with railways. About 170 miles of the Eastern Bengal State Railway, all broad gauge, lie within its borders. The main line from Calcutta to Siliguri passes through the district, roughly from south to north; the distance from Kanchrapārā on the southern boundary to Dāmukdiā on the Padmā is about 92 miles, and this section has 21 stations. The Lāl Golā branch takes off from Rānāghāt junction; it passes in a north-westerly direction; the portion within the district is about 48 miles in length, and there are 8 stations upon it. This branch traverses the Kālantar, which is the tract that is most liable to famine in the district and generally contains the lowest stock of food grains. In the 1896-97 famine the supply of food suddenly gave out in this tract, and, in the absence of the railway, which had not then been constructed, the greatest difficulty was experienced in importing enough grain to prevent deaths from starvation. If another famine should unfortunately occur, this line will save the District Officer much of the anxiety which his predecessors had to bear. The central branch of the Eastern Bengal State Railway also takes off from Rānāghāt junction; only about nine miles of it (with two stations) lies within the boundaries of the district; it passes in an easterly direction through the Rānāghāt subdivision into the Bangāon subdivision of the Jessore district. The Goalundo branch takes off from Poradah

junction, and passes in an easterly direction for about 21 miles, when it crosses the boundary of the district near Khoksā into Faridpur; there are five stations on this portion of the line. The light railway which runs from Aistolā Ghāt, on the right bank of the Churni about two miles from Rānāghāt, to Krishnagar viâ Sāntipur, is about 20 miles in length, and has seven stations. This line was constructed by Messrs. Martin and Company at a cost of Rs. 7,00,000, upon a guarantee by the District Board of 4 per cent. interest on the capital expenditure. The line was opened in the year 1898, and was worked by the company until it was taken over by the Eastern Bengal State Railway on 1st July 1904. During the intervening years it never worked at a profit of more than 3 per cent., and the District Board in consequence lost a considerable sum annually in making good the guarantee which it had given. The arrangements for crossing the river at Aistolā Ghāt were defective, especially during the rainy season, and it was this and the fact that the stations at Sāntipur and Krishnagar are at some distance from the centre of the town, that caused the receipts to fall below the figure which it was expected that they would reach. Orders have recently been issued for the preparation of detailed plans and estimates for the construction of an extension of this line from Ghorālia station to Kalna Ghat viâ Sāntipur city, and from Sāntipur city to Sāntipur station on the light railway; also for the construction of a new bridge over the Churni, and the conversion of the present broad gauge siding from Rānāghāt station to Aistolā Ghāt to 2 feet 6 inch gauge.

A detailed project and estimate amounting to Rs. 15,36,522, as finally revised, have been prepared for constructing a 2 feet 6 inch light railway, 56 miles in length, from Krishnagar to Jalangi, viâ Meherpur.

A rough project and estimate have also been prepared for a branch from Shibnibāsh station on the Eastern Bengal State Railway to Kotchāndpur in Jessore. The Manager of the Railway has recommended a line viâ Khālispur, Kāliganj and Jhenidah; the length of this would be about 55 miles, and the estimated cost is Rs. 52,49,115. From statistics which have been taken it appears probable that this line could count upon gross earnings of Rs. 90 per mile per week from the date of its opening.

The total rail-borne imports into, and exports from, the district during the year 1908-09 amounted to 1,374,277 and 1,642,660 maunds respectively. Among imports the most important items were—paddy 622,399 maunds; salt 212,124 maunds; kerosene oil 116,369 maunds; and rice 113,207 maunds. Among exports the most important items were—raw jute 755,324 maunds; gram and pulses 474,934 maunds; "other food-grains" 114,456 maunds; and *gur* (molasses) 84,189 maunds.

Roads.   The District Board maintains 107 miles of road of class I, metalled, bridged and drained throughout; 230 miles of class IIA, unmetalled but bridged and drained throughout; 392 miles of class IIB, unmetalled and partially bridged and drained; 21 miles of class IV, banked but not surfaced, partially bridged and drained; and 52 miles of class V, cleared, partially bridged and drained. Village roads to an aggregate length of about 526 miles are also maintained by the Board.

The chief roads in class I are described below.

Bagula to Krishnagar.— Until Krishnagar obtained a direct railway service this was the most important road in the district, as it connected the head-quarters with the railway. It is about 9½ miles in length, and a metalled surface 12 feet wide was formerly kept up; the width is now being gradually reduced to 8 feet, as the traffic along the road has greatly decreased since the advent of the railway. At the third mile the Churni river has to be crossed by a ferry.

Ránághát to Sántipur.—This is about eight miles in length. A metalled surface nine feet wide is maintained. The Churni river has to be crossed by a ferry in the 1st mile.

Krishnagar to Sántipur.—The total length of this road, including four miles within municipal limits and maintained by municipalities, is 14 miles; the metalled surface is 9 feet wide. This road is not interrupted by any ferries. According to local tradition this road was originally constructed by Mahárájá Rudra Rai of Nadiá.

Chuádángá to Meherpur.—This road is 17½ miles in length, and has a metalled surface eight feet in width. It is interrupted by two rivers, one of which has to be crossed by a ferry. It is of importance, in that it furnishes the nearest outlet to the railway from the Meherpur Subdivision.

Chuádángá to Jhenida.—This is in continuation of the last-mentioned road. It is ten miles in length, with an 8 feet wide metalled surface. It is an important feeder road for the railway.

Other roads of this class are: (1) Kushtiá to Salgamedia, 8 miles, not now of much importance; (2) Kushtiá to Daudpur, 5 miles; (3) Kissengunge to Hánsada on the Jessore boundary, 11 miles; (4) Krishnagar to Nabadwip, 7 miles; (5) Chákdaha to Balia on the Jessore boundary, 10 miles.

Among the class IIA roads the longest are : (1) Krishnagar
to Plassey, 31 miles, of diminished importance since the opening
of the Lālgolā extension of the Eastern Bengal State Railway ;
(2) Krishnagar to Jāguli, 32 miles ; (3) Meherpur to Gopālpur
viâ Māmdagāri, 23 miles ; (4) Darsana railway station to
Kedārganj *viâ* Kapāsdāngā, 17 miles.

In class IIB the three longest roads are Krishnagar to Meherpur, 25 miles ; Meherpur to Kāliganj *viâ* Plasipārā and Mirā,
29 miles ; and Nischintapur to Hāt Boāliā, 23 miles.

The District Board maintains eight major and three minor Ferries.
ferries. The most important ferries are those at (1) Subalpur over
the Mātābhāngā on the Darsana railway station to Kedārganj road ;
(2) Nonaganj, over the Ichhāmati, on the Bagula to Chankhāli
road ; (3) Meherpur, over the Bhairab, on the Meherpur to
Nandanpur road. The total income which the Board derived
from ferries during the year 1908-09 was Rs. 5,486.

The district contains altogether 143 post offices, and 529 miles Postal
of postal communication. The number of postal articles deli- communi-
vered in the year 1908-09 was 187,697, including 109,800 cations.
post cards and 49,828 letters. The value of money-orders issued
in that year was Rs. 15,87,646, and of those paid Rs. 25,59,647.
The total number of Savings Bank deposits was 16,300, the
amount deposited being Rs. 13,18,196. There are eight postal-
telegraph offices situated at Krishnagar, Kumārkhāli, Kushtiā,
Kushtiā Bazar, Meherpur, Nabadwip, Rānāghāt and Sāntipur ;
8,794 messages were issued from these offices in 1908-09.

CHAPTER X.

LAND REVENUE ADMINISTRATION.

THE revenue system of the Mughal Empire was never strictly introduced into that part of Bengal in which the Nadiā district lies. The country was only partially under the sway of Delhi during the 13th century, and in 1340 the governor declared himself independent. For the next two hundred years it was nominally ruled by independent Muhammadan Kings, but their power was never sufficiently absolute to render them secure from invasion or re-conquest without the assistance of the local Rājās and zamindārs, who were, more or less, given a free hand in the revenue administration of their own territories. During the sixteenth century Lower Bengal passed from the hands of the Afghāns into those of the Mughals, but Akbar's detailed revenue settlement did not extend to so distant a part of his empire. During the seventeenth century Lower Bengal was in a great state of disorder, and each Rājā and zamindār endeavoured to make himself as independent as he could. It was not until the advent of Murshid Kuli Khān as governor in 1704 that any real attempt was made to enforce the regular payment of the land revenue. Murshid Kuli Khān was a strong and despotic ruler, and during his governorship, which lasted till 1726, many zamindārs were forcibly dispossessed for non-payment of their dues to the state.
In the year 1722 Murshid Kuli Khān drew up a " Jumma Caumil Toomary, or more perfect standard account of the imperial revenues of Bengal." In this account the whole province was divided into " Chucklahs " or large divisions of territory constituting an equal number " of separate foujedari and aumildary zelahs of civil and military jurisdictions—a compound of the 34 ancient districts of circars which nevertheless were still to be distinguished." In this account two-fifths of the district of Nadiā, which was then known as " Oukerah," were included in the Murshidābād Chāklah, and the remaining three-fifths in the Hooghly, or Sātgaon Chāklah. A further " Toomar Jumma " of Bengal was drawn up by Sujah Khān who succeeded Murshid

Kuli Khān and in the abstract of this as given by Mr. J. Grant in his "Analysis of the Finances of Bengal," written in 1788, the following passage is to be found :—

"Nuddeah, properly Oukerah, and more recently called Krishnagar from the propensity of Indian landholders to derange the ancient established system of Government ascertaining their own relative situation, and hence attribute princely consequence to themselves by deriving local designations from their proper names, was originally bestowed in the beginning of this century on Ragooram, a Bramin, descended from Bobanand, the first conspicuous man of the family distinguished by the title of Mazumdar as holding the office of temporary substitute, recorder of the Jumma or rental of the circar of Sātgaon. The district though large and wonderfully fertile in all the dearer productions of Indian soil capable of an easy, quick transportation by the river Hooghly to all the great foreign settlements in Bengal hath yet, from the tolerated corrupt practice of zamindari defalcations, heightened in the present instance by fraudulent alienations of lands or exemption in the payment of the established dues of Government in favour of inferior brother members of the same religious caste, ever remained prodigiously underrated in the general assessment of the province, and in the proportional one of the Ausil Toomary, only set down perghs. 73, valued at Rs. 5,94,846."

According to the "Jumma Bandobust teshkhees kool", an account which appears to have been rendered officially by the kanungos to the Naib acting on behalf of the East India Company as sovereign representative of the Mughal Emperor, the total net revenue of the district was nearly eleven lakhs in the year 1763, and at this rate it was settled with Mahārājā Krishna Chandra. At the first settlement after the acquisition of the *Diwāni* by the East India Company, the *jama* was reduced by Muhammad Reza Khān to Rs. 3,74,964. On this point, and on subsequent variations, Mr. J. Grant wrote as follows in his "Analysis of the Revenue of Bengal" :—"No *hustabood* seems to have been then formed of the modern actual value of the district. It was assessed generally on the Ausil by towfeers and abwabs. In this state it might have been expected that, if remissions had really been necessary, the amount would have fallen upon the new additional increases. Yet the contrary happened, and the deductions were made from the standard toomary jumma or the old well-established profits accruing on the jageer lands. From this time forward the ostensible formal bundobust seems to have been slowly decreasing until the year 1778 immediately after the famine and on dismission of the Naib Dewan, when suddenly it was raised, no doubt, on very sufficient grounds, beyond all former example to a gross annual demand of Rs. 12,66,266.

* * * *

" To conclude, in 1190 (1783 A. D.), the clear revenue stipulated for, notwithstanding a formal increase of one lack of rupees, stated to have been brought on at the institution of the Committee in 1188, did not much, if at all, exceed eight lacks of rupees, so that, in right and moderation equitable policy, three lacks ought to be regarded as the recoverable defalcation or effective increase capable of realization on the latter jumma, payable to the exchequer, forming the comparison with the rent roll originally established before the reduced settlement of M. R. Khan in 1765. Considering, indeed, the vast known resources of this fertile extensive district (exclusive of arable lands turned into pasture, to evade payment of the expedient dues of Government, of fraudulent alienations of territory, with collusive reductions chiefly in favour of Brahmins, of the ancient rates of assessment specified in the Pottahs of the ryots), the improvement of which its finances are immediately susceptible, might fairly be stated at seven lacks."

Generally speaking, Mr. Grant formed the opinion that the resources of the country had been much under-estimated. Mr. Shore, however, in his minute of June 1789, contended that this proposition was a fallacy, and that the then assessment was nearly equal to what it should be. The opinion of the former prevailed, and in the permanent settlement the land revenue for the district was fixed at Rs. 12,55,325.

The *Diwáni* of Bengal was assigned to the East India Company on 12th August 1765. It was not considered advisable at first to take the administration of the revenue out of the hands of the native officials, but the attempt to maintain the old system was found disastrous from all points of view, and, therefore, in 1769 British Supervisors were appointed to superintend the local collection of revenue. The Supervisors acted under the control of two Provincial Councils at Murshidábád and Patna. The reports which were submitted by the Supervisors showed that the whole country was in a state of great disorder ; so, in 1772, the Court of Directors determined upon a radical change, under which the whole control was taken over by the Company. The chief revenue office was removed from Murshidábád to Calcutta, and a Collector assisted by a native officer called *Diwán* was appointed for each district. The system of mixed European and native agency in the districts produced only a partial

improvement, and was in its turn abolished, the European Collectors being recalled from the districts in the year 1774, and the
collection of revenue being entrusted to native agents, called
Amils, under the superintendence of six Provincial Councils.
In course of time it was found that the work of supervision could
not be adequately carried out by these Provincial Councils, and
in 1781 they were abolished, their place being taken by a Committee of Revenue (subsequently the Board of Revenue), with
headquarters at Calcutta, and European Collectors were again
placed in charge of each district.

The first regular settlement after the assumption of the *Diwāni*
was made for a period of five years from 1772. It was concluded
with the highest bidders, whether they were the previous zamindārs
or not. This system led to great speculation, as a result of which
most of the old families in Bengal were more or less ruined, and
the remissions and irrecoverable balances reached an enormous
figure. The annual settlements which were in force from 1777
till the time of the Decennial Settlement in 1790, were based on
no proper data, and were little less disastrous in their effects. By
1790 the district, which 30 years before had been settled with a
single zamindār, the Mahārājā of Nadiā, had been split up into
261 separate estates, held by 205 registered proprietors. This
partition was due, first to the selling off of portions of the Raj
to cover defaults in the payment of land revenue, and second
to the creation of *tāluks*, or subordinate zamindaries. The
Mahārājā, when anxious to raise money had made over portions
of his estate to those who were willing to oblige him, either
rent free, or on nominal rent, and the portions so made over
were called *tāluks*; for a time the *tālukdārs* continued to pay the
land revenue due upon their *tāluks* through the Mahārājā, but
it was subsequently ordered that these grants were to be treated
as separate estates, and the land revenue due upon them was to
be paid to Government direct, and not through the Mahārājā.
The great Rāj, which once covered the whole district, has, by
mismanagement and misfortune, been so greatly reduced that it
now (1909) produces only about one-fifteenth of the total land
revenue of the district.

In 1793 the Decennial Settlement was made permanent.
The effect of this was to place all classes of zamindārs on a
uniform legal basis, and so "in a short time to obliterate the
previous differences in the customary status which had grown
out of differences in origin. Even before the permanent settlement, the revenue farming system adopted by the East India
Company from 1769 to 1788 had tended to obscure such

[margin note: DECEN-NIAL SETTLE-MENT.]

[margin note: PERMA-NENT SETTLE-MENT.]

differences. For the effect of the farming system was to'level down the ancient zamindārs."* The only condition common to all zamindaries before the permanent settlement was that each zamindār held a *sanad* from the state authorizing him to collect the land revenues. The essential portions of the *sanad* which was granted to the Rājā of Bishnupur in 1780 are reproduced below, because they represent the form of title under which the Bengal zamindārs held in the eighteenth century, a form very similar to that under which certain parganas were settled with the East India Company itself in 1757-58. "The office of zamindar of the aforesaid pargana has been bestowed, agreeable to the endorsement from the beginning of the year 1187, Bengal era, to the cream of his peers, Chaitan Singh the grandson of Gopal Singh, zamindar, deceased, on his consenting to pay the royal *peshkash*, etc., of 186 goldmohars and 2 annas. It is required of him that, having executed with propriety the duties and functions of his station, he be not deficient in the smallest respect in diligence and assiduity, but observing a conciliatory conduct towards the ryots and inhabitants at large, and exerting himself to the utmost in punishing and expelling the refractory: Let him pay the revenue of Government into the treasury at the stated periods, let him encourage the body of the ryots in such manners that signs of an increased cultivation and improvement of the country may daily appear, and let him keep the high roads in such repair that travellers may pass and repass in the fullest confidence and security.

"Let there be no robberies or murders committed within his boundaries: but (God forbid) should any one notwithstanding be robbed or plundered of his property, let him produce the thieves, together with the stolen property, and, after restoring the latter to the rightful owner, let him assign the former over to punishment. Should he fail in producing the parties offending, he must himself make good the property stolen. Let him be careful that no one be guilty of misconduct in his behaviour, or commit irregularities of any kind. Let him transmit the accounts required of him to the *Huzur* (Chief Revenue Officer), under his own and Kanungo's signature, and, after having paid up the whole revenues completely to the end of the year, let him receive credit for the Maskurat (allowance to the zamindar), agreeably to usage, and finally let him refrain from the collection of any of the *abwab* abolished or prohibited by Government."

The counterpart which was executed by the Rājā, is, *mutatis mutandis*, in almost identical words. Every such *sanad* was

---

*, Hunter's Bengal Miscellaneous Records.

granted to the person named in it, and no mention was made of his heirs or successors. It is true that a transfer was generally recognized, and a fresh *sanad* issued on payment of *peshkash*, or transfer fee, but the zamindár had no absolute right to sell or bequeath his estate; such right, however, he obtained under the permanent settlement, and this resulted in some instances in the zamindár having to part with the whole or portions of his estate, in order to satisfy his creditors. Other forces of disintegration came into play. The Government demand, as fixed at the permanent settlement, was one which left but a small margin of profit; punctuality of payment was insisted upon; the rights of the ryot to hold at customary rates were secured by law, but the power of the zamindár over them was limited, and he had no power to enforce punctuality of payment to himself. The result of all these disabilities was that by the close of the century the greater portion of the Nadiá Ráj had been alienated.

Some few remarks are necessary in connection with the status of the ryots. By section 7 of the Permanent Settlement Regulation of 1793 the zamindárs were required "to conduct themselves with good faith and moderation towards the dependent talukdars and ryots." In section 8 it was declared that "it being the duty of the ruling power to protect all classes of people, and especially those who from their situation are most helpless, the Governor-General in Council will, whenever he may deem it proper, enact such Regulations as he may think necessary for the protection and welfare of the dependent talukdars and ryots and other cultivators of the soil." But though the rights of the landlords were defined, the rights of the tenants against the landlords were only reserved, and were not defined. It was intended that there should be an interchange of *pattahs* and *kabuliyats* between the zamindárs and the ryots, under which the rent payable should be definitely fixed in perpetuity, but there was a general refusal on the part of both classes to carry out this intention. In the meantime the necessity of securing the landlords in the realization of their dues from the ryots resulted in the enactment of the Regulations of 1799 and 1812, under which the landlords obtained practically unrestricted power over the property, and even over the person, of their ryots, and it was many years before the ryots were relieved of these disabilities. "The failure of all the attempts made to control agrarian relations led the Court of Directors in 1824 to sanction a proposal to make a survey and record-of-rights of the permanently settled districts of Bengal, as being the only means of defining and maintaining the rights of the ryots. More than sixty years, however, were to elapse before this vast undertaking was begun. But for temporarily settled areas, Regulation VII of 1822 provided that all future settlements of the land revenue should be preceded by a record of "the rights and obligations of various classes and persons possessing the interest in the land or in the rent or produce thereof." And this course was followed in the resumption to revenue of lands held revenue-free under invalid titles. These proceedings were carried out mainly between 1830 and 1850, and in many districts covered considerable areas. * * * The work done in connection with these resumption proceedings supplied Government for the first time with a really detailed account of the rights and obligations of different classes of landlords and tenants."* These proceedings finally eventaated in Act X of 1859, which is entitled an Act to amend the law relating to the recovery of rent, and which has been described as the first effective step taken by the Legislature to discharge the duties in connection with the ryots undertaken at the Permanent Settlement.

LAND TENURES ESTATES. At the time of the permanent settlement there were four classes of Zamindārs in Bengal. They are thus described in the introduction to Hunter's Bengal Manuscript Records. "The first class of Bengal zamindārs represented the old Hindu and Muhammadan Rājās of the country, previous to the Mughal conquest by the Emperor Akbar in 1576, or persons who claimed that status. The second class were Rājās, or great landholders, most of whom dated from the 17th and 18th centuries, and some of whom were, like the first class, *de facto* rulers in their own estates or territories, subject to a tribute or land tax to the representative of the Emperor. These two classes had a social position faintly resembling the Feudatory Chiefs of the British Indian Empire, but that position was enjoyed by them on the basis of custom, not of treaties. The third and most numerous class were persons whose families had held the office of collecting the revenue during one or two or more generations, and who had thus established a prescriptive right. A fourth and also numerous class was made up of the revenue farmers, who, since the *diwāni* grant in 1765, had collected the land tax for the East India Company, under the system of yearly leases, then of five years' leases, and again of yearly leases. Many of these revenue farmers had, by 1787, acquired the *de facto* status of zamindārs." The original differences in the holdings of these four classes of zamindārs were obliterated by the Permanent Settlement, and from 1793 onwards all estates, whatever their origin, were placed on a uniform basis.

---

* Introduction to Rampini's Bengal Tenancy Act.

The proprietors of estates are known as zamindārs or tālukdārs. The latter originally paid their quota of land revenue through the zamindārs from whose estates their properties had been carved out. But, partly at their own request, in order that they might receive protection from the exactions of the zamindārs, and partly for other reasons, the tāluks were finally completely separated from the parent estates, and recognized as separate estates with land revenue payable direct to the State. In the year 1790-91 the total number of estates in the district was 261, held by 205 registered proprietors, paying a total land revenue of Rs. 12,55,325, the average payment by each estate being Rs. 5,210, and by each proprietor, Rs. 6,630. By 1799-1800 the number of estates had increased to 737, and the registered proprietors to 413, paying a total land revenue of Rs. 12,45,815 ; the average payment for each estate being Rs. 1,830, and for each proprietor Rs. 3,260. By 1850-51 the number of estates had increased to 3,064, with a total land revenue of Rs. 11,74,490 ; the average amount paid by each estate being Rs. 380. The current land revenue demand for 1908-09 was Rs. 9,02,228, due from 2,455 estates, the average demand from each estate being Rs. 368. The falling off in the total demand, and in the number of estates, is due to reductions in the area of the district. Out of these, 2,245 estates, with a revenue of Rs. 8,09,902, are permanently settled ; 194 estates, with a revenue of Rs. 73,768, are temporarily settled, and 16 estates paying Rs. 18,558, are managed by the Collector direct. In addition, there are 298 revenue-free estates, and 9,213 rent-free lands, which pay road and public works cess. The gross rental of the district has been returned at $33\frac{2}{3}$ lakhs, and of this the Government revenue demand represents 26·7 per cent. The incidence of the land revenue demand is Re. 0-15-3 per acre of cultivated area.

The only classes of tenures which call for special remarks are Tenures. (1) Patni tāluks, and (2) Utbandi tenures.

The Patni tāluk had its origin in the estate of the Mahārājā of Patni Bardwān. At the Permanent Settlement the assessment of this Taluks. estate was very high, and in order to ensure easy and punctual realization of the rent, a number of leases in perpetuity, to be held at a fixed rent, were given to middlemen. These tenures are called Patni (*i.e.*, dependent) tāluks, and are in effect leases which bind the holder by terms and conditions similar to those by which a superior landlord is bound to the State. By Regulation XLIV of 1793 the proprietors of estates were allowed to grant leases for a period not exceeding ten years, but this provision was rescinded by section 2 of Regulation V of 1812, while by Regulation XVIII of the same year proprietors were declared competent to grant leases for any period, even in perpetuity. Finally, Regulation VIII of 1819, known as the Patni Sale Law, declared the validity of these permanent tenures, defined the relative rights of the zamindārs and their subordinate tālukdārs, and established a summary process for the sale of such tenures in satisfaction of the zamindār's demand of rent. It also legalized under-letting, on similar terms, by the patnidārs and others. Since the passing of this law this form of tenure has become very popular in Nadiā with zamindārs who wish to divest themselves of the direct management of their property or part of it, or who wish to raise a lump sum of money. It may be described as a tenure created by the zamindār to be held by the lessee and his heirs or transferees for ever at a rent fixed in perpetuity, subject to the liability of annulment on sale of the parent estate for arrears of the Government revenue, unless protected against the rights exerciseable by auction-purchasers by common or special registry, as prescribed by sections 37 and 39 of Act XI of 1859. The lessee is called upon to furnish collateral security for the rent and for his conduct generally, or he is excused from this obligation at the zamindār's discretion. Under-tenures created by patnidārs are called darpatni, and those created by darpatnidārs are called sepatni tenures. These under-tenures are, like the parent tenures, permanent, transferable and heritable, and have generally the same rights, privileges and responsibilities attached to them. The first effect of this system was to introduce a class of middlemen who had no interest in the ryot, except to extract as much from him as they possibly could. By degrees, however, the sons and grandsons of the original tenure-holders acquired something of the sense of duty to their tenants which the hereditary possession of landed property gives, and it is probable that the ryot is no worse off now than he would have been, had the system never been introduced.

Utbandi tenure.   The particular tenure which is known by the name *Utbandi* apparently had its origin in the Nadiā district, from which it has spread to neighbouring districts, though in no district is it as common as in Nadiā, where about five-eighths of the cultivated lands are held under it. The literal meaning of the term is "assessed according to cultivation." In 1861 Mr. Montresor, who had been deputed to investigate locally certain complaints of some European proprietors in the district, described the system as follows:—

"The *Utbandi* tenure apparently has its origin in this district and is peculiar to Nadiā. There is, in almost every village, a certain quantity of land not included in the rental of the ryot, and which, therefore, belongs directly to the recognized proprietor of the estate. This fund of unappropriated land has accumulated from deserted holdings of absconded tenants, from lands gained by alluvion, from jungle lands recently brought into cultivation by persons who hold no leases, and from lands termed *khās khamār*, signifying land retained by the proprietor for his household.

" In other districts lands of the three first descriptions are at once leased out to tenants, but in Nadiā it appears to be different. Owing either to the supineness of the landlord or to the paucity of inhabitants, a custom has originated from an indefinite period of the ryots of a village cultivating, without the special permission of the landlord, portions of such land at their own will and pleasure. This custom has been recognized and established by the measurement of the lands at the time the crop is standing, through an officer on the part of the landlord styled *halsana*, and when the assessment is accordingly made.".

In the report of the Government of Bengal on the Bengal Tenancy Bill (1884), the *utbandi* holding was described as follows :—

" A tenancy from year to year, and sometimes from season to season, the rent being regulated not, as in the case of *hālhāsili*, by a lump payment in money for the land cultivated, but by the appraisement of the crop on the ground, and according to its character. So far it resembles the tenure by crop appraisement of the *bhāoli* system, but there is between them this marked difference, that while in the latter the land does not change hands from year to year, in the former it may."

The Bengal Government, when the Tenancy Bill was under consideration, proposed to treat *utbandi* lands as ordinary ryoti lands were treated, *i.e.*, to presume that tenants of *utbandi* lands were settled ryots if they had held any land in the village for 12 years, and to declare that they had, as settled ryots, occupancy rights in all lands held by them in the village. The Select Committee did not, however, agree to this proposal, and applied the provisions relating to *Char* and *Diāra* lands to *utbandi* lands also. Accordingly by section 180 of the Bengal Tenancy Act, it was laid down that an *utbandi* tenant can acquire no rights of occupancy until he has held the same land for 12 years continuously, and that, until he acquires such a right, he is liable to pay the rent agreed on between him and the landlord. Under these circumstances it is of course practically impossible for a tenant to acquire a right of occupancy, except with the consent of the landlord. The most authoritative ruling of the law courts as to the nature of this tenancy is that delivered by the Chief Justice (Sir W. C. Petheram) and Tottenham, J., in the case of Beni Madhab Chakravarti *versus* Bhuban Mohan Biswas (I. L. R., 17, Cal. 393). This ruling concludes with the following words :—

" The description of *utbandi* seems to refer rather to particular areas taken for cultivation for limited periods, and then given up, than to holdings of which parts are cultivated and other parts lie fallow, while the rent for the whole is assessed year by year with reference to the quantity within the holding under cultivation in that year. A holding of the latter description hardly seems to answer to the general conception of *utbandi*."

The subject of this particular tenure came prominently before the Government of Bengal during the years 1900-1903. In the annual report for the year 1900 the Collector remarked that advantage had been taken of the prevalence of the *utbandi* system to extort excessive rents. The remark attracted the attention of Government, and an enquiry was held chiefly with a view to ascertain whether any amendment of the law was necessary. After considering the matter in all its bearings the Lieutenant-Governor came to the conclusion that "the system, though theoretically unsound, is practically unobjection-able ; it is of great antiquity ; it has its champions ; and no one contends that the need for change is acute "; there was no need for immediate legislation, but the Commissioner should continu-ously direct his attention to the system, and promptly bring to the notice of Government any signs of its abuse.

CHAPTER XI.

GENERAL ADMINISTRATION.

THE administration of the district is in charge of the Collector under the Commissioner of the Presidency Division, whose head-quarters are in Calcutta. For some years until 1860, Krishnagar was the head-quarters of the Division, but as it was found more convenient that the Commissioner should reside in Calcutta, the head-quarters of the Division were transferred there, and have remained there since.

For general administrative purposes the district is divided into five subdivisions with head-quarters at Krishnagar, Rānāghāt, Meherpur, Chuādāngā and Kushtiā. The head-quarters of the Rānāghāt Subdivision were at Sāntipur until the year 1863, when they were transferred to Rānāghāt, where they have remained since. For five years, *viz.*, from 1892 to 1897, the Chuādāngā Subdivision was abolished, the area covered by it being amalgamated with the Meherpur Subdivision; but in the latter year it was re-established in deference to the petitions filed by the inhabitants of the eastern portion complaining of the distance which they had to travel to reach the Court at Meherpur.

The head-quarters subdivision is under the direct superintendence of the Collector, who has a staff of four Deputy Collectors, one Probationary Deputy Collector, and one Sub-Deputy Collector. A Deputy Collector is in charge of each of the four outlying subdivisions, and he is, as a rule, assisted by a Sub-Deputy Collector.

The total revenue of the district in 1880-81 was Rs. 16,68,000, REVENUE. with the Bangāon Subdivision included. In 1890-91, the Bangāon Subdivision having in the meantime being transferred, it was Rs. 14,93,000. In the course of the following ten years it rose to Rs. 16,58,000, and in the year 1908-09 it was Rs. 21,71,586.

As elsewhere, the land revenue forms by far the most important Land item of receipt in the district. According to the best information Revenue. now available, the land revenue payable in the year 1790-91 amounted to Rs. 13,59,935; in 1799-1800 to Rs. 13,49,633; in 1850-51 to Rs. 11,74,492; and in 1871-72 to Rs. 10,17,550. These successive declines were not due to any alteration in the rate of levy, but to transfers of outlying portions of the district to other districts. There has not been much variation in the land revenue demand since the Bangāon subdivision was transferred to Jessore in 1883. The current demand for the year 1908-09 was Rs. 9,02,228, of which about 90 per cent. was due from the proprietors of permanently settled estates. There were 2,245 such estates with a current demand of Rs. 8,09,902 ; 194 temporarily settled estates, with a current demand of Rs. 73,768; and 16 estates, held direct by Government, with a current demand of Rs. 18,558. The Government estates are scattered throughout the district, but the most important ones are in the Meherpur and Kushtiā subdivisions. The total cost of management in 1908-09 was Rs. 1,321, equal to 7 per cent. of the demand. The gross rental of the district was returned at Rs. 27,76,530 when the Road Cess Act was introduced in 1880. It is now estimated to have risen to Rs. 33,64,219, showing an increase of Rs. 5,87,689. There has been but little extension of cultivation during these years, and nearly the whole of this substantial increase in the gross rental must be attributed to increase in the rate of rent.

Cesses.

Road and Public Works cesses are, as usual, levied at the maximum rate of one anna in the rupee. The average collections during the quinquennium ending with the year 1899-1900 amounted to Rs. 1,54,684; during the following quinquennium (ending with the year 1904-05) they amounted to Rs. 1,69,093; in .the year 1908-09 the collections were Rs. 1,83,697. The current demand in the year 1908-09 was Rs. 1,83,111 ; of this sum Rs. 1,57,878 was due from 3,383 revenue-paying estates ; Rs. 2,382 was due from 298 revenue-free estates; and Rs. 22,851 from 9,213 rent-free lands. The number of estates assessed to cesses is 12,894, and the number of recorded shareholders is 18,075. There are 21,081 tenures assessed to cesses, with 34,386 shareholders. The current demand of cesses is equal to about one-fifth of the current demand of land revenue.

Stamps.

Next to land revenue, the sale of stamps forms the most important source of revenue. The receipts upon this account have been steadily increasing since the year 1896-97 ; they averaged Rs. 3,37,000 for the quinquennium ending with that year ; during the following quinquennium they averaged close on Rs. 3,70,000 ; in 1904-05 judicial stamps alone furnished Rs. 3,73,473, and in the year 1908-09 judicial stamps to the value of Rs. 3,87,022, and non-judicial stamps to the value of Rs. 83,842 were sold. The increase in the revenue from stamps is almost entirely due to the greater sale of judicial stamps, caused by the growth in the number and value of rent and civil suits.

The income from excise has been steadily increasing for many Excise. years. In 1894-95 it was Rs. 1,21,293. During the next five years it increased to Rs. 1,30,081. By 1904-05 it had reached Rs. 1,52,828, and in the year 1908-09 it was Rs. 1,74,188, which works out at the rate of one anna eight pies per head of the population for the year. There are three main sources of the excise revenue, viz., country spirits, ganja and opium. Up till the close of the year 1906-07 the outstill system was in force. The country liquor shops had ifallen into the hands of monopolists, and the liquor sold was both bad in quality, and expensive in price. With effect from 1st April 1907 the contract distillery system was introduced. Under this system the local manufacture of country spirits is prohibited, and a contract is made with a firm of distillers for all the liquor which is required for consumption in the district. The contractors are forbidden to hold any retail licenses for the sale of the spirit, but are allowed the use of the distillery and depôt buildings for the storage of liquor. The spirit is brought from the distillers to the various depôts, and is there blended and reduced to certain fixed strengths, at which alone it may be supplied to retail vendors, and sold by the latter to consumers. A maximum price is fixed for retail sale. The Collector reported as follows at the close of the first year after the introduction of this system :—" The sale of country liquor of fixed strengths at a fixed price has induced people to use country liquor in preference to cheap imported liquor. Under the old system the vendors diluted and adulterated the liquor and fixed their own prices, and so many preferred to buy cheap imported liquor from Calcutta. The Excise Officers have been exercising a salutary check by testing the strengths of liquor in the shops, and in the custody of consumers, and so the public are assured of getting liquor of full strength. While the new system has increased the number of consumers, there has been no tendency to increase of drunkenness. The Excise Deputy Collector and the subordinate inspecting staff made it a point during the year under report to visit all fares and festivals, but they have seldom come across any drunken and disorderly people."

After country liquor the next most important source of excise revenue is that derived from the sale of ganja, *i.e.*, the unimpregnated dried flowering tops of the cultivated female hemp plant (*Cannabis Indica*), and the resinous exudation on them. The revenue under this head also has been steadily rising of late years. In 1898-99 it was Rs. 32,380, and in 1908-09, Rs. 43,807. The incidence of license fees on consumption is usually high in Nadiā.

Opium is the third article important from an excise point of view. The revenue under this head was Rs. 39,178 in 1908-09;

118   NADIA.

it has remained almost constant during the last twenty years, between Rs. 38,000 and Rs. 40,000.

The other items which go to make up the excise revenue are the receipts from *tāri, pachhwāi*, imported wines and liquors, and *charas*, which in the year 1908-09 amounted respectively to Rs. 4,123, Rs. 4,132, Rs. 6,382 and Rs. 1,744. There are also a few petty miscellaneous items, none exceeding Rs. 100.

Income-
tax.

The receipts under the head of income-tax amounted in 1892-93 to Rs. 44,372 payable by Rs. 2,021 assessees. By 1901-02 the receipts had risen to Rs. 61,514 payable by 2,587 assessees; but in the year 1902-03 the steady increase, which had up till then been maintained, received a severe check by the exemption of incomes between Rs. 500 and Rs 1,000, and in the year 1908-09 the net collections amounted to Rs. 46,563 only, payable by 1,046 assessees. As regards revenue from income-tax, Nadiā takes the third place among the districts in the Presidency Division, producing less than the 24-Parganas and Murshidābād, and more than Jessore and Khulnā.

Registra-
tion.

There are 11 offices for the registration of assurances under Act III of 1877, including the Registrar's office at Krishnagar. In the five years 1895—99 the average number of documents registered per annum was 23,687, and in the next quinquennium (1900- —04) it was 26,123. In 1908 the number of registrations rose to 31,783. The following statement gives a list of the registry offices in the district, and the salient statistics for the year 1908 :—

NAME.	Documents registered.	Receipts.	Expenditure.
		Rs.	Rs.
Krishnagar	4,878	10,481	6,355
Kushtiā	3,181	3,365	2,820
Meherpur	1,764	2,915	1,749
Chuādāngā	2,976	3,514	2,590
Rānāghāt	2,649	3,262	2,027
Sāntipur	1,049	1,328	1,809
Kumārkhāli	6,131	5,763	2,777
Mirpur	2,970	3,563	2,810
Birohi (at Chākdaha)	3,510	3,681	2,178
Rāmnagar	1,775	1,965	2,032
Shikārpur	900	1,245	1,728
Total ...	31,733	41,082	28,875

ADMINIS-
TRATION
OF
JUSTICE,
Civil
Justice.

The average number of civil suits disposed of annually during the quinquennium ending with the year 1899 was 19,737, and during the following quinquennium 23,848. During the year 1908 the number of suits disposed of rose to 30,133, of which 389 were on the file of the District Judge, 773 on that of the Subordinate Judge, and 28,971 on the files of the Munsifs. The increase in civil litigation is more marked in the Nadiā district than in any other district in the Presidency Division. In 1905 the Collector remarked in his annual report that "the public complaint continues of the cumbrous Civil Court procedure and delay in the disposal of cases and consequent heavy expenses incurred by the parties." The Judicial staff in 1908 consisted of the following officers :—One District Judge, one Subordinate Judge and two Munsifs at Krishnagar ; one Munsif at Rānāghāt; two Munsifs at Chuādāngā; three Munsifs at Kushtiā; and two Munsifs at Meherpur.

Criminal justice is administered by the District Magistrate and the various Magistrates subordinate to him, under the appellate authority of the District and Sessions Judge. The sanctioned staff at Krishnagar consists, in addition to the District Magistrate, of three Deputy Magistrates of the first class, and one Deputy Magistrate of the second class or third class. Besides these officers there is generally one Sub-Deputy Magistrate with second or third class powers at head-quarters. The four Sub-divisional Officers are invariably Magistrates of the first class, and they are generally assisted by a Sub-Deputy Magistrate vested with second or third class powers. In addition to the Stipendary Magistrates, there is a Bench of Honorary Magistrates at each of the subdivisional head-quarters, and at Nabadwip, Jamsherpur and Sāntipur ; and there are also Honorary Magistrates with powers to sit singly at Kumārkhāli, Meherpur, Chuādāngā, Kushtiā and Rānāghāt. *Criminal Justice.*

For police purposes the district is divided into five administrative subdivisions each in charge of an Inspector. In the Krishnagar Subdivision there are 7 thānās, *viz.,* Kotwāli, Nabadwip, Chāprā, Hānskhāli, Kāliganj, Nakāsipārā and Kissengunge. In the Rānāght subdivision there are 4 thanas, *viz.,* Haringhātā, Rānāghāt, Sāntipur and Chākdaha. In the Kushtiā Subdivision there are 6 thānās, *viz.,* Kushtiā, Mirpur, Daulatpur, Dāmukdiā, Khoksā and Kumārkhāli. In the Meherpur Subdivision there are 4 thānās, *viz.,* Meherpur, Karimpur, Gāngni and Tehata. In the Chuādāngā Subdivision there are 4 thānās, *viz.,* Chuādāngā, Dāmurhudā, Alamdāngā and Jibannagar. There are thus 25 thānās in the district, exclusive of the town outposts in the nine municipalities. The present (1909) sanctioned strength of the district police force is 1 Superintendent, 1 Deputy Superintendent, 7 Inspectors, 58 Sub-Inspectors, 63 head-constables, and 598 constables, exclusive of 29 town chaukidars. The total strength of the force is therefore 757 men, *Police.*

representing one policeman to every 3·7 square miles, and to every 2,203 of the population. The total budget grant for the maintenance of the force is Rs. 1,64,222. The town police, employed in the nine municipalities consist of 16 head-constables, 183 constables and town chaukidars. The rural police, for the watch and ward of villages in the interior, consist of 3,485 chaukidars working under 346 dafadars, representing one rural policeman to every 435 inhabitants.

Crime.   At the beginning of the eighteenth century the district was notorious for the crime of gang-robbery or dacoity. Stern steps were, however, taken during the viceroyalty of Murshid Kuli Khán (1704—1725) to suppress the crime, and he succeeded to a great extent. The following extract is taken from Stewart's History of Bengal, published at the beginning of the nineteenth century :—" Moorshud Cooly was indefatigable in the extirpation of robbers. Whenever a robbery was committed, he compelled the Foujedar, or the zemindar, either to find out the thief, or to recover the property. The goods or their equivalent in money were always restored to the persons who had been robbed, and the thief, whenever caught, was impaled alive. At Cutwah and Moorshudgunge he erected guard-houses for the protection of travellers ; and gave the command of the police guards to one of his slaves, named Mohammed Jan, who was of a savage disposition, and who was always attended by a band of executioners ; and, whenever he caught a thief, used to have the body split in two, and hung upon trees on the high road ; from which circumstance he was nick-named the Kolhareh or axe. By these severe means, during Murshud Cooly Khán's government, travellers were protected on the roads, and every man slept securely in his own house."

Under the less vigorous government of Murshid Kuli Khán's successors dacoity again became prevalent, and great disorder reigned for some years after the English obtained the *Diwáni* in 1765. It was not until the beginning of the nineteenth century that real efforts were again made to put it down. The vigorous administration of Mr. Blaquiere, first as Magistrate of Nadiá, and later as Superintendent (or Inspector-General) of Police, had the effect of practically ridding the district of dacoits by the end of the first decade of the nineteenth century. Since then, though the crime has not been extirpated, Nadiá no longer bears the unenviable reputation which it bore for the greater part of a century. At present there is no form of crime which is specially prevalent in the district. River dacoity, which is characteristic of the eastern districts of the Division, is practically unknown in Nadiā. Professional cattle thefts are fairly common, but not to any very marked extent. In the year 1908 the proportion of cognizable crime to population was one offence to 438 persons. Burglaries and thefts formed about 65 per cent. of the total cognizable crime reported. Among heinous offences there were 11 murders and 10 dacoities.

There is a district jail at Krishnagar and a subsidiary jail at Jails. each of the outlying subdivisions. The head-quarters jail has accommodation for 180 prisoners in all. There are barracks with separate sleeping accommodation for 125 male and 12 female convicts; the hospital holds 18 beds; there are four separate cells; the undertrial ward has accommodation for 19 persons; and the separate ward for civil prisoners, for 2 persons. This jail is generally over-crowded, and a proposal has been submitted for increasing the accommodation by the erection of new barracks. The Meherpur Subsidiary Jail has accommodation for 11 males and 3 females; at Kushtiā there is accommodation for 20 males and 4 females; at Rānāghāt for 9 males and 2 females; and at Chuādāngā for 9 males and 3 females. The mortality in the head-quarters jail frequently compares unfavourably with the average jail mortality of the Province. In 1907 it amounted to 50 per mille. In this connection the following remarks are extracted from the annual administration report of the Inspector-General of Prisons for the year 1907 :—" There were nine deaths in this jail with a daily average population of 171·87. I made a special enquiry into the health of the prisoners at Krishnagar Jail. The district has been unhealthy during the year, and an epidemic of pneumonia affected the jail, and caused five deaths out of the nine in this jail. The other fatal cases were (1) acci-dental, (2) a hill boy received into jail in a dying state, and a third, a sudden death from peritonitis. The arrangements now in vogue for the early detection and prompt treatment of the sick and weakly are satisfactory, and have greatly improved during the past year. I have reason to hope that the jail will show a better record soon, but it always receives a very high percentage of prisoners suffering from enlargement of the spleen and from malaria."

The industries carried on in the district jail are mustard-oil pressing, *surkhi* making, wheat grinding, weaving and spinning. In 1907 the average earning per head of persons sentenced to labour was Rs. 10. According to Hunter's Statistical Account the average earning amounted to Rs. 17 in 1854-55; to Rs. 8 in 1857-58; to Rs. 8 in 1860-61; and to Rs. 11 in 1870. During the last 30 years it has varied between Rs. 8 and Rs. 15.

CHAPTER XII.

LOCAL SELF-GOVERNMENT.

DISTRICT BOARD. The premier institution of Local Self-Government in the district is the District Board, which was constituted under Act III (B. C.) of 1885. Under the same Act five Local Boards were simultaneously constituted, viz., one in each of the five subdivisions of the district. Elections for the Local Boards were held, for the first time, in 1886, and the 31 elected members fell under the following classes: zamindārs, 16; pleaders, 9 ; traders, 3; and other occupations, 3. On an average for the whole district, the attendance of the electors was fair, the percentage of those who recorded their votes varying from 20 in the Kotwāli Thānā to 83 in the Gāngni Thānā. As soon as each Local Board was completed by the appointment of the nominated members, it met to elect two members to represent it on the District Board ; the ten members thus elected were supplemented by ten nominated by Government, and the District Board, thus constituted, took the place of the late District Road Committee on 1st October 1886. The constitution of the District Board has remained unaltered since. At the general election which was held in the year 1905-06, the attendance of the electors left a good deal to be desired, and elicited from Government the remark that "it is still the case that, except in the neighbourhood of Calcutta, little or no interest is taken in the elections." At the last general election, held in 1908-09, the attendance of the electors was small, and little interest was taken in the proceedings.

During the year 1895-96 four Union Committees were constituted, namely Murāgāchhā and Kissengunge in the Sadar Subdivision ; Poradah in the Kushtiā Subdivision; and Chuādāngā in the subdivision of the same name. These same four committees are still working, and their number has not been added to. The committees have been entrusted with the control of pounds, village roads, sanitation and water-supply ; in regard to Primary Schools their authority is restricted to inspection, and no power of control has been given to them.

The District Board consists of 20 members, exclusive of the District Magistrate who is *ex-officio* Chairman. As already stated, ten of the members are elected by the five Local Boards, and of the remainder five are *ex-officio* members and five nominated. Nadiā is a poor district for its size, and the sources of income of the District Board are more inadequate than in the other districts of the Presidency Division. Its average annual income, including provincial grants, for the seven years ending with 1904-05 was Rs. 1,55,350, and the average annual expenditure for the same period on major heads was Rs. 1,04,910 made up as follows: civil works, including public works establishment, Rs. 63,512; sanitation and water-supply, Rs. 2,400; medical relief, Rs. 2,966; and education, Rs. 36,032. In 1907-08 the total income, excluding opening balance, was Rs. 1,96,149; the principal receipts were Rs. 88,680 from rates, Rs. 47,567 from civil works (including Rs. 40,010 from contributions and Rs. 6,042 from tolls on ferries and roads), Rs. 34,423 from pounds (which are more profitable in Nadiā than in any other district in the Division), and Rs. 21,192 contributed by Government. The incidence of taxation per head of the population was ten pies. The total expenditure in the same year was Rs. 2,31,324, of which Rs. 1,51,820 was spent on civil works; Rs. 47,543 on education; Rs. 8,516 on medical relief; and Rs. 8,477 on famine relief.

The Board maintains 107 miles of metalled, and 716 miles of unmetalled roads, in addition to a large number of village roads with an aggregate length of about 526 miles. The cost of maintaining these roads in 1907-08 averaged Rs. 313, Rs. 29 and Rs. 17 per mile, respectively. The following extract is taken from the quinquennial administration report of the Presidency Division for the period ending with 1904-05:—"The District Board of Nadiā expended Rs. 57,857 on the improvement of roads and construction of bridges, of which the metalling of the Krishnagar-Plassey road, the improvement of the Bhairāmārā-Tārāgoniā road, the bridging of the Hānsdāngā and Bhangā *khals* on the former road, and of the Arangsdrisha *khāl* on the Krishnagar-Meherpur road, were the most important. For all these special grants were given from provincial revenues. The Board could not spend much on new works, and in all such enterprises they had to be materially assisted by Government, as the district is large, while its cess income is limited, and it contains a number of district and feeder roads originally constructed from provincial funds before District Boards came into existence." In 1871, according to Hunter's Statistical Account of the district, there were in it 284 miles of roads (number of

miles metalled unspecified), regularly kept up, besides minor
tracks and routes from village to village, and 44 roads maintained
by the landholders and peasantry. The annual cost of maintenance of these was about Rs. 45,000 ; whereas Rs. 1,13,000 was
spent on roads in 1907-08.

The Board leased out 250 pounds, from which it derived the
substantial income of Rs. 34,423 in the year 1907-08. Its
expenditure on education during the same year was Rs. 47,543,
the greater part of this sum, *i.e.*, Rs. 37,090, falling under the
head of grants-in-aid to primary schools, and Rs. 2,114 only
going towards secondary education. It maintained three Middle
schools, and 45 Aided : it also aided 97 Upper Primary, and 643
Lower Primary schools. Its expenditure on hospitals and dispensaries was Rs. 6,255 (for which sum it maintained two and
aided nine dispensaries), and on sanitation Rs. 864.

Local
Boards.
The five Local Boards at Krishnagar, Rānāghāt, Chuādāngā,
Meherpur and Kushtiā exercise jurisdiction over the subdivisional charges of corresponding names. They were among the
first Local Boards to be established in the Province. The
Krishnagar Local Board has 12 members, of whom 2 are
elected and 10 nominated. The Rānāghāt Local Board has nine
members, of whom 6 are elected and 3 nominated. The Chuādāngā Local Board is similarly constituted. The Meherpur
Local Board has nine members, of whom 6 are elected, 2 nominated and one is *ex-officio*. The Kushtiā Local Board has nine
members of whom 4 are elected and 5 nominated. The functions
of these bodies are unimportant, consisting mainly of the
administration of village roads, the control of pounds and
ferries, and the distribution of grants-in-aid to Primary schools.

Union
Commit-
tees.
There are four Union Committees, as noted above. They
each have jurisdiction over 10 square miles, with an aggregate
population of 42,890, ranging from 13,197 in the Murāgāchhā Union to 8,545 in the Poradah Union. Murāgāchhā
has nine members, and the other three seven members each.
Each Committee received a grant of Rs. 300 from the District
Board in 1907-08, and each expended its full income. The duties
at present entrusted to these Committees consist of attention to
village sanitation, and the up-keep of village roads and drains
within their respective jurisdictions.

MUNICI-
PALITIES.
There are nine Municipalities within the district, viz.,
Krishnagar, Sāntipur, Rānāghāt, Nabadwip, Kushtiā, Kumārkhāli, Meherpur, Birnagar and Chākdaha. In 1907-08 the total
number of rate-payers was 26,340. The percentage of rate-
payers to total population within municipal limits varied from 23·1

in Meherpur to 36·1 in Nabadwip, the corresponding percentage for the whole of the Presidency Division being 19·8. The average incidence of taxation per head of population was Re. 1-4-7, ranging from 8 annas 3 pies in Meherpur to Re. 1-10-2, in Krishnagar; the Divisional average for the same year was Re. 1-8-9.

The Krishnagar Municipality was established in the year Krishna- 1864, and its affairs are administered by a committee consisting gar. of 21 members, of whom 14 are elected, 3 nominated and 4 *ex-officio*. The area within municipal limits is about 7 square miles, and there are 6,226 rate-payers, their percentage on the total population being 25·3. The average annual income for the five years ending with 1905-06 was Rs. 48,129 and the expenditure Rs. 45,107. In 1907-08 the total income, exclusive of the opening balance, was Rs. 48,317, and the incidence of taxation was Re. 1-10-2 per head of the population. The main source of income was a tax on holdings, which was levied at the rate of $7\frac{1}{2}$ per cent. on the annual valuation, and yielded the sum of Rs. 23,389. Part IX of the Act is in force, and latrine fees are levied in accordance with a sliding scale on the annual valuation of the holdings; the tax collected under this head amounted to Rs. 11,836. The only other item of any importance on the receipt side was the rent of pounds, which yielded Rs. 869. The total expenditure during the same year amounted to Rs. 48,479. The largest item in this was Rs. 17,748 (equal to 36·6 per cent. of the total expenditure) for conservancy. Public works accounted for Rs. 11,728 (24·1 per cent.); medical relief, for Rs. 8,480 (17·4 per cent.); education, for Rs. 950 (1·9 per cent.); while Rs. 923, or 1·9 per cent. of the total expenditure, was devoted to water-supply.

The Sāntipur Municipality was established in 1865 with 24 Sāntipur. Commissioners of whom 16 were elected and the remainder nominated. The Subdivisional Officer of Rānāghāt was the *ex-officio* Chairman.

This constitution continued till the year 1903, when the Commissioners were superseded by Government for contumaciously refusing to introduce Part IX of the Act, and give proper attention to the conservancy of the town. The municipality was, however, re-established in September 1904, with nine Commissioners appointed by Government, and the same *ex-officio* Chairman as before. The elective system has not, however, been restored up to date (1909).

The area within municipal limits is about 7 square miles, and the number of rate-payers is 7,824 or 29·1 per cent. of the population.

The average annual income for the five years ending in 1904-05 was Rs. 30,386, and the average expenditure Rs. 29,725. In 1907-08 the total income, exclusive of the opening balance, was Rs. 43,646, and the incidence of taxation was Re. 1-5-2 per head of the population. The tax on holdings is in force; it is levied at the rate of 7 per cent. on the annual valuation of the holdings, and in the year mentioned it yielded Rs. 19,775. The latrine tax, which was introduced during the year in which the Commissioners remained superseded, is levied at the rate of 7 per cent. on the annual valuation of the holdings, and it yielded an income of Rs. 11,871. Pounds produced Rs. 704. No other item on the receipt side calls for notice. The total expenditure in this same year was Rs. 49,822, the largest item on this side being Rs. 18,588 (37·3 per cent. of the total expenditure) for conservancy. Rs. 8,078 (16·2 per cent) was expended on education ; Rs. 5,732 (11·5 per cent). on public works; Rs. 2,933 (5·8 per cent.) on medical relief, and Rs. 647 (1·2 per cent) on water-supply.

Rānāgbāt. The Rānāghat Municipality was established in the year 1864 with 14 Commissioners, of whom 5 were appointed *ex-officio*, and the remaining 9 nominated by Government. When Act III (B.C.) of 1884 came into force, the number of the Commissioners was raised to 18, of whom 12 were elected and 6 nominated ; there has been no change in the constitution since then. The area within municipal limits is about $2\frac{1}{2}$ square miles, and the number of rate-payers is 7,824, or 29·1 per cent. of the total population. The average annual income for the five years ending with 1904-05 was Rs. 11,810, and the average expenditure Rs. 11,775. In 1907-08 the total income, excluding the opening balance, was Rs. 14,128, and the incidence of taxation was Re. 1-6-5 per head of the population. The tax on holdings is in force, and it was levied at the rate of $6\frac{1}{4}$ per cent. of the annual valuation. The latrine tax is also in force and is levied at the rate of $5\frac{1}{2}$ per cent. on the annual valuation of the holdings. The income from the former of these two sources was Rs. 6,252, and from the latter Rs. 4,283. There is no other item on the receipt side which calls for notice. The total expenditure in this same year was Rs. 15,004. Rupees 6,217 or 41·4 per cent. of the total expenditure, was devoted to conservancy ; the next most important item was public works, on which Rs. 2,558 (17·04 per cent.) was expended. On medical relief Rs. 2,576 (17·1 per cent). was expended, on education Rs. 368 (2·4 per cent.), and on water-supply Rs. 303 (2·01 per cent.)

Nabudwip. The Nabadwip Municipality was constituted in the year 1869. There were originally 12 Commissioners, of whom 8 were elected and the remainder nominated. But in January 1904 the Commissioners suffered the same fate as those of Sāntipur, and for the same reason. They were superseded until March 1905 when the Municipality was re-established with 9 Commissioners appointed by Government. In September 1907 the elective system was restored, and the town has now (1909) 12 Commissioners, of whom 8 are elected and the remainder nominated. The area within municipal limits is about 3½ square miles, and the number of rate-payers is 3,931, or 36·1 per cent. of the total population, The average annual income for the five years ending with 1905-06 was Rs. 12,777, and the average expenditure Rs. 11,535. In 1907-08 the total income, excluding the opening balance, was Rs. 14,801, and the incidence of taxation was Re. 1-2-4 per head of the population. The tax on holdings is in force, and it is levied at the rate of 6¼ per cent. on the annual valuation of the holdings ; it produced an income of Rs. 6,227. The latrine tax is also in force, and it is levied at the same rate as the tax on the holdings ; it produced an income of Rs. 5,577. The income derived from fees paid under the Puri Lodging House Act, which is in force in this town, is not included in the above figures; the sum realized under this head amounts to about Rs. 3,000 per annum. The total expenditure during the year 1907-08 was Rs. 15,214. The principal items of expenditure were as follows :—Rs. 6,955 (45·7 per cent. of the total expenditure) on conservancy ; Rs. 2,737 (17·9 per cent.), on public works ; Rs. 1,886 (12 3 per cent.) on medical relief, and Rs. 498 (3·2 per cent.) on education. The expenditure on water-supply was only Rs. 23, or 1 per cent. of the total expenditure.

The Kushtiā Municipality was established in the year 1869, Kushtiā with 12 Commissioners, 8 of whom were elected and the rest nominated. There has been no change in the constitution since then. The area within municipal limits is about 3 square miles, and the number of rate-payers is 1,290, or 24·2 per cent. of the population of the town. The average annual income for the five years ending with 1904-05 was Rs. 9,258, and the average expenditure was Rs. 8,534. In 1907-08 the total income, exclusive of the opening balance, was Rs. 9,236, and the incidence of taxation Re. 1-6-1 per head of the population. Both of the main systems of taxation are in force, viz., that on holdings, which is levied at 6¼ per cent. of their annual valuation, and that on persons, for which there is no fixed rate. The former produced Rs. 1,600 and the latter Rs. 1,556. The latrine tax is also in force, and the income from it was Rs. 2,343 ; it is levied at the rate of 5 per cent. on the annual valuation of the holdings. In

the year under reference the total expenditure amounted to
Rs. 10,785, out of which the chief item was conservancy, which
accounted for Rs. 3,200, or 29·6 per cent. of the total expenditure.
Other important items were public works Rs. 3,084 (28·6 per
cent.) and medical relief Rs. 1,116 (10·3 per cent). The expenditure on water-supply was Rs. 634 (5·8 per cent.) and on
education Rs. 297 (2·7 per cent.).

Kumār-
khāli.

The Kumārkhāli Municipality was established in the year 1869
with 6 Commissioners, all appointed by Government; the number of
Commissioners was raised to 9 in 1875 ; in 1884 the privilege of
the elective system was conferred upon the town, 15 Commissioners being allotted for it, of whom 10 were elected and the
remainder nominated. There has been no change in the constitution since then. The area within municipal limits is about 2½
square miles, and the number of rate-payers is 1,176, or 25·5
per cent. of the population of the town. The average annual
income for the five years ending with 1904-05 was Rs. 5,876, and
the average annual expenditure Rs. 5,702. In 1907-08 the total
income, exclusive of the opening balance, was Rs. 6,092, and the
incidence of taxation Re. 1-2-9 per head of the population. The
main source of income is the tax on persons which is levied at no
fixed rate; this tax produced Rs. 2,789. The latrine tax is also
in force, and is levied at the rate of 7½ per cent. on the annual
valuation of the holdings; the income from this source was
Rs. 2,094. The total expenditure during the same year was
Rs. 6,342. Conservancy accounted for the expenditure of
Rs. 2,248, which represents 35 4 per cent of the total expenditure.
The other main items on this side of the account were:—public
works, Rs. 1,476 (23·2 per cent.) ; medical relief, Rs. 530 (8·3 per
cent.) ; and water-supply Rs. 170 (2·6 per cent.). The expenditure on education was only Rs. 120, or 1·8 per cent. of the total
expenditure.

Meherpur.

The Meherpur Municipality was established in the year 1869
with 9 Commissioners, of whom 6 were elected and the rest nominated. There has been no change in its constitution since then.
The area within municipal limits is about 7¼ square miles, and
the number of rate-payers is 1,334 or 23·1 per cent. of the total
population. The average annual income for the five years ending
with 1904-05 was Rs. 3,841, and the average expenditure
Rs. 3,440. In the year 1907-08 the total income, exclusive of the
opening balance, was Rs. 4,324, and the incidence of taxation
was 8 annas 3 pies per head of the population. The main source
of income was the tax on persons (not levied at any fixed rate),
which produced Rs. 2,370. Part IX of the Municipal Act is not

in force. The income from pounds was Rs. 441, which represents the large proportion of over ten per cent. of the total income. The total expenditure during the same year was Rs. 3,958, of which Rs. 1,156, or 29·2 per cent. of the total expenditure, went on medical relief. Rs. 528 (13·3 per cent.) was spent on waterworks; Rs. 915 (23·1 per cent.) on public works; Rs. 284 (7·1 per cent.) on conservancy; and Rs. 181 (4·5 per cent.) on education.

The Birnagar Municipality was established in the year 1869 Birnagar. with 12 Commissioners, of whom 8 were elected, and the remainder nominated; there has been no change in the constitution since then. The area within municipal limits is about 2 square miles, and the number of rate-payers is 790, or 25·2 per cent. of the total population. The average annual income for the five years ending with 1904-05 was Rs. 3,993, and- the average expenditure Rs. 2,875. In the year 1907-08 the total income, exclusive of the opening balance, was Rs. 3,535, and the incidence of taxation was 15 annas 3 pie per head of the population. The main source of income was the tax upon persons, which is levied at no fixed rate; this produced Rs. 2,768. Part IX of the Municipal Act is not in force, and latrine tax is consequently not levied. The total expenditure during the same year was Rs. 4,287, of which Rs. 1,504 (35 per cent. of the total expenditure) was devoted to public works; Rs. 844 (19·6 per cent.) to medical relief; Rs. 590 (13·7 per cent.) to water-supply; Rs. 350 (8·1 per cent.) to conservancy; and Rs. 114 (2·6 per cent.) to education.

The Chākdaha Municipality was established in the year 1886, Chākdaha. with 12 nominated Commissioners; there has been no change in the constitution since then. The area within municipal limits is about 5 square miles, and the number of rate-payers is 1,340, or 24·4 per cent. of the total population. The average annual income for the five years ending with 1904-05 was Rs. 3,739, and the average expenditure Rs. 3,605. In 1907-08 the total income, exclusive of the opening balance, was Rs. 4,293, and the incidence of taxation was 11 annas 1 pie per head of the population. The main source of income was the tax upon persons, which is not levied at any fixed rate; this produced Rs. 2,592. The latrine tax is not in force. A comparatively large income, Rs. 1,056, accrued from the tax on animals and vehicles. The total expenditure was Rs. 5,148. Rs. 1,093, or 21·2 per cent. of the total expenditure, was devoted to medical relief; Rs. 1,368 (26·5 per cent.) to public works; Rs. 854 (16·5 per cent.) to water supply; Rs. 274 (5·3 per cent.) to conservancy; and Rs. 174 (3·3 per cent.) to education.

CHAPTER XIII.

EDUCATION.

THE Nadiā district has for centuries been famed for its learning, but in early days literacy was confined to a few privileged castes, and even now it cannot be said to have diffused among the masses to the extent which would have been expected. It is true that the census of 1901 showed that there had been a relatively large improvement in this respect during the preceding twenty years, but the percentage of males recorded as literate was only equal to that for the whole of Bengal, which is certainly not in keeping with the reputation of the district, especially considering its proximity to the metropolitan area, which is naturally the most favoured part of the Province from the point of view of education. There are no statistics to show what proportion of the people could read and write at the time when the first census was taken in 1872, but the Subdivisional Officer of Chuādāngā made a detailed enquiry into this point over the greater part of his subdivision in the year 1871-72, and from the figures obtained by him it appears that at that time only 2·4 per cent. of the people were sufficiently literate to be able to read and write. The percentage of literate males was 5·5 in 1881, as is evidenced by the figures of the census of that year. The censuses of 1891 and 1901 showed 7·1 and 10·4 of the male population respectively as literate, 10·4 being the exact percentage of male literacy of the Province as a whole in 1901. The percentage of male literacy thus increased nearly twofold in the 20 years ending with 1901.

In the year 1856-57 there were only 19 Government and aided schools in the district; these were attended by 1,865 pupils. By 1871 the number of such schools had increased to 252, attended by 9,120 pupils. In addition to these there were 255 private schools attended by 6,406 pupils. There were thus in all 507 schools attended by 15,516 pupils. In comparing these figures with those of subsequent years, it must be remembered that in 1871 the Bangāon subdivision of the Jessore district was still included in Nadiā, it not having been transferred to Jessore until 1883. By 1895 the number of schools had increased to 973, and the attendance to 31,304. In 1908-09 the corresponding figures were 1,175 and 41,505 respectively. Of these latter schools 46 were maintained or aided by Municipalities and 738 by the District Board. Included in the above were one High English school with 216 pupils, 4 Middle English schools with 517 pupils, and 41 Primary schools with 2,052 pupils, which were chiefly maintained by the Church Missionary Society.

There is one Arts College in the district, namely, that at COLLE-Krishnagar. It was founded by the Government in 1845 and is GIATE EDUCA-under the control of the Director of Public Instruction, Bengal. TION. Any person who has passed the University Entrance Examination may be admitted. Students pay a monthly fee of Rs. 5.

The College stands upon an enclosed compound of upwards of 100 bighas. It occupies two buildings. The larger one, which is the main College building, is a handsome structure covering about three bighas, or one acre. It was erected in 1856 at a cost of Rs. 66,876, of which about Rs. 17,000 was contributed by private persons. There are thirteen free studentships which are within the gift of the subscribers to the cost of the building, each donation of Rs. 1,000 having entitled the donor to nominate to one free studentship in perpetuity, and each additional Rs. 500 to one further similar nomination. The smaller building is a later addition, in which parts of the Physical and Chemical Laboratories are located. Part of the ground occupied was purchased by Government; for the remainder the College is indebted to the munificence of the Mahārājā of Nadiā and Mahārāni Swarnamayi of Cossimbazar.

In 1871 the B.A. classes were abolished by Sir George Campbell, then Lieutenant-Governor of Bengal, and for some years the College only afforded instruction up to the First Examination in Arts. In 1875, however, Sir Richard Temple, on the petition of the chief inhabitants of the district, consented to restore the College to its former status, provided that a considerable share of the increased cost was subscribed by the community. A sum amounting to more than Rs. 40,000 was subscribed during the year, and with this endowment B.A. classes in the B course were opened. Classes for the A course for the B.A. were opened in June 1888.

The College, which was affiliated in 1857, has been affiliated in Arts up to the B.A., and in Science up to the B.Sc. Standard, under the new regulations.

A prize of Rs. 80, founded by Babu Mohini Mohan Ray in 1883, and called the Mohini Mohan Ray prize, is awarded annually to the student who most successfully passes the B.A. Examination with honours, or to a graduate of the College who passes the M.A. Examination in any subject.

Another prize of Rs. 8, founded by Babu Syama Charan Maitra, and called the "Smith and Macdonell Prize," is annually awarded to the student who most successfully passes the F.A. Examination and prosecutes his studies for the B.A. Examination in the Krishnagar College.

The College endowment funds now amount to Rs. 46,500.

There is a Hindu Hostel attached to the College, which is under the direct control of the Principal, and is managed by a Superintendent who is also the Gymnastic Master of the College.

The College has been very sparsely attended by Muhammadans (during the five years ending on 31st March 1907 there was never at one time more than one Muhammadan on the rolls), and in 1905 the Principal reported that the Muhammadans of the town and district could not afford to give their children a proper education. It was thought that the absence of a Muhammadan boarding house in Krishnagar was partly responsible, and, in July 1906, the funds necessary for opening a hostel for them were sanctioned, and it was arranged that one of the College Maulvis should reside in it as Superintendent. However, up to the end of 1907, no application for accommodation in this boarding-house had been received, and the funds sanctioned had not been utilized.

In 1909 the staff consisted of the Principal, five Professors, four Lecturers, and an Assistant for each of the Laboratories. The number of students on the rolls was 124.

SECON-
DARY
EDUCA-
TION.
In the year 1856-57 there were only three aided Higher and Middle schools in the district. The number of Higher schools, had increased to 11 by the year 1871-72. In the year ending on 31st March 1899 there were 16 High English schools. Ten years later, i.e., on 31st March 1909, there were 25 High schools in the district. Of these, one, Krishnagar Collegiate School, was maintained by Government; one, Sāntipur Municipal school, was maintained by a municipality; 17 were aided by the District Board and municipalities; and 6 were unaided. These 25 schools were attended by 4,813 pupils, giving an average of 192 pupils per school. The average cost of these schools for the year was Rs. 4,047. The names of the two schools which are supported entirely from the public funds have already been given. The following schools are aided by Government:—
Amlā Sadarpur, Belpukur, Bhajanghāt, Chuādāngā, Gosāin

Durgāpur, Harināráyanpur, Kumārkhāli, Kushtiā, Mājdiā Rail-
bāzār, Murāgāchhā, Meherpur, Rānāghāt, Sudhākarpur, Shikārpur, Krishnagar Church Missionary Society, Jāmserpur. The
Nabadwip Hindu school is aided by the Nabadwip |Municipality·
The following are private and unaided schools, which, however,
have been recognized by the Calcutta University :-- Krishnagar
Anglo-Vernacular school, Khoksā Janipur, Sutrāgarh (Mahārājā
of Nadiā's) High English school, Sāntipur Oriental Academy,
Juniādaha, Natudaha. None of these unaided schools were in
existence even ten years ago.

In 1898-99 there were 48 Middle English schools, and the
same number were in existence on the 31st March 1909. The
average cost of these schools was Rs. 949, and the average
attendance at them was 78 pupils. The number of Middle
Vernacular schools was, in 1871-72, 31, including 4 unaided;
in 1898-99 28 (none unaided); and on 31st March 1909, 13
only. The average expenditure on these schools in the year
1908-09 was Rs. 588, and they were attended on the average by
64 pupils. The falling off in the lowest of these three classes of
schools, and the increase in the highest, are a clear indication of
the desire of the people for an English education rather than a
purely vernacular one.

The number of Primary schools, including *pāthshālās*, was 229 PRIMARY
in 1871-72. In 1898-99 there were 85 Upper Primary and 615 TION. EDUCA-
Lower Primary schools. On the 31st March 1909 there were
123 Upper Primary and 706 Lower Primary schools. The
total number of pupils at the three periods mentioned were 4,836,
20,824 and 26,117 respectively; the latter figures do not, however,
include the pupils who are attending the Primary classes of
secondary schools; taking these in, the total number of pupils
reciving primary education on 31st March 1909 was 31,235. The
spread of primary education has more than kept pace with the
increase in the population during the last 30 or 40 years, and
this notwithstanding the fact that there has recently been some
falling off in the number of schools owing to the insistence upon
greater efficiency in the teachers.

The progress of female education has been more marked than FEMALE
that of male primary education. In the year 1871-72 there TION. EDUCA-
were only 21 girls' schools; by the year 1898-99 their number
had increased to 103; and on 31st March 1909 there were 152
primary schools for girls only, in addition to which 589 girls
were attending at primary schools for boys. During the year
1908-09 the number of girls and women attending classes at
public institutions increased from 4,275 to 4,753, the increase

being made up of 10, or 6·2 per cent, in the number of pupils in special schools, and 468, or 11·3 per cent., in secondary and primary schools. The number of girls in the middle stage of education was 10, and in the primary stage 4,572. There are two Model Primary Schools in the district, one at Sāntipur and the other at Nabadwip; each of these is attended by more than 50 pupils and has three qualified teachers; they are shortly to be recognized as Government institutions. One female teacher was employed during the year at a cost of Rs. 389 to impart instruction in zenānās; she had 25 pupils.

TECHNI-CAL EDU-CATION. There is no public technical institution in the district, but an Industrial School is maintained at Chapra by the Church Missionary Society. This was attended by 33 pupils in 1908.09, and the cost was Rs. 1,050. The school received no direct assistance from either Government or the District Board, but the latter paid the sum of Rs. 588 for special scholarships for boys leaving the school for further training in the Kānchrāpāra workshops and elsewhere. The Divisional Commissioner has recently (1909) given this school special grants for the purchase of a steam engine and of a screw-turning lathe.

TRAINING SCHOOLS. The Church Missionary Society maintains a first grade Training School at Krishnagar. It had 27 pupils on the rolls on 31st March 1909. The total expenditure was Rs. 9,069, of which Rs. 2,800 was met from provincial revenues, and the balance by the Society. There are ten Guru Training Schools, which are attended by 134 pupils; they are maintained at a cost of Rs. 14,709 which is met from provincial revenues and fees. A Training School for females is maintained at Krishnagar by the Church of England Zenana Mission Society; it is attended by 36 pupils, and six-sevenths of the cost is borne by the Society, the balance being covered by a contribution from provincial revenues.

MUHAM-MADAN EDUCA-TION. Although the ratio of Muhammadans to Hindus in the district is about 6 to 4, the ratio of Muhammadan pupils at the schools to Hindus is about 1 to 2. The Muhammadans of the district cannot therefore be described otherwise than as backward in education; but they are steadily improving their position in this respect. In 1871-72 the ratio of Muhammadan pupils to Hindu was 1 to 8, and in 1898-99 it was 1 to 4; the fact that during the last ten years the disparity has been further reduced to 1 to 2, gives hopes that the advantages of education are receiving wider recognition among the Muhammadan community.

SANSKRIT EDUCA-TION. This has been dealt with in the article upon the town of Nabadwip in the Gazetteer Chapter of this volume.

There are small libraries at Rānāghāt, Kānchrāpārā, Sāntipur, LIBRARIES AND NEWS-PAPERS.
Meherpur, and Haradhām. There is a useful library attached
to the Krishnagar College, but this is not available to the public.
One weekly newspaper, *Banga Ratna*, is printed in Calcutta and
published in Krishnagar, but it has a very small and purely
local circulation. A weekly paper, *Banga Lakshmi*, and a
monthly magazine, *Jubak*, are printed in Calcutta and published
in Sāntipur ; they also have a very restricted circulation.

CHAPTER XIV.

CHRISTIAN MISSIONS.

ACCORDING to the last (1901) census, there are 7,912 Indian Christians in the Nadia district. This number is exceeded only in three districts in the Province, namely, 24-Parganas, Santal Parganas and Ranchi. Out of the total number of Indian Christians returned, 5,715 belong to the Anglican Church, and 2,125 to the Roman Catholic Church. In the following pages a short account is given of the work of the different Missions in the district.

CHURCH MISSIONARY SOCIETY. The first recorded visit of Church of England missionaries to the district occurred, in 1822, when Messrs. Hill, Warden and Trawin of the London Missionary Society went to Sāntipur to see whether it would make a suitable mission station. They reported that "the people have much simplicity and received the truth more earnestly than the Bengalies generally." They recommended the establishment of a station here for various reasons, among which was "the favourable disposition of the moral feelings of the people, which, we conceive, has been cherished materially by the general instruction which has been diffused by the Company's school." No specific action, however, appears to have been taken upon this report.

In 1832, a Mr. Deerr, who was then stationed at Kālnā in the Bardwān district, went to Krishnagar for a change of air, and, while there, opened two schools in the town of Nabadwip and one at Krishnagar itself. For the next few years work consisted mainly in the establishment of more schools, but, in 1838, 560 persons were baptised at Krishnagar, Rānābandha, Bhabarpārā, Solo and Anandabāsh, and a mud church was built at Bhabarpārā. In 1840 mission houses were built at Kapāsdāngā, Chāprā and Ratnapur, and another church was built at Solo. The following year the foundation-stone of the present church at Chāprā was laid, and the church at Krishnagar was commenced. The plans of the latter were drawn up by Captain Smith, and the cost was met from subscriptions from the residents and others, on condition that the Church Missionary Society should hold English as well as Bengali services in it. Both these churches were opened in 1843, and have been maintained ever since. By 1843 the Christian community numbered 3,902, and free boarding-schools had been started in which 42 boys and 22 girls were being fed and taught. During the next few years one or two other churches were built and mission houses opened, and the work spread over the greater part of the district; but most of the missionaries engaged in it appear to have been disheartened at the progress: the general trend of the reports submitted by them was that they distrusted the motives of the converts. There can be little doubt that the large access to the community in 1838 was caused mainly by the distress which resulted from the great inundation of that year and the hope that admission to the church would secure some relief from temporal necessities. The question of caste had also begun to give trouble. In 1850 the school at Chāprā was commenced, and in the following years some attempts were made to impart industrial training. The conditions that prevailed in the church about this time were not considered satisfactory, as may be seen from the following extract from a report submitted by the Revd. S. Hasell in 1859:—

"It is of course possible to sketch a very dark picture of any of the congregations in this zillah, and perhaps one of the darkest might be Chupra, but still there is another view, and the people are not, I firmly believe, so much to blame as would appear on the first glance. They|have been trained to be what they are, by the over-anxiety, kindness and liberality of England.

"I will try to explain. There has always been an anxiety to get a number of Christians and to get all their children to school. There has been no lack of funds for the erection and maintaining in efficiency the machinery as schools, churches, etc. The poor have been, until very recently, liberally provided for. The Missionary has been all things to all men, always ready to listen to any tale of distress or suffering, and always anxious to assist to the utmost of his power every applicant. The teachers have always been employed, when necessary, in pleading the cause of any oppressed by zemindar, and in every possible way the whole mission establishment has been at the service, so to speak, of the Christian, and they have not failed to perceive that in some way or other are they of some importance. The education provided for their children they neither want nor appreciate, and the anxiety for their spiritual welfare, which leads the missionary to beseech them in Christ's stead to be reconciled to God, they regard as the result of fear lest they should leave the Mission; in short, many put on the profession of Christianity as a means of 'improving their worldly condition, and it is not surprising, after the number of years during which they have realized that as a fact that they should avail themselves of any new opportunities which may arise apparently tending to that end. To be more explicit, it may be put thus: for years my predecessor here, with untiring zeal and self-denial, devoted himself wholly to the people. He made their care his own, and wearied 'himself to provide for their temporal wants and necessities, in the hope of securing their attention to spiritual things. Many, now the heads of families, have grown up under his kind, fostering care, and treasure up his name among their household treasures. Surely neither he nor they can be blamed; but he leaves for Europe, I take charge, and gradually reveal my inability to follow in his footsteps. I have no money to lend. I cannot, and will not, superintend the many modes of employment which his ingenuity had devised to assist them. They are told over and over again that they must now begin to help themselves. The style of living in the schools is reduced almost to the standard of that of the parents of the children; clothes are no longer dealt out with a liberal hand to those women who called themselves poor. The burden of supporting the really poor is thrown at once and for ever on the congregation, and, in short, everything by degrees is being cut off that in any way partakes of the nature of support. As a natural consequence, the people are displeased; the teachers, who are so intimately mixed up with the people, that they have scarcely an independent opinion, secretly agree with them, whatever they may say to me openly; and thus the whole community is prepared to murmur, and the least spark leads to an explosion. There is, however, still enough left, and more than enough, to keep the congregation together: unless some greater inducement present itself . . . . They would join any man, be he Baptist, Independent, or Papist, if he came and really paid down enough to render it worth their while to leave us. The Gospel has not taken such a hold upon them as yet, as to render them proof against temptations, especially when the zemindar is pressing them hard for money. This must be considered before any judgment is passed upon them. The Mission has been very like a damp hothouse, and it is no wonder that some of the plants should fade and look sickly for a time, now that they are exposed to the influence of a more natural atmosphere.

"I believe, however, that in time they will be healthier and more independent; but it will take time, it may be years;

meanwhile we may go on gradually withdrawing aid, and wait, and watch and pray."

In 1863, the Christian community was reckoned to be about 3,800. In the following year the Training or the Normal School, which had first been established at Solo, then transferred to Kapāsdāngā, then located for a time at Sāntipur, was finally moved to Krishnagar, where it has remained and been maintained ever since. There is nothing special to record of the next ten years or so, but towards the end of the seventies the caste question had become acute. The following extract from a report submitted by Mr. Vaughan in 1878 may be quoted:—

"When fifteen months ago I arrived in this district, my first anxiety was to understand the actual state of things. I had a general impression that the condition of the mission was far from satisfactory. I am bound to say that the reality has proved to be worse than my fears.

"The standard of education throughout the whole district was found to be mournfully low; a painful state of ignorance marked great numbers of our Christians; a general neglect of religious ordinances, disregard of the sabbath, or other inconsistencies were all too apparent. The lack of earnestness and piety in too many of the Society's agents was also a very disheartening feature. Then, again, the fact that, for a long series of years, not a single convert had been made from the surrounding heathen, was strange and anomalous. The outer circle of darkness and death had derived neither light nor life from the Church in its centre. Indeed, a bare idea of the church being an aggressive and evangelizing agency seems to have never entered the minds of the Christians.

"Not a little struck was I the other day in coming upon an entry made by Bishop Milman in a church book here. His Lordship had made a visitation of the district just two months before his death. His words are, 'the Church has come to be looked upon as a kind of "jāt," (caste), which is well enough in its way and may be acquiesced in, but not to be wondered at, or attractive to others.'

"And yet there are elements of better things in the Church. The people are affectionate and trustful, they are intelligent, they are industrious and fairly energetic, nor are godly souls wanting among them.

"But the elements of good spoken of are no new thing; they have existed all along in the mission; yet, notwithstanding, a living death has for 40 years characterized the Church. This state of things has led some persons to ask whether there might

not be some hidden evil, some radical error, operating to the
prejudice of the Mission, and nullifying every effort to raise and
improve it. This conjecture, I am convinced, was a true one:
and God in His goodness has brought the root-evil to light.
Within the last few months strange facts have been revealed, that
the whole body of our Christians, the Society's agents included,
have for 40 years been fast bound in the bonds of caste: indeed,
at no period has caste ever been renounced; it was brought over
bodily with the people at the time of their baptism, and for all this
time has that heathenish and deadly institution maintained its
sway in the Mission.

"The first thing which awakened my surprise and suspicion
was the discovery that the Christians were spilt up into sections
bearing distinctive names, answering to their caste-standing
prior to their conversion. Thus the Hindu converts and their
descendants have ever called themselves 'Hindu Christians.' In
the same way the converts from the Musalman pale have ever
clung to the term 'Musalman Christians.' And as in their
unconverted state it was unlawful to mingle their blood, so to this
day the 'Hindu' and 'Musalman' Christians, respectively, refuse
to intermarry. Nay, the very sub-castes of the former standing
have been maintained in unbroken integrity. Thus the
Christians are subdivided into two sections called 'Satgeya' and
'Soterapera,' answering to Musalman sects in this district.
These again kept up the traditions of their Moslem forefathers
and refuse to intermarry. The grandchildren of the first
converts as rigidly maintain their caste prejudices and exclusive-
ness as did their ancestors ages ago. The hallowed fusing power
of the Gospel has been lost, and the glorious oneness of that
family which is the Church and household of God has never been
realized.

"But it is in relation to other sections of the Christian community that the worse aspect of caste feeling presents itself. The
members of this section are called 'Moochie Christians.' As their
name implies, they were converts from one of those despised castes
who occupy the lowest place in the Hindu system. As dealers in
skins and leather, they were abhorrent to orthodox Hindus, who
worship the cow. Hinduism thus fixed its unmerited stigma upon
them. Christianity has not removed that stigma ; for although
baptised and grafted into the Church of Christ, their Christian
brethren have ever regarded them with loathing and animosity.
Besides personal dislike, a selfish consideration had actuated the
other sections in their treatment of these brethren. They found
that by denouncing the moochies they obtained perfect toleration,

and even caste recognition, among their heathen neighbours; but to own the moochies, and treat them as brethren in Christ, would have severed the dubious tie which they wish to maintain with the outer circle. Accordingly for all these years their effort has been to ostracise those poor brethren, and even to drive them beyond the pale of Christianity. If a native Pastor ventured to baptise a moochie infant, he was threatened with desertion by the rest of his people ; when a poor moochie brother ventured into a church, the congregation indignantly protested; if they presumed to approach the holy table, the other communicants declared they would withdraw. It is a sad and strange story, and one ceases to wonder that under such a state of things the Church's life was faint and slow."

In 1880 Mr. Vaughan wrote :—

"It will soon be two years since the outbreak at Bollobhpore, with its strange revelations, startled us. That unlooked-for event brought to light hidden evils of which hardly any one had dreamt, and went very far towards accounting for the past history of this Mission. It largely explained the strange enigma that, despite all effort to the contrary, the Church in these regions had remained lifeless and inactive, and had made for well nigh forty years hardly any accessions from the outer mass of heathen darkness.

"It showed that caste, with all its deadly and deterrent influences, had been imported into the church by the first converts, and had lived on in unbroken integrity for all those years ; that the same impassable barriers, as Hindus, Mussalmans and moochies before their conversion, continued still, to divide them as fellow Christians ; so to divide them that not even would they meet at the Holy Supper of love.

"But it is important to guard against too sanguine expectations: indeed, few persons who rightly comprehend the nature of the evils which have oppressed this Mission, would look for a speedy triumph. To suppose that caste prejudice, which is burnt into the very nature of the people, will expire in a day, is a great mistake. . . . .

"Sombre, therefore, as the general aspect of things may be, it is not unbroken gloom; streaks of light and hope cheer us on every way. For these we are most thankful, but I am particularly anxious that too much should not be made of the signs of good which have been vouchsafed us. I have seen more than once the statement that 'the caste struggle is well nigh over, and that signs of spiritual awakening are appearing throughout the district.' I cannot bear out such a statement. The caste struggle is not over, and we could not make a greater mistake than to assume that it was."

In 1881 Mr. Vaughan reported that for some time no outward expression of caste feeling had given trouble, and the following year Mr. Clifford, who succeeded him, reported to the same effect, but added that the feeling was not eradicated, but only suppressed, and that the hope lay in the next generation. This hope appears to have been fulfilled, for there is no further reference to the matter in later reports, and it is to be presumed that, the caste question has now ceased to cause trouble.

After a period of financial difficulties, which led to the closing of some outstations, work was resumed with vigour, and in 1885 the Bishop visited the district and remarked that "the wonderful improvement effected during the last five or six years shows how much depends upon wise, systematic supervision and mutual confidence: there is now no more hopeful and interesting mission in North India than that in the Nadiā district." In the same year the Church of England Zenana Mission Society commenced work in the district.

In 1886 was held at Balabhpur the first meeting of the Nadiā District Native Church Council, which, together with a sister council in Calcutta, had been constituted in accordance with a resolution of the Bengal Native Church Council held at Krishnagar in May 1884. The ultimate object of the District Council is to provide the native Christian community, which inhabits 65 villages, distributed among the nine parishes of Balabhpur, Chāprā, Ratnapur, Kapāsdāngā, Solo, Joginda, Rānabandha, Bahirgāchhi, and Krishnagar, with a self-supporting, self-governing, and self-extending system, thus giving the scattered congregation a federal union throughout the district. The council has a Chairman (also known as Superintendent), Vice-Chairman, Secretary and Treasurer, and the body is composed of all the pastors under the District Council and two delegates from each of the Church Committees in the district. The income of the Council is derived from the grant from the Church Missionary Society; from a fixed rate paid compulsorily every month by the workers under the Council; and from contributions from friends and from the members of the Churches. The Chairman, or Superintendent, has to be constantly on the move, visiting the parishes, keeping the workers up to the mark, examining schools, checking accounts and aiding Pastors and Committees with advice. The Council has provided many native Christians for work in Bengal and other parts of India, and has certainly influenced missionary work in India.

Steps were taken in 1886 for evangelizing the northern part of the district, in the commencement of the system known as the

Associated Band of Evangelists' scheme, with head-quarters at Shikārpur, at which place a house, church, and hospital and dispensary were subsequently built. In 1891 the Church Missionary Society Girls' School was put on a satisfactory basis, and has done excellent work since. During subsequent years great improvements were effected in the large school at Chāprā and in the Training School at Krishnagar.

In 1906 the Society took over the Rānāghāt Medical Mission, of which an account has been given below. It is reported that in 1907 the numbers attending the dispensary continued at about 800 a week up till August, when the increase became rapid and the numbers nearly doubled during September. The plan of having two days a week at the dispensary at Rānāghāt was adhered to, and from February till the end of June the outstation at Kāliganj was open at first two days a week, and thereafter one day a week, on account of the small staff and the difficulty of reaching the place during the rains: the total attendances at Kāliganj were about 37,000. In the Rānāghāt hospital 282 in-patients were treated, and 37 major and 76 minor operations were performed.

The following extract is taken from the report of the Superintendent of the Chāprā School for 1907 :—

" Last year two hundred and fifty-two pupils were on the roll, divided roughly into—

Christian boys 150 (114 are boarders).
Mohammedan boys 20.
Hindu boys 20.

" One boy died of fever, but the general health of the school was good. We stood first and second both in the Middle Vernacular and Middle English sections amongst the Church Missionary Society Schools of the district at the annual examination in September, though we did not get a coveted Government scholarship.

" The Industrial Department needed further arranging and development and its funds replenishing, and I found it necessary to collect money for it from Home friends who sent £160. One believer in industrial work, living in Calcutta, sent me £100 unsolicited. In my letter I also mentioned the need of a European Manager or Foreman for the Department. I have just found a man with experience, who, I trust, by giving his undivided attention to it, will carry out the purpose of its establishment, viz., the proper training of the boys, now 30 in number, who are learning carpentry and smithwork. A new opening for boys appeared in the newly established Rifle Factory at Ichāpur, not far from Kanchrāpārā, and there a hostel was opened and placed under the care of a catechist last April. It has suffered the ups and downs of every new project, and has added much to the financial burdens which the missionary at Hāt Chāpra seems always bound to bear."

The report for the year 1907 of the Chairman of the Native Church Council of the district contains some remarks of general interest, and a portion of it is reproduced below :—

" To take the year as a whole, its characteristics have been very sober. It has been one of the unhealthiest years I have ever experienced, and many of my workers have been laid aside with protracted illness, and more with occasional spells of sickness, incapacitating them for work ; so that in many places it has meant leading the sick and wounded to the fight. Cholera and malaria are still laying many low all round me as I write

"In addition to this, it may be said that temporally I have never known a worse year. Famine prices have ruled and for persons of small fixed income, it is specially hard to have food-stuffs of all kinds doubled in price right through the year. It has meant real privation to many, and at such a time as this, it has been especially trying that a diminished income from home has kept us from granting increases urgently needed, and made it necessary to reduce our staff while straining every nerve by urgent appeals to friends, withholding special help, and spending every pice that came to our hands to keep the existing work going. It has also been a year of political unrest. The growth of the nationalist movement is having a marked effect upon the Missionary cause, for it spurns and repudiates all European connexion, including religion, and seeks to cling to all indigenous things, including Neo-Hinduism. Throughout the educated classes all over the country there is a growing impatience toward European authority and control, and dim perception, or foreshadowing of a national life and spirit, among races and creeds hitherto absolutely separated and aloof, and an utter absorption in political questions to the exclusion of all else. The Native Christian community has been also stirred by this movement; its spirit has penetrated the churches, and several members have been prominent in it. Through all its trials the year has been a year of grace, and in many cases one is able to report more than usual patience, unmurmuring loyalty and growth in grace. Writing of the workers, brings the work to my mind. I read in your pamphlet on the Bengal Mission 'that the post of a European Superintending Missionary is no sinecure ; he has to be daily in the saddle (whether supported by bicycle or horse), visiting the different villages (he has nine parishes having an average of seven villages attached to each), examining the schools, one in each village, and generally seeing that each one of his 75 or 80 workers is doing his share of the work faithfully and zealously', and, it might well be added, this in a climate almost as deadly as West Africa, that invalids men home, stricken down by fever year by year, so that a really old Missionary is not to be met with in this plain that either drowns or burns, a desert and a swamp, by turns."

According to the returns for 1907 five European and eight Indian Clergymen were at work in the district at the end of that year. There was one boarding-school for girls, at Krishnagar, attended by 76 pupils, all Christians, and maintained at an annual cost of Rs. 5,700. There was one High School, also at Krishnagar, attended by 233 boys, of whom 50 only were Christians, and maintained at a cost of Rs. 5,402, of which sum Rs. 1,540 was provided by Government. Throughout the district 43 day schools were maintained at a cost of Rs. 10,717 (Rs. 1,400 being provided from public funds), and were attended by 1,241 boys (including 200 Christians) and 412 girls (including 282 Christians). The above figures will show that a large proportion of the expenditure of the Society in the district goes towards providing secular education to non-Christians.

The Rānāghāt Medical Mission was established in 1893 by Mr. James Monro, c.b., a retired member of the Bengal Civil Service. During his service Mr. Monro had been struck with the need for Mission work in Bengal, and the members of his family resolved to join their parents in the work. The district of Nadiā was well known to Mr. Monro, who at one time was in charge of it, and when, in 1892, the Secretary to the Calcutta Committee of the Church Missionary Society suggested Rānāghāt as a suitable place for the work of Mr. Monro and his family, the suggestion was accepted. The Mission is conducted in accordance with the principles of the Church of England, and the sphere of its operations was in 1901 constituted a Missionary district by the Lord Bishop of Calcutta. It was carried on by Mr. Monro and his family, assisted by various workers who joined them from time to time, until the end of 1905, when, owing to various difficulties, chiefly in the matter of staff, it was made over to the Church Missionary Society, by which it is now being maintained on the same lines as those conceived by its founder.

The Mission opened a dispensary and a hospital in Rānāghāt in July 1894, and in the first nine months gave free medical

RĀNĀ-GHĀT MEDICAL MISSION.

advice and medicine to nearly 28,000 out-patients, subject only to the condition that they attended a short service which was held before the medical work commenced. During this same period 49 in-patients were treated in the hospital. In the cold weather evangelistic visits were paid to a good many villages in the neighbourhood of Rānāghāt. In 1895 the medical work was continued in the same manner, except for a period of one month, during which it was necessary to give the much overworked staff a short rest. In this year, the enormous number of 68,000 out-patients, coming from 1,349 villages, were treated at the dispensary and 122 in-patients received into the hospital. A small school was started in connection with the Mission, and bible-classes and services on Sundays were commenced. Itinerating work was carried on to a certain extent, so far as the exigencies of the medical work allowed. The record of 1896 was much the same as in the preceding year, but the work in 1897 was interrupted by the great earthquake which played havoc with the buildings occupied by the Mission. Between 1898 and 1902 the medical work was extended by establishing out-dispensaries at three or four outlying villages, and a considerable number of patients were attended by the members of the Mission while on tour. In 1902 the head-quarters of the Mission was removed to a site about a mile from Rānāghāt, where a village has now been built, to which the name of Dayābāri (home of mercy) has been given. The settlement at Dayābāri contains a dispensary building, which, with the waiting sheds attached, is capable of affording accommodation for 1,000 out-patients; hospitals (with operation-room and store-houses attached) with room for 40 beds; barracks for the unmarried subordinate staff; accommodation for women attached to the Mission; school for girls and infants; seven bungalows containing an aggregate of 44 rooms for the accommodation of the members of the Mission ; and a small church with mud walls, which it is now intended to replace with a masonry building. Four-fifths of the cost of this settlement, which was considerable, was borne by the members of the Mission, and the balance was met by contributions received from friends. The work was carried on with full vigour during 1903 and 1904, but operations had to be limited during 1905 owing to illness among the staff and other difficulties, which led, as has been stated above, to the handing over of the Mission to the Church Missionary Society on 1st January 1906.

During the 12 or 13 years of its existence as a separate entity, the Mission did an enormous amount of good, as may be gathered from the following statistics; at the head-quarters dispensary over 250,000 out-patients were treated, and 100,000 at out-stations; about 30,000 patients were treated by members of the Mission when on tour; and well over 2,000 in-patients were received in the hospital. This is indeed a noble record of human suffering relieved, and the poor of the Ranaghat subdivision owe a deep debt of gratitude to Mr. Monro and his family.

In 1855, at the request of the Right Reverend Dr. Carew, ROMAN Archbishop of Calcutta and Vicar-Apostolic of Western Bengal, CATHOLIC MISSION. the Sacred Congregation for the Propagation of the Faith sent out three missionaries from the Seminary of St. Calocera in Milan, namely Fathers Albino Parietti, Antonio Marietti and Luigi Limana. They arrived in Calcutta on 17th May 1855, and on 15th June following they reached Berhampore, which they made their head-quarters. They worked in the districts of Murshidabad, Rajshahi, Malda, Bogra, Nadia and Jessore, and in a part of the Sundarbans. In 1857 Father Limana went to Krishnagar and settled down in a small house, which served also as a chapel for the few Catholic residents who had hitherto been receiving occasional visits from a Calcutta priest. These converts having left the place or died, the house was let to the Municipality, and was used as a small hospital. In 1860 the Mission was re-started by Father Limana with the help of another Father and four Sisters of Charity. They founded a boarding-school for boys and another for girls. Four years afterwards other missionaries and nuns joined them, and they were able to start work in the interior of the district. In 1866 the first village mission was started by Father de Conti and Father Brioschi at Dariapur in the Meherpur subdivision. Not being very successful there, Father Brioschi moved to Fulbari, where he built a church, and commenced working in the neighbouring villages. In September 1886 the Diocese of Krishnagar was constituted, comprising the districts of Nadia, Jessore, Khulna, Murshidabad, Faridpur, Dinajpur, Bogra, Malda, Jalpaiguri, Rangpur, Rajshahi and Cooch Behar. Monsignor Pozzi, the first Bishop, died in October 1905, and he was succeeded by the present (1909) Bishop, Monsignor Taveggia.

At Krishnagar there is the Cathedral Church of the Divine Saviour, built in 1898. There is also a boarding-school and orphanage for Bengali boys, and the Convent and Orphanage for Bengali girls. Attached to the Convent is a home for widows and catechumens, and also a refuge for the aged and incurable under the care of the Sisters of Charity. There are churches at Bhabarpara, Fulbari, Meliapota, Ranabandha and Pakhura, with resident clergy at Bhabarpara and Ranabandha. At Bhabarpara the Sisters of Charity maintain a school and an orphanage for Bengāli girls. The Catholic population of the district is about 3,350 and of the Diocese about 6,300. The girls at the Convent in Krishnagar make beautiful Italian hand-made lace of any design or pattern. Attached to the Mission there are many primary schools, some of which receive stipends from the District Board.

CHAPTER XV.

THE NADIA RAJ.

The following account is based mainly upon an article which appeared in the Calcutta Review of July 1872. It was repro- duced almost verbatim by Sir W. W. Hunter in his Statistical Account of Bengal, and he remarked that the incidents related rest chiefly on local traditions, which vary in different districts, and that some of them must be received with caution.

The Nadiā family derives its descent directly from Bhatta- nārāyan, the chief of the five Brahmans who were imported from Kanauj by Adisur, King of Bengal, for the performance of certain purificatory rites. The following are given as the successive Rājās of Nadiā :—

Bhattanārāyan.	Rām Samuddhār.
Nipu.	Durgā Dās (Mājmuā-dār
Halāyudh.	Bhabānand.)
Harihar.	Sri Krishna.
Kandarpa.	Gopāl.
Biswambhar.	Rāghab.
Narahari.	Rudra Rai.
Nārāin.	Rāmjiban.
Priyankur.	Rām Krishna.
Dharmāngar.	Rāmjiban.
Tārāpati.	Raghu Rām.
Kām.	Krishna Chandra.
Biswanāth.	Siva Chandra.
Rām Chandra.	Iswar Chandra.
Subuddhi.	Giris Chandra.
Trilochan.	Sris Chandra
Kansāri.	Satisa Chandra.
Shashthidās.	Ksitish Chandra.
Kāsināth.	

Interesting particulars are related of the career of some of the above-mentioned Rājās, but generally overlaid by tradition

Sifting the wheat from the chaff, it appears that Bhattanārāyan built up his estate from the villages which Adisur had in part sold and in part granted to him. These villages were enjoyed by him exempt from taxation for twenty-four years. The legends by Sanskrit writers of the Rājās, commencing from Nipu, the son of Bhattanārāyan to Kām are of little consequence. They are said to have been wise and virtuous rulers, but it appears that their administrations were sterile of recorded events. Biswanāth was the first Rājā who proceeded to Delhi, and was confirmed in the Rāj by the Emperor, in consideration of an annual tribute. He made additions to his ancestral zamindaris by the purchase of Parganā Kāmkādi and other properties. The next Rājā whose administration deserves to be chronicled was Kāsināth. He was the first of his race who met with conspicuous misfortune. During his government it happened that from a troop of elephants, which had been sent from the Rājā of Tripurā to Akbar, Emperor of Delhi, being his annual tribute, one large elephant escaped, and straying about in a great forest, broke into villages and alarmed their inhabitants. The Rājā of Nadiā learning that the elephant had broken into one of his villages and done considerable mischief, hunted the animal to death. This circumstance having been reported to His Majesty, peremptory orders were issued to the Mussalmān Governor of Bengal to take the Rājā prisoner, and send him to Delhi.

On the invasion of the Musalmāns, the Hindu prince, Kāsināth, having received timely information of the proceedings of the enemy, fled towards the banks of the Bhāgirathi, but the army of the Governor followed and captured him. He was there put to death. His wife who was with child went to live in the house of Harikrishna Samuddhār. Her child, when born, was named Rām. He acquired much learning, and became a great favourite with Harikrishna, owing to his many amiable qualities, and his descent from an illustrious family. Harikrishna died, bequeathing to Rām his little kingdom of Patkābāri, which is supposed to have been situated between Plassey and Jalangi, on the banks of the river Jalangi. In consequence of Rām being born in the house, and having inherited the kingdom of Samuddhār, he was called by the name of Rām Samuddhār. His wife bore him four sons, called Durgā Dās, Jagadis, Hariballabh, and Subuddhi. Durgā Dās, the eldest Rāj Kumār, was once amusing himself on the banks of the river witnessing sports and dances, when a Muhammedan chief arrived from Delhi in a large fleet and with a numerous retinue. His arrival was the signal for the stoppage of the dances and the disappearance of the spectators. Durgā Dās was the only person who maintained his place. The chief asked him : " Tell me, Brahman, how many *kros* is it from here to the city known by the name of Hugli?" Durgā Dās gave the required information, at which the chief said to him: "I am highly pleased with your fearlessness and other virtues; come with me, then, to the country of Hugli." Durgā Dās readily obeyed, and, accompanying him to Hugli, was appointed Kānungo. The young Rājā at first demurred to the appointment, and said: "We are kings by inheritance, and know not how to serve others." The chief replied: "Then I will write to the Sultān of Delhi, that he grant you a title and a kingdom; but now do as I bid you." Durgā Dās obeyed this injunction, and entered upon the duties of his office as Kānungo. On the recommendation of his superior, the Emperor conferred upon him, in due time, the title of Majmuādār Bhabānand. Some time after, he retired from the service, and built a palace at Ballabhpur, and having inherited the kingdom of his father, Rām Samuddhār, ruled for twenty years. His other brothers lived in happiness, each building a palace of his own, Hariballabh at Fathipur, Jagadis at Kodālgāchhi, and Subuddhi at Patkābāri. The family originally resided in a palace in Pargaṇā Bāgnā, constituting the largest zamindari of the Nadiā Rāj. But after Kāshināth paid the forfeit of his life for killing the elephant, his son Rām lived and ruled in Patkābāri.

At this time, of all the contemporaneous Rājās, Pratāpāditya, the chief of Yasohara, or Jessore, was the most powerful. He had subdued, or rather humbled, eleven Rājas; Bengal being now supposed to have been divided into twelve principalities or large *zamindaris*. He defied even the authority of the Emperor, refusing him tribute, and vanquishing more than once the Mughal troops. The Sundarbans placed him for a time in an impregnable position, and enabled him to carry on a guerilla war. He was an usurper, having banished the rightful Rājā, his nephew Kachu Rai. In spite of his adverse circumstances, Kachu Rai contrived to acquire a respectable knowledge of the Sastras and of the military art as then practised.

Fortified with this knowledge, and relying upon his rights, he proceeded to Delhi, for the purpose of moving the Emperor to recognise his claim to the Jessore Rāj. On reference being made to the Subahdār of Jahāngirā (Dacca) and the Faujdār of Hooghly, they reported favourably on the claim of Kachu Rai. The Emperor, already enraged against Pratāpāditya for his insolence and rebellion, determined to punish this refractory vassal

152 NADIA.

for his usurpation, and appoint his nephew to the Rāj. Accordingly he deputed his general Mān Singh to Jessore for the purpose of bringing the rebel Rājā to subjection. The avenging Muhammadan army with their general arrived by boat at Chākdaha, on the road to Jessore. But their arrival was the signal for the flight of all the neighbouring Rājās. Majmuādār Bhabānand was the only Rājā who remained at his post. He paid his homage to the general, and offered a golden ring and other ornaments as his *nazar*, declaring : " Lord of great power ! on your arrival all kings of this land have fled ; only I, lord of a few villages, have remained here to see your grace, the king of Justice ; if you desire me, who am here to congratulate you, to do any thing for you, be pleased but to order it." To· this Mān Singh replied : " Well, then, Majmuādār, make the necessary preparations for passing the river, that my soldiers may safely reach the opposite bank." " My Lord," answered the Majmuādār, "although I have but a small retinue, yet at the orders of your grace all shall be performed." He then collected a large number of boats and transports, and led the whole army across the river. When Mān Singh himself had reached the opposite bank, he offered his thanks to Majmuādār for the seasonable aid. But at this time the further march of his army was arrested by stormy weather, which lasted for a whole week. What between this untoward event and the shortness of rations, the army was nearly ruined, but Majmuādār became the Commissary-General, and fed the troops from his own stores. When the weather cleared up, Mān Singh thus addressed the Majmuādār, " Tell me after how many days or on what day can I arrive from here at the capital of Pratāpāditya ? and on which side is the entrance of the army practicable ? Write it down accurately, and give it to me." Majmuādār prepared and submitted the required statement. Mān Singh was much pleased with the information supplied to him, and spoke to him thus : " Oh, high-minded Majmuādār, when I return again from the subjugation of Pratāpāditya, you shall utter a wish, and I will certainly grant it. But come yourself along with me to the capital of Pratāpādiyta." Prātāpaditya defended himself boldly, but after showing a great deal of courage, was overcome. His fort was stormed, and he was captured, pinioned, and shut up in an iron cage to be taken up to Delhi.* He died on the way at Benares. Mān Singh, on his triumphant return, thus addressed the Majmuādār : " I have been pleased by the zeal you have manifested in this war, and

* Compare the account of the downfall of Pratāpāditya given by Mr. O'Malley in vol. XV (Khulna), Bengal District Gazetteers, p. 31.

you also saved the lives of my soldiers during the foul weather which lasted without interruption for seven days. Utter therefore any wish you please, and I will certainly fulfil it." Majmuādār then narrated his antecedents, informing Mān Singh of the flight of his grandfather Kāshināth, and his subsequent capture and violent death, with the settlement of his grandmother and father at Patkābāri; and expressed a wish to be reinstated in his ancestral possessions. Mān Singh promised to further his petition, and took him up to Delhi. He then presented the Majmuādār to the Emperor Jahāngir, and brought to His Majesty's notice the services rendered by him in the expedition against Pratāpādiyta. His Majesty was much pleased with the conduct of Majmuādār, and in compliance with the recommendation of his General, restored him to his Rāj, and conferred on him the title of Mahārājā. These events are popularly assigned to the end of the 16th, or first years of the 17th, century.

According to Bhārat Chandra, the author of Annadā Mangal, who flourished in the time of Rājā Krishna Chandra, the Emperor Jahāngir held an animated discussion with the Majmuādār on the comparative merits of the Muhammadan and Hindu religions. His Majesty dwelt on the evils of idolatry. He pointed out the absurdity of worshipping images of stone, wood, and clay, instead of the one true and living God. He condemned the law under which the Hindu women losing their husbands are precluded from re-marrying, and deplored their perpetual widowhood as unnatural and revolting. He also condemned the shaving of the beard, and the expression of homage by prostration and lowering of the head, as undignified. He characterized the Brāhman priests as a crafty tribe, doing one thing and teaching another. He lamented the future of the Hindus who were wedded to a debasing and demoralizing idolatry, and inculcated that God was not incarnate, but formless. The Majmuādār attempted a feeble and inconclusive reply, arguing that the Purānas and Kurān inculcated substantially the same cardinal doctrines; that whether God was incarnate or not, those who worshipped Him were equally entitled to salvation; that all objects, whether stone or clay, were pervaded by the spirit of the Creator. The only remarkable idea to which Majmuādār gave utterance in the course of the discussion, was that there was not much to choose between Muhammadanism and Hinduism, but that the religion of the Feringhis (Europeans) was better than both, inasmuch as it acknowledged neither the rite of circumcision practised by the Muhammadans, nor that of *Karnabedh*, or ear-boring, practised by the Hindus; but that it recognized only one God, ignored all distinctions of castes, and laid no restrictions on eating and drinking.

Majmuādār returned to his palace at Ballabhpur, and took possession of the 14 Parganās which the *farmān* of Jahāngir had awarded him. He erected a palace in the city called Matiāri, and removed there because it was more central than Ballabhpur with reference to his newly acquired and extended dominions. He also built another palace in the village called Dinliyā, and set up an image there.

About this time the Subahdār of Jahāngirā (Dacca) began to cast eyes on the kingdom of the Majmuādār, and with a view to obtain the government of it, sent a messenger called Murād to call him into his presence. Majmuādar obeyed the summons, and proceeded to Jahāngirā, accompanied by his grandson Gopiraman. On his arrival he was treacherously cast into prison. But the grandson so pleased the Subahdār by the exhibition of his extraordinary prowess, that he persuaded His Excellency to liberate his grandfather. On his arrival at home, the Majmuādār showed his gratitude to the gods by *pujās* and sacrifices.

After this the Majmuādār announced to his three sons, Sri Krishna, Gopāl and Gobind Rām, his intention to divide his Rāj among them. "Take my kingdom; I have divided it into equal shares." But the eldest, Sri Krishna, objected. "No, the kingdom shall not be divided; to the eldest according to custom, belongs the whole." "You are very wise and learned," replied the Majmuādār angrily, "why do you not procure yourself another kingdom?" "If Your Highness's feet permit me the observation," answered Sri Krishna, "what is there wonderful in that?" Fired by this ambition to win his way to a kingdom, he proceeded straight to Delhi, and obtained with much difficulty an audience from the Emperor, to whom he communicated his circumstances and wishes. His Majesty, pleased with his self-reliance and enterprise, conferred on him a *farmān* assigning over the government of two valuable Parganās, Kushdah and Ukhad. Some time after he acquired this estate, he returned home and delighted his old father with the recital of his adventures. After the death of the Majmuādār, Gopāl and Gobind Rām governed the divided Rāj of their father, and Sri Krishna ruled over the Parganās he had gained for himself. Sri Krishna died childless of small-pox : his brother Gopāl, too, after seven ye dars,eparted this life. He was succeeded by his son Rāghab, who erected in the village called Reui a large residence, containing magnificent palaces and a seraglio. Rāghab also excavated an immense lake, and celebrated its dedication to Siva with sacrifices and a public festival.

Rãghab was scrupulously punctual in the payment of the tribute to the Emperor; and his punctuality was rewarded by a donation of elephants from His Majesty. He was succeeded by his son Rudra Rai, whose career was eventful. Rudra Rai erected at Nabadwip a temple dedicated to Siva. He changed the name of the place Reui, where his father had built a royal residence, into Krishnanagar (Krishnagar), in honour of Krishna. He also constructed a canal extending northward and southward, and connected it with the moat surrounding Krishnagar. The Emperor having heard of his public spirit and enterprise, conferred upon him by *farmān* the government over the two Parganās Khari and Juri; and as a token of further favour, confirmed his title of Mahārājā. Moreover His Majesty accorded to him a concession which none of his predecessors, and in fact no other Rājā of Bengal, had been able to obtain, to erect upon his palace a turret, which is called the Kangarh, and also made a donation of arrows, flags and drums. In acknowledgment of these favours, the Mahārājā sent to the Emperor a *nazar* of 1,000 head of cattle, a mass of gold equal to his own weight, and other valuable gifts.

Basking in the imperial favour, the Mahārājā did not think it worth his while to conciliate the Governor of Jahāngirā (Dacca), or to send him tribute. The Governor being highly irritated at his conduct, wrote to the Faujdārs of Murshidābād and Hooghly and other subordinate authorities, to inform them that Rudra Rai, affecting equality with himself, would neither pay the tribute nor obey his orders, and directed them to contrive to take him prisoner and send him to the city. In compliance with these orders, Rudra Rai was enticed by some stratagem to the vicinity of Hooghly, and thence brought to Jahāngirā (Dacca). Rudra Rai paid the Subahdār his respects, and observed the etiquette due to the Nawāb, thereby disarming his anger. His Excellency was much pleased with him, and showed him great attention. He obtained his permission to return home and brought with him from Jahāngirā an architect named Alam Khān, by whose aid he erected a new palace at Krishnagar. He also built a separate *nāch-ghar* or concert-hall, and also a *pilkhānā* or stables for his elephants and horses. But the most useful public work carried out by him was a broad and high causeway between Krishnagar and Sāntipur, connecting his new capital with one of the most populous towns and celebrated cloth-marts of his Rāj. The grave of the Musalmān saint Alam Khān is still found in Krishnagar Chauk. He himself is canonized and is generally called Allāldastur Pir. Though fond of magnificent buildings the

Mahārājā Rudra lived a very simple and primitive life. His personal wants were few, but his donations were many and large. He governed his Rāj with justice and impartiality, tempered of course by his recognition of the prescriptive rights and privileges of the Brahmanical class. He was succeeded by his son Rāmjiban. The latter having incurred the displeasure of the Faujdār of Jahāngirā, was displaced in the Rāj by his brother Rāmkrishna, who had a long and prosperous reign. During his time, the Rājā of Bardwān plundered the capital of Sobhā Sinh, Rājā of Chituā, a *pargana* in the district of Midnapore. The latter, resenting his attack, and being resolved to revenge himself, led his army through a wood by an unknown route, passed the river Dāmodar, and took up his station before Bardwān. He attacked the Bardwān chief and slew him, and established his authority over Bardwān. Jagadrām, the son of the Rājā of Bardwān, took refuge in the court of the Rājā of Nadiā. Emboldened by his success, and strengthened by the co-operation of Rahman Khān of Orissa and the Marhattās, Sobhā Sinh sent his Generals against several royal cities, and attacked the authority of the Delhi Emperor in Bengal The latter was greatly enraged by the intelligence of the conquest of Bardwān by Sobhā Sinh. He immediately organized an expedition for the purpose of punishing the rebel Rājā of Chituā, and placed at his head the General Azim-us-Shān When the Mughal army arrived at Murshidābād, news reached them of the death of Sobhā Sinh. He was killed while in a fit of drunkenness by the daughter of Krishna Rām, the late Rājā of Bardwān, in defence of her honour. Upon this Himmat Sinh, the younger brother of Sobhā Sinha, came with a great army to Bardwān, and began to plunder that city as his brother had done. He also attacked Rām Krishna, the Rājā of Nadiā but was defeated. At this time Prince Azim-us-Shān arrived from Murshidābād at Plassey. Having heard there of the outrages committed by Himmat Sinh, he hastened with his army to Chituā, where he attacked Himmat Sinh, and defeated him. The prince is said to have used in the battle fire-arms called Jelala or Jinjal, a short of musket fixed on a swivel. Prince Azim-us-Shān remained for some time in Bengal for the purpose of regulating the affairs of Bardwān and other districts. The Rājās of Bengal waited upon and paid homage to His Highness, but most of them came attended with only a few followers, not daring to show their wealth. Rām Krishna came surrounded by a stately retinue, on which the Prince declared : "These are no princes, but offspring of low families, else they would have been attended by retinues.

But Prince Rám Krishna is the offspring of a great family, for he alone has a stately retinue, comparable to my own ; he himself, too, appears like a second Kandarpa, and shines before one like the sun, and is like Vrihaspati in his spirit ; he is surrounded by numerous soldiers, waited upon by hosts of ministers, who themselves are honoured by retinues in splendid carriages. Thus he is a man gladdening the eyes of such a person as I am, and certainly the first among the Princes of Gaur and those of other countries." The result of this interview was the growth of a great intimacy between the prince and the Rájá. The prince repeatedly declared the great pleasure he had derived from his intercourse with Rám Krishna, and expressed the opinion he had formed of his ability and character. The prince having settled the affairs of Bardwán and the neighbouring districts, proceeded to Jahángirá, where he resided for some time. While he was at Jahángirá (Dacca), the prince reported to the Emperor the valuable services rendered by Rám Krishna.

Rám Krishna administered the affairs of Nadiá Ráj for a long time, living happily at the new capital Krishnagar, and receiving from the prince Azim-us-Shán valuable support in the discharge of his duties. He also lived on terms of amity with the then Governor of the English settlement at Calcutta ; the latter, in token of his regard for the Rájá, placed at his disposal a garrison of 2,500 soldiers. He was of a stirring and aggressive nature. A violent difference having arisen between Rám Krishna and the Rájá of Yasohara (Jessore) in regard to the boundaries of certain villages, he marched to Jessore and vanquished the Rájá. This achievement, as well as the favour he enjoyed at the Court of Delhi, established his power on a solid foundation, enhancing his influence over the neighbouring Rájás and securing him against the extortions and oppressions of the Subahdár. But the Subahdár, being determined to do him an injury, allured him to Jahángirá (Dacca), where by treachery he was closely confined. He died in prison of small-pox. The news of his death greatly grieved Azim-us-Shán, who instructed Jafar Khán to confer the Ráj on the lineal descendant of Rám Krishna. His Highness wrote to the Subahdár to ask if there was a son, a foster-son, a grand-son, or any such relation of Rám Krishna, in order that the Ráj should be conferred on him. Jafar Khán replying that there was no such relation, the prince ordered, " Then give it to any minister of Rám Krishna who is fit for the government and who will protect the wife and family of Rám Krishna." Jafar Khán replied, " Your Highness, there is no such minister ; Rám Krishna's elder brother, however, Prince Rámjiban,

lives in prison here. If you command, I will commit the kingdom
to him." No other alternative being left to him, the prince sanctioned the proposal of Jafar Khān. Rāmjiban was thus entrusted
with the Rāj for a second time. He had, of course, to pay the
full price for the favour thus shown by Jafar Khān. He was
fond of poetry, and especially of the drama. He patronized
the *nātaks* and his court was frequently enlivened by dramatic
performances. He had a son, Raghu Rām, who combined a
benevolent heart with a genius for warlike pursuits, and rendered
signal service to Jafar Khān by assisting his General, Lāhurimall,
in vanquishing the army of the Rājā of Rājshāhi. The latter, in
consequence of a quarrel with the Subahdār, had taken up his
position with a considerable force near the village of Birkati. In
recognition of this service, his father Rām Jiban, who had been
a second time imprisoned by Jafar Khān, not at Jahangira
(Dacca) but at Murshidābād, his new head-quarters, was liberated.
Raghu Rām, during the lifetime of his father, had a son born to
him, for whom a glorious future was predicted. When the child
had reached the age of six months, Rām Jiban celebrated with
great pomp his *Annāprāsan*, or the ceremony of feeding him with
rice for the first time. He invited learned pandits and powerful
Rājās from Anga, Banga, Kalinga, Kāsi, Kānchi and the
adjacent provinces. The child whose *Annaprāsan* was celebrated
with such splendour was named at that ceremony Krishna
Chandra.

Rāmjiban was at this time summoned by Jafar Khān to
Murshidābād, to settle the accounts of the tribute due from him
and he died at that city.

Rāmjiban was succeeded by his already celebrated son Raghu
Rām. Having governed the Rāj for two years at Krishnagar,
he was arrested by orders of Jafar Khān, carried to Murshidābād, and kept there in confinement. He was a very benevolent
man, and dispensed his charities from the jail.

After some time he was released and allowed to resume the
management of the Raj. He, however, survived his liberation for
only four months. He died on the banks of the Bhāgirathi in
1782, and the same year Krishna Chandra was anointed as
Mahārājā.

One of the first acts of the Mahārājā Krishna Chandra Rai
was the celebration of *yajnas*, or festivals called *Aginhotra* and
Rāj-peya. He spent twenty lakhs of rupees in the ceremony.
Learned pandits from different parts of Bengal and from Benares
came by invitation to assist in the performance of the *yajnas*. They
were rewarded with valuable presents, according to their respective

ranks, and in turn for the same, as well as for the recognition of the merits supposed to inhere in the performance of the *yajnas*, they conferred upon him the title of *Aginhotri Bájpei Sriman` Mahárái Rájendra Krishna Chandra Rai.*

He' was 'fond of sport and delighted in hunting, being a fearless rider and a good shot. On one occasion he set on foot a great hunting expedition, and went in pursuit of game to a place now'-known as Sibnibās. He was so struck with the beauty of the place and its pleasant situation on the banks of the river, that he built a palace there for his occasional residence He called the palace the 'Sibnibās Rājbāri, and the river Kankanā. He established in connection with the palace an asylum for the infirm and the aged poor, and also several *pathsálás* and *tols* for the benefit of Sanskrit scholars

Krishna Chandra is described in the Annadā Mangal as the patron of the four *Samájs*, viz., Nadiā, Kumārhatta, Sāntipur and Bhātpārā, all of which towns were noted for learning, and as the seats of scholars. In order to encourage the cultivation of Sanskrit learning, he fixed a monthly allowance of Rs. 100 as stipends to students who came from a distance to study in the *tols* of Nadiā. This allowance was perpetuated by his grandson Iswar Chandra, who made arrangements with the Government for its punctual payment, and Rs. 100, subsequently increased to Rs. 300, is now paid every month from the Collectorate of Nadiā. The munificent patronage accorded by him to various branches of learning formed a leading glory of his administration, and still renders it famous. There is a Bengali proverb still current in the country, that any one who does not possess a gift from Krishna Chandra cannot be a genuine Brahman. The custom of inviting and giving pecuniary presents to learned Brahmans on occasions of *sráddhas*, marriages, etc., received encouragement from him.

The political condition of Bengal during the time of Mahārájā Krishna Chandra Rai was extremely critical and unsatisfactory. It was complicated by the dissensions of the Subahdārs and their principal officers, arising from the tyranny of the former, and culminating in civil wars. It was further complicated by incessant warfare waged by the Marhāttas. The evils attending this state of things were the destruction of crops, with the consequent scarcity of grain, the depression of foreign and inland trade, and the prevalence of universal oppression.

In A D. 1739 Sarfrāz Khān became Subahdār of Bengal. His oppression had alienated from him his chief officers and the leading noblemen of the country. Among the former were the

Topkhānā Dāroga and Hāji Hamit, brothers of Ali Vardi Khān, Governor of Patnā, and Alam Chānd. Among the latter was Fāthi Chānd, who had received from Aurangzeb the title of Jagat Seth, and who was esteemed the greatest banker and the most opulent subject in India. His indignation against the public misgovernment was intensified by a private wrong perpetrated‑ by Sarfrāz Khān. He had about this time married his grandson, Mahtāb Rai, to a handsome girl, and the fame of her exquisite beauty having reached the ear of Sarfrāz Khān, the latter longed for the possession of her person. He sent for Jagat Seth, and demanded a sight of her. The Seth remonstrated against his demand as a gross violation of his honour and caste, but Sarfrāz Khān insisted on committing this outrage She was carried off by force to the palace of the Subahdār at night, and sent back after a few hours. This indignity rankled in the heart of Jagat Seth, and his whole family influence was exercised with a view to the dethronement of Sarfrāz Khān. He was joined in this pro- ject by Hem Chānd and Hāji Hamit, the latter not only wanting to get rid of the oppressor, but to place his brother, Ali Vardi Khān, on the throne. The triumvirate arrived at the resolution " that none could be secure in their lives, honour, or property whilst Sarfrāz Khān remained invested with the Subadārship." They further resolved that " Ali Vardi Khān was the only one capable of rescuing the provinces from apparent and inevitable ruin, and that he should be immediately advised of their sentiments, and entreated to concur with their proposal, by preparing for a speedy march to Bengal to take upon himself the government."

The events which followed belong to the general history of the Province. Ali Vardi dethroned the tyrant and was himself suc- ceeded by his adopted son Sirāj-ud-Daula, |whose violence and perfidy ended with the battle of!'Plassey. The part taken'by Krishna Chandra of Nadiā in the establishment of the English power reflected credit on his foresight, and in recognition of the services rendered by him, Lord Clive conferred on him the title of Rājendra Bahādur. He was also presented with a dozen guns used at Plassey. They may be still seen in the Rājbāri.

The Mahārājā was a scholar, and fond of the society of scholars. He also patronized musicians of the upper provinces, and was a great connoisseur in matters regarding oriental music. As a patron of architecture, he constructed a large building for pujā in the Rājbāri, and built a marble staircase for going down the sacred well Gyān Bāpi in Benares, for the benefit of the pilgrims. He was universally considered the head of Hindu society, and the arbitrator on all questions of caste.

In 1758, the Nadiā Rāj became a defaulter to the English Government, on which Mr. Luke Scrafton proposed to send a trusty person into Nadiā to collect the revenues for the Mahārājā, and to deprive him of all power in his district, allowing him Rs. 10,000 for his subsistence. It appears from the proceedings of the Government, dated 20th August 1759, that the revenue of the Mahārājā Krishna Chandra for the Parganā Nadiā was nine lakhs of rupees, less Rs. 64,048, being the revenue of Nadiā lands included in East India Company's land, so that the net amount was Rs. 8,35,952. This amount was payable by monthly *kists* or instalments. For its punctual payment the Mahārājā entered into the following agreement :—"I promise to pay the above sum of Rs. 8,35,952, agreeable to the *kistbandi*, without delay or failure. I will pay the same into the Company's Factory. I have made this that it may remain in full force and virtue. Dated the 23rd of the moon Tulhaide (*sic*), and the 4th August, of Bengal year 1166."

Mahārājā Krishna Chandra died at the good old age of 70, and left six sons and one daughter.

Siva Chandra, the eldest son of the deceased Mahārājā, succeeded to the title and estate of his father, in accordance with the provisions of the will of the latter. Krishna Chandra was one of the first Hindus who adopted the custom of making written wills, a practice unknown to the *sāstras*.

Siva Chandra retained in his employ the old officers of the Rāj and availed himself of their experience. He managed the affairs of his estate with great tact and judgment. He was a more profound scholar in Sanskrit than even his father. A manuscript work of his composition has been lately discovered. He was a religious man and spent a large portion of his time in performing ceremonies. He celebrated the Soma Yāga, and died at the age of 47, leaving one son and one daughter.

Siva Chandra was succeeded by his son, Iswar Chandra, a generous and extravagant prince, who diminished the estate to the extent of three lakhs of rupees. He built a villa called Sriban, situated in a romantic spot about two miles from the Rājbāri. Iswar Chandra died in the fifty-fifth year of his age, leaving one son and one daughter. The son, Girish Chandra, a young man sixteen years of age, succeeded to the title and property. During his minority the estate was managed by the Court of Wards. Like his father, he was a very extravagant man, and a considerable part of the property was in his time sold, owing to the non-payment of the Government revenue.

The *debottar* lands which had been expressly set aside for the worship of the family idols, yielding an income of about a lakh of

rupees a year, and some zaṃindāris heavily encumbered, were alone,
left to him of an inheritance which at one time embraced a vast
extent of country, and comprised eighty-four *parganas*, the seat of
great manufacturing industries, and rich in agricultural resources.

Girish Chandra, like his predecessors, was a great encourager
of Sanskrit learning, and delighted to reward the learned men of
his time. During his administration the celebrated poet, Rasa-
sāgar flourished, and was for a long time an ornament of his
Court. Girish Chandra had two wives, but left no issue at the
time of his death, which took place in the sixtieth year of his
age. Before his decease he adopted a son named Srisa Chandra,
who succeeded him.

Srisa Chandra was only 18 years of age, and had scarcely
passed his minority, when he took charge of the estate. By tact,
sagacity, and judgment he managed to clear off the encumbrances
and increased the income to some extent. He was an intelligent,
affable man, and very popular with all who came in contact
with him.

Srisa Chandra, though representing the most orthodox family
in Bengal, emancipated himself from the fetters of bigotry, and
caught the spirit of innovation characteristic of the present age.
He introduced European customs, and observed no distinction of
caste in eating and drinking. When the first petition for
legalizing the re-marriage of Hindu widows was prepared, he
headed the list of subscribers to the document. He also opposed
the system of Hindu polygamy, and heartily joined in the
movement for abolishing it, except in certain cases. He established an Anglo-Vernacular school at his own residence, with a head
master, three assistant masters and two pandits, without aid
either from Government or subscriptions from private sources.
He also presented to the Government the tract of land on which
the Krishnagar College stands, and subscribed a large sum for
its erection. Though not a scholar he was a great admirer of
learning, and had his two sons educated at the Government
College. He was tolerably conversant with Persian and Sanskrit;
a patron of Hindu music, and himself a good singer; his name
was known to all the celebrated singers of the day, and they
came to him even from distant places like Delhi and Lucknow.

The Government recognised and confirmed his title of Mahārājā Bahādur, and bestowed upon him the usual *khilat* and other
honours appertaining to the same. Srisa Chandra died in the
thirty-eighth year of his age, leaving one son and one daughter.

Satisa Chandra succeeded his father at the early age of
twenty, and carried still further his imitation of English habits.

He died at Masuri on the 9th October 1870 in the thirty-third year of his age, and was succeeded by his adopted son, the present (1909) Mahārājā Kshitish Chandra, during whose minority the estate was again managed by the Court of Wards. He came of age in May 1889, and was installed by Sir C. S. Bayley, the then Lieutenant-Governor of Bengal, at Krishnagar in July 1890. He has maintained the tradition of his house as a supporter of learning.

At present the total land revenue payable by the estate is Rs. 62,542, while its annual value, according to the Road Cess returns, is Rs. 2,17,790. The largest compact block within the estate lies in the Chāprā thānā: the remainder consists of smaller blocks, scattered over the thānās Kotwāli, Sāntipur, Kissengunge, Chākdaha, Rānāghāt, Gāngni, Tehata, Hānskhāli and Jibannagar.

CHAPTER XVI.

GAZETTEER.

Amghāta—Gangavās:—Gangavās is the name given to a portion of the village of Amghāta, which is situated about 6 miles west of Krishnagar. It lies on the Alakānanda, which was an off-shoot of the Jalangi falling into the Bhāgirathi, but has now silted up. The waters of this stream, owing to its connection with the Ganges, were considered holy, and a palace was built on the banks by Māhārājā Krishna Chandra, and named Gangavās, *i.e.,* residence on the Ganges. Temples were also erected in which the images of Hari and Hara and six other gods and goddesses were installed, and provision was made on a liberal scale for their worship. As a consequence the fame of Gangavās spread far and wide, and it became a place of pilgrimage, at which a large number of persons assembled on the Paush Sankrānti, Bārun and Dasāhara days, to bathe in the sacred waters of the Alakānanda, and pay their homage at the various shrines. When the stream silted up, the place gradually lost its importance, and the temples were neglected and fell into ruins. Only those of Hari Hara and Kal Bhairav have withstood the ravages of time, and now one Brahman, on a small pittance allowed by the present Mahārājā of Krishnagar, performs the daily *pujā* to the idols. The Rām padak (*i.e.,* footprint of Rām) which is still to be seen here is said to have been brought from the Chitrakuta hills.

Aranghātā—Village situated in the Rānāghāt Thānā about 6 miles north of Rānāghāt. It lies on the main line of the Eastern Bengal State Railway and has a station called after its name. The population is about 600, most of whom are low class Muhammadans. The river Churni passes by the village and on its bank is the Hindu temple of Jugal Kishwar, which is believed to have been constructed about 1728 A.D., and which contains the images of Krishna and Rādhā. According to tradition the former was brought from Brindāban and first installed at Samudragarh (near Nabadwip), whence it was transferred to Aranghātā by Gangā Rām Dās, the first mahanth of the temple. The image of Rādhā is said to have been brought from the palace of Krishna Chandra, the famous Mahārājā of Nadiā, who made a grant of 125 bighas of rent-free land for the support of the temple. A big fair is held here annually throughout the month of Jaista, and is attended by pilgrims from all parts of Bengal: among the visitors females predominate, owing to the belief that any woman who visits the temple will escape widowhood, or, if she be already a widow, will be spared from that fate in her next birth. To the south of this temple there is another, and a more ancient one, containing the idol of Gopi Nāth, but this possesses no special fame or sanctity.

Bagulā.—A small village and a station on the Eastern Bengal State Railway. Until Krishnagar received a direct railway service, it was the nearest railway station to that place, with which it is connected by a metalled road 11 miles in length. It is now of little or no importance. It was for some time, from 1862 onwards, an outstation of the Church Missionary Society.

Bāmanpukur.—A village in the Kotwāli Thānā on the east bank of the Bhāgirathi opposite Nabadwip. There seems no doubt that a portion of the old Nabadwip of the Hindu kings of Bengal lay within this village: the remainder of the site now lies under the waters of the Bhāgirathi. In the village there is a large mound which is called Ballāldhibi and is believed to be all that is left of the palace of Ballāl Sen; and near by is a tank which is called Ballāldighi.

Birnagar.—The ancient name of this small town was Ulā. It is in the Rānāghāt Subdivision about five miles from Rānāghāt and 13 from Krishnagar, and is situated in 23° 15′ N. and 88°34′ E. Its population was 3,124 in 1901 as compared with 3,421 in 1891, and 4,321 in 1881. Its present (1901) population is made up as follows:—Hindus, 2,380; Muhammadans, 735; and Christians, 9. The town was constitued a Municipality in 1869, with 12 Commissioners, 8 of whom are elected and the remainder nominated. The Subdivisional Officer of Rānāghāt was *ex-officio* Chairman until 1901, but since that year there has been a non-official Chairman. The average annual income and expenditure was from Rs. 3,500 to Rs. 4,000 until 1906-07. In the last two years the figures on both sides of the account have increased, and in 1908-09 the income was Rs. 5,483 and the expenditure Rs. 5,735. The public buildings are (1) the Municipal Office, (2) the Municipal Charitable Dispensary and (3) the Municipal Market.

One of the earliest traditions connected with this town is that it was once visited by Srimanta Saudāgar, the mythical Hindu merchant-prince. At that time the Ganges flowed past the place, and as Srimanta was sailing up to it, a terrific storm came on. In response to divine inspiration he called upon Ulai Chāndi, one of the wives of Siva, the destroyer, to help him. She answered his prayer and protected his fleet; whereupon he instituted a special worship of her in this place, which has been carried on to the present day. The Ulai Chāndi festival is celebrated here annually in the month of Baisākh, and is attended by 10,000 pilgrims, who, it is said, are housed and fed by the residents. According to tradition the present name of Birnagar (anglicé, town of heroes) was conferred upon the town in recognition of the bravery of its inhabitants in capturing noted dacoits on two occasions. The first capture was that of a notorious bandit, who was known as Shena Shani, a native of Sāntipur, and a Goālā by caste: it is said to have been effected by Anādi Nāth Mustafi, of the Mustafi family of Ula. The second capture was that of the gang of dacoits who were headed by Baidya Nāth and Biswa Nāth, and ravaged the district during the latter part of the eighteenth century. Bābu Mahādeb Mukbapādhyāy is said to have effected this capture, though this is somewhat at variance with the account of the destruction of the gang which has been given by Sir William Hunter.*

*Since the above was written, the following letter, dated 29th October 1800, from Mr. J. Lumsden, Registrar, to the Secretary to the Government in the Revenue and Judicial Departments, has been traced, and may be quoted *in extenso*, "Sir,—In a trial before the Third Judge of the Calcutta Court of Circuit at the last Jail delivery for Zilla Nuddea which came under reference before the Nizamat Adawlut, it appeared in evidence that a night attack having been made on the house of Mahadeo Muckerjee, a respectable resident in the village of Ooloo, by a large Gang of armed Dacoits, the Inhabitants of the Village immediatedly assembled, surrounded the House, and after a desperate Resistance in which nine of the Villagers were wounded, apprehended on the spot eighteen of the Robbers, who were tried and convicted and sentenced to perpetual Imprisonment and Transportation.

2. The Judge of Circuit considered the Inhabitants of Ooloo as entitled to some mark of Distinction for their Behaviour on this occasion, and the Nizamat Adawlut concurring in this Opinion, desired him to propose some specific Recompense which might with propriety be made to them.

3. I have now received the Orders of the Court to transmit to you the enclosed copies of two letters from the 3rd Judge of the Calcutta Court of Circuit on this subject, and to request that you will lay them before the Most Noble the Governor-General in Council, with their recommendation that his Lordship will be pleased to authorize the Magistrate of Nuddea to pay a reward of twenty sicca Rupees to each of the nine Villagers who were wounded in apprehending the Robbers, and to change the name of the Village from Ooloo to Beernagur, as proposed by the Judge, notifying the same by Proclamation in the manner suggested in Mr. Camac's Letter of the 25th instant.

4. The timid Behaviour of the Natives of Bengal in general, in deserting their Habitations and Property when attacked by Gangs of Dakoits, is to be ascribed, in the opinion of the Court, more to the horrid acts of Barbarity which are often perpetrated by the Robbers, than to any want of personal Courage, and it is believed that the occasional notice and approbation of an Opposite Line of conduct by Government, may operate as a spur to excite others to follow the example, and by creating a Spirit of Emulation throughout the Country, may prove the most effectual means of checking the Depredations of the banditti, and raising up opponents to them in every village."

The Mustafi family was founded by one Rāmeswar Mitra, who visited Delhi in the time of Aurangzib, and who is said to have much impressed the Emperor with his scholarship and personal appearance, and to have obtained from him an introduction to Murshid Kuli Khān, then Nawāb of Bengal. The Nawāb gave him a high post in the Accounts Department, in which he so distinguished himself and did such good work, as to earn for himself the title of Mustafi. This title has been retained in the family during the eight generations which have passed since it was conferred. Owing to partition and litigation the fortunes of the family have greatly declined and they are no longer well off.

The Mukhopādhyāy family, whose founder is alleged to have been instrumental in the capture of the gang of Baidya Nāth and Biswa Nāth, are the local magnates of Birnagar, and keep open house for all who care to avail themselves of their hospitality when visting the town.

Birnagar was once a large and prosperous town, but the epidemic of malarious fever in 1857 caused great ravages in the place, and it has been steadily declining ever since.

The following account of the place is taken from an article by Revd.' J. Long which appeared in the *Calcutta Review* in 1846. "Not far from Ranighat is Ula, so called from Uli, a goddess whose festival is held here, when many presents are made to her by thousands of people who come from various parts. There are a thousand families of Brahmans, many temples and rich men living in it. As Guptapara is noted for its monkeys, Halisbar for its drunkards, so is Ula for fools, as one man is said to become a fool every year at the *mela*. The Baruari Puja is celebrated with great pomp; the headmen of the town have passed a bye-law that any man who, on this occasion refuses to entertain guests, shall be considered infamous, and, shall be excluded from society. Saran Siddhanta of Ula had two daughters, who studied Sanskrit grammar and became very learned. In 1834 the Babus of Ula raised a large subscription and gave it to the authorities to make a pukka road through the town."

Chākdaha.—A town in the Rānāghāt Subdivision on the main line of the Eastern Bengal State Railway, situated in 23° 6′ N. and 88° 33′ E., not far from the left bank of the Hooghly river. Tradition says that Bhāgirath, when bringing the Ganges from Himālaya to Ganga Sāgar to water his forefathers' bones, left the traces of his chariot wheel (*chakra*) here; hence the name. Not much appears to be known of the ancient history of the town, but it is believed that the army of General Mān Singh was weatherbound here for some days, on its way to the subjugation of Pratāpāditya at the close of the sixteenth century. Chākdaha, as well as Bānsbāria and Ganga Sāgar, was once notorious for human sacrifices by drowning. In Hamilton's "Description of Hindostan," London, 1820, it is stated that "this town was formerly noted for voluntary drownings by the Hindoos, which however latterly have become a mere ceremony of immer-sion without any fatal result." Stavorinus, 1785, writes, "The village of Chagda, which gives its name to the channel, stands a little inland, and there is a great weekly market or bazar here: the channel terminates about three Dutch miles inland, and on its right has many woods in which are tigers and other wild beasts; on entering the woods a little way, we soon met with the traces of tigers in plenty, and therefore we did not think it prudent to venture further; we met in the way the remains of a Bengali who had been torn in pieces by a beast of prey." There is other evidence to show that tigers were not uncommon in the district in the latter part of the eighteenth century; it is said that during that period persons travelling in the neighbour-hood of Nabadwip were compelled to sound instruments to frighten these animals away; in 1802 expeditions were made to Krishnagar to hunt them, and as late as 1825, a tiger was killed at Dhogāchhiā 6 miles west of Nabadwip. Tigers have long since disappeared, but leopards are still found occasionally in the district, especially in the Meherpur Subdivision.

At the beginning of the nineteenth century, dacoits committed great havoc in the neighbourhood of Chākdaha. At the trial of some men who had committed a dacoity in the town, one of the witnesses stated that "the country is in the hands of the dacoits, and they do not scruple to plunder in broad daylight." In 1809 one Hanif, with eight companions, was hanged in the town for dacoity.

Chākdaha used to be an important trade centre, but a change in the course of the river affected it adversely in this respect. The only public buildings now in the town are the Municipal office, dispensary and hospital, and the office of the Sub-Registrar. The town was constituted a Municipality in 1886, with 12 Com-missioners, all of whom are nominated. The population in 1901 was 5,482 as compared with 8,618 in 1891. Its present (1901) population is made us as follows:—

Hindus	. 4,300
Muhammadans	. 1,181
Christian	. 1

The average annual income for the quinquennium ending with the year 1894-95 was Rs. 3,844, and the expenditure Rs. 3,984. There was but little variation during the following ten years, but from the year 1905-06 there was a considerable increase in the figures on both sides of the account. In 1908-09 the income was Rs. 4,669, and the expenditure Rs. 4,259.

Chāprā.—A village about ten miles north of Krishnagar on the road between that town and Meherpur. It has been a centre of work of the Church Missionary Society for nearly 70 years. A church was built here in 1841, and a school was started in 1850: the latter is now a most useful institution; in 1908, there were 202 boys on the rolls, and teaching was carried on up to the Middle English Standard. There is a thānā in the place, and not far off, on the banks of the Jalangi, is the village of Bangāljhi, which was once an important river-mart, and in which there is still a certain amount of local trade.

Chuādāngā Subdivision—Forms the central portion on the eastern side of the district, and lies between 23° 22′ and 23° 50′ N., and 88° 38′ and 89° 1′ E., with an area of 437 square miles. It is bounded on the north-east by the Kumār or Pāngāsi river; on the north-west by the Meherpur subdivision; on the south-west by the head-quarters subdivision; and on the south-east and east by the Jessore district. It has no natural boundaries except upon the north-east. It is traversed by the Mātābhāngā or Haulia river, upon which lies its head-quarters. The subdivision consists of a flat widespread plain intersected by numerous streams, which have now in many instances silted up. The population which suffered a decrease of 3·5 per cent. in the decade ending in 1891, more than made up the loss by an increase of 3·74 per cent. in the following decade, and was, in the census of 1901, returned at 254,589, which gives a density of 583 persons to the square mile. The variations in the decade ending in 1901 ranged from an increase of 1·54 per cent. in the Jibannagar thānā to an increase of 9·65 per cent. in the Dāmurhudā thānā. The subdivision contains 485 villages, but no towns, Chuādāngā being its head-quarters. From 1st April 1892, it was amalgamated with the Meherpur subdivision under one Subdivisional Officer, but on 1st April 1897 it was re-established in response to a petition from the inhabitants of the villages on the east, complaining of the great distances which they had to travel to reach the Court. For police purposes, it is divided into four thānās, viz., Chuādāngā, Dāmurhudā, Alamdāngā, and Jibannagar.

Chuādāngā.—This village is the head-quarters of the subdivision to which it gives its name. It is situated in 23° 39′ N. and

88° 51′ E., ꞏon the left bank of the Mātābhāngā river. It is traversed roughly from north to south by the main line of the Eastern Bengal State Railway, which has a station here; and from west to east by a metalled road from Meherpur over the boundary into the Jessore district. It is an important trade centre. It contains the usual public offices of the head-quarters of a subdivision. Its population was returned at 3,147 in the census of 1901.

Dāmukdiā.—A village on the Padmā in the extreme north of the district, and within the Kushtiā Subdivision. It is the southern transhipment station for the crossing on the Ganges on the Eastern Bengal State Railway. There is a police outpost in the village.

Ghoshpārā.—A village situated in the Chākdaha thānā of the Rānāghāt subdivision, about five miles north-west of the Kānchrā-pārā Railway station. It is also known under the name of Nityādhan. This village is the head-quarters of the *Kartābhājā* sect, of which an account has been given in Chapter III above. According to Babu Gopāl Krishna Pāl, who has witten an interesting note on the sect, festivals are held at Ghoshpārā at the Dol Jātrā, in the month of Fālgun; at the Rath Jātrā in the following month; on the anniversary of the death of Rāmdn Lāl, or Dulāl Chānd, the son of the original founder of the sect, in the month of Chaitra; on the anniversary of the death of the founder, in the month of Asārh; and on the anniversary of the death of the founder's wife in Aswin. The places visited by the pilgrims are the room where the founder's wife was buried, the room containing the relics of the founder, and the room containing the relics of his son; in each of which places daily prayers are also offered. In addition to the above, two tanks, named Dālimtālā and Himsāgar, are also visited by the pilgrims: both of these tanks are associated with the name of the Fakir who assisted in the founding of the sect. Except for its connection with the sect, the village of Ghoshpārā is of no interest or importance.

Ghurni.—The north-eastern suburb of the town of Krishnagar, famous for the manufacture of clay figures and models of remark-able excellence. The industry is carried on by a few men of the Kumār or potter caste, and specimens of their work have received medals at the London and Paris exhibitions. Ghurni is said to have been the birthplace of Gopāl Bhar, the celebrated jester of the court of Mahārājā Krishna Chandra.

Gosain-Durgāpur.—A village in the Kushtiā Subdivision about 5 miles to the south-east of the Hālsā railway station. A fair is held here annually on the full moon day in the month of Kārtik, in honour of the idol Rādhā Raman, which is installed in a temple in the village. According to local tradition, this idol was stolen by a band of outlaws and presented by them to the saint Kamalā Kānta Goswāmi, in return for his having miraculously quenched their thirst with a small *lota* full of water. Shortly afterwards, the saint, who was young and good-looking and deeply learned in the Sāstras, was seen by the princess Durgā Devi, who had accompanied her father to the spot on a hunting expedition. The father consented to their marriage, and made a grant of several villages as a dowry. The temple bears an inscription to the effect that it was erected by Rājā Sri Krishna Rai in 1674 A.D., and was dedicated to the idol which it contains.

Hānskhāli.—A village on the Churni river at the point where the metalled road from Bagulā to Krishnagar crosses that river. It was, before the advent of the railways, a river-mart of some importance, but has now greatly declined, especially since Krishnagar obtained a direct railway service. It is a station for the collection of Nadiā Rivers tolls. There is a thānā on the right bank of the river by the ferry.

Kānchrāpārā.—A fairly large village in the extreme south of the district, and about 3 miles west of the station on the main line of the Eastern Bengal State Railway, to which it has been given its name. It is about a mile to the west of the Hooghly, and is on the road to Ghoshpārā, the seat of the Kartābhājā sect. At one time Kānchrāpārā was a big and important village, and was very largely attended by visitors on the occasion of the celebration of the Rath Jātrā festival. It is now, however, on the decline, and is being depopulated by malaria. The village temple of Krishna and Rādhikā is said to have been built by the Malliks of Calcutta in 1708.

Kapāsdāngā.—A village in the Dāmurhuda thana of the Chuādāngā subdivision, about 7 miles from the Rāmnagar railway station on the Eastern Bengal State Railway. An out-station of the Church Missionary Society was established here in 1840, and has been maintained since. Kapāsdāngā was visited by a Mr. Innes in 1841, and he described the Bhairab river, on which it stands, as " a beautiful river whose banks are richly ornamented with fine trees, and the water of which is truly excellent and wholesome." This description is very far from representing present conditions; the place has been notoriously unhealthy for years, and there seems no doubt that this unhealthiness is directly attributable to the stagnancy of the river. In 1843 a church was built, which was replaced by a somewhat larger building in 1893.

There is a school in the village. About a mile away is a cemetery.

One mile to the east of Kapāsdāngā is Nischintapur, the head-quarters of a concern which formerly used to cultivate indigo but now does zamindari only. The property was once known as the "Katchee Katta" Concern, and it lay along the line of the Eastern Bengal State Railway from near Munshiganj to Porādah. The following extract from a letter written in 1860 by the then Manager is of interest :—"In the year 1849 I joined the Katchee Katta Concern as an Assistant in the Pykeparrah Division. Owing to high inundations and the crops having failed some years pre-vious to my coming, the whole of the country was nothing but waste lands and jungles all round my four factories, and I may say for miles together. It used to be a favourite hunting-ground of the Nawab of Murshidabad, when he gave large parties in Mr. Torrentine's (?) time; his last was 1851, as the country after that began to clear up. In 1850 the villages were mostly deserted and the few houses that were left were in a most miserable condi-tion. Mr. Montresor, who was then Magistrate of Nadia, can prove the above, as he was with me in Pykeparrah in March 1850 and saw the state the country was in then. Now I can say that in the 10 years that I have managed the Concern, from 1849 to 1860 (I took the management of the whole Concern in 1850), the whole of these jungles and waste lands have been brought into cultivation, and for miles now around Katchee Katta, Pykeparrah and Doorgapore Divisions not a bigha of waste land is to be seen. Mr. Forlong, who has been over all that part of the country lately, can swear to the truth of what I assert. Not less than 40 to 50,000 bighas of lands were brought into cultivation in the Katchee Katta Concern while I had the management of it. Numbers of large and prosperous villages now existing were formed by me, and this was done by my cultivating a portion of lands, *neezabad*, for one year, and then abandoning them to the ryotts; in many instances I dug the lands with my own coolies, and after this was done, the ryotts used to pay me my expenses, and they took the land for paddy. That is the system I pursued for several years."

In 1857 the Manager wrote thus with reference to the mutiny. " Since these unhappy disturbances began, the factory business everywhere has gone on as regularly and quietly as if mutiny in the country had never taken place. I wish only the want of rain had frightened me as little as the mutiny or disbanded sepoys have done, and I should have had little indeed to make me anxious."

Khoksā.—A village in the Kushtiā Subdivision in the north-east corner of the district about 3 miles to the south-west of the railway station which is named after it. It is situated on the banks of the Sirājpur river or *khāl*, an off-shoot of the Garai. A fair is held here in honour of the goddess Kāli, during the month of Māgh every year. It was established by one of the Rājās of Naldāngā, who is said to have discovered there a stone sacred to the goddess. There is a thānā in the village.

Krishnagar Subdivision.—Head-quarters subdivision of the district, lying between 23° 17′ and 23° 49′ N. and 88° 9° and 88° 48° E. It has an area of 701 square miles, and consists of a wide alluvial plain, bounded on the west by the Bhāgirathi, and intersected by the Jalangi which flows past the head-quarters station, and, eight or nine miles further on, joins the Bhāgirathi opposite Nabadwip. The population, which had decreased by 6·9 per cent. in the decade ending in 1891, increased in the following decade, by 3·5 per cent., and, in the census of 1901, was returned at 361,336, which gives a density of 515 persons to the square mile. The variations in the decade ending in 1901 ranged from an increase of 15·38 per cent. in the Kissen-gunge thānā to a decrease of 5·69 per cent. in the Kotwāli thānā, which was the only thānā which did not show an increase. The subdivision contains two towns, Krishnagar (population 24,547), the head-quarters of the district, and Nabadwip (popula-tion 10,880); and 740 villages. For police purposes it is divided into seven thānās, viz., Kotwāli, Chāprā, Hānskhāli, Kāliganj, Nakāsipārā, Nabadwip and Kissengunge. The famous battle-field of Plassey lies in the extreme north of the subdivision, in the Kāliganj thānā.

Krishnagar.—Head-quarters of the district, situated in 23° 24′ N. and 88° 31′ E., on the left bank of the Jalangi, about 9 miles above its junction with the Bhāgirathi.

The town covers an area of about 7 square miles, and its population was 24,547 in 1901, as compared with 25,550 in 1891 and 26,750 in 1872; this steady decline is probably due to the ravages of malarial fever, for which the town is notorious. A few years ago the municipality took a loan from Government to re-excavate the stagnant bed of the Anjana river, which passes through the town and is believed to be one of the causes of the prevalence of fever; but the scheme has not been a success. The present (1901) population is made up as follows:—Hindus, 16,220; Muhammadans, 7,449; Christians, 864; and other religions, 14.

174

The original name of Krishnagar is believed to have been Reni. In this village a palace was erected by Mahārājā Rāghab, whose son Rudrā Rai changed the name to Krishnagar or Krish-nanagar, in honour of Krishna. Since then the town has remained, almost continuously, the residence of the Mahārājā of Nadiā. A municipality was constituted in 1864 with 21 Muni-cipal Commissioners, two-thirds of whom are elected and the remainder nominated.

The income during the year 1883-84, which is the first year for which records are now available in the Municipal office, was Rs. 23,539, and the expenditure Rs. 25,482. There was not much variation until the five years ending with 1900-01, during which the average annual income was Rs. 43,609, and the average expenditure Rs. 39,391. Since then there has been a steady advance in both income and expenditure, the figures for which, for the year 1907-08, were Rs. 58,541 and Rs. 58,117 respectively, including advances and deposits. There is only one major building which belongs to the municipality, namely the Municipal office.

Up till 1898 the town was without the benefit of a railway service, and the nearest railway station was Bagulā, on the Eastern Bengal State Railway, with which it was connected by a metalled road about 11 miles in length, broken at Bānskhāli by the Churni river, which was unbridged and had to be crossed in open ferry boats. In 1898 a light 2½ feet gauge railway was constructed from Krishnagar *viá* Sāntipur to Aistolā Ghāt, on the right bank of the Churni, near Rānāghāt, and the Eastern Bengal State Railway ran a siding down to the opposite bank from Rānāghāt station. Finally in 1906 the Rānāghāt-Lālgola branch of the Eastern Bengal State Railway, with a station at Krishnagar, was opened, and the town was at last placed in direct railway communication with Calcutta.

Krishnagar contains the usual public offices, including the District Jail, which has accommodation for 189 prisoners, the manufactures being mustard oil, mats and surkhi or brick-dust, all of which are sold locally. In addition to these buildings there is a Government College affiliated to the Calcutta Univer-sity, which was attended by 82 pupils in 1907-08 : the total expenditure in that year was Rs. 29,983. Attached to the college is a Collegiate school. The attendance at both these institutions has shown a steady increase since 1881.

The town is a centre of Christian evangelistic enterprise : it is the head-quarters of a diocese of the Roman Catholic Church, and an important station of the Church Missionary Society, each of these bodies having its own church and schools. The Church of England Zenānā Mission also maintains here two dispensaries, a hospital and two schools.

The great Hindu Swinging festival (Barādol) is celebrated in Krishnagar annually in March or April, when 12 idols, belong-ing to the Mahārājā of Krishnagar and representing Sri Krishna in twelve different personalities, are brought together to the Rājbāri from different parts of the district and worshipped. Some 20,000 pilgrims assemble every year for this festival, and a fair lasting for three days is held simultaneously.

The town suffered somewhat severely in the great earthquake of 1897 : some masonry buildings were destroyed and many were seriously damaged, including the Collectorate office, the main entrance of which collapsed.

Kuliā.—Small village, situated in the Chākdaha thānā of the Rānāghāt subdivision, about 3 miles north-east of the Kānchrā-pārā Railway station. A fair is held here annually on the 11th day of Paush: it is called the *Apradh Bhanjan Mela*. There are various legends as to the origin of this fair: that which, perhaps, obtains the greatest credence is that the place was once visited by Chaitanya, who was well entertained there by one Debananda, after having been refused hospitality in the neighbouring village of Kānchrāpārā, and he was so pleased with the treatment which he received, that he sanctified the place and declared that all who worshipped there on the 11th day of Paush would be absolved of all their sins. There is a temple in the village, known as Debanandapat : it is of comparatively recent date and is said to have been built by Babu Kanai Lāl Dhar of Calcutta. Adjoin-ing the temple are some tombs, among which is alleged to be that of Debananda.

Kumārkhāli.—A town in the Kushtiā subdivision, situated in 23° 52′ N. and 89° 15′ E., on the left bank of the Garai river. It is a station on the Poradah-Goalando branch of the Eastern Bengal State Railway, and is a trading centre of some importance. During the mercantile days of the East India Company, a Commercial Resident was stationed at Kumārkāli, and a large business in silk was carried on : the only relic of those days now to be found is a cemetery with a few tombs, the earliest dating from 1790. The town was originally included in the Pabnā district, and it had a Munsif's Court, subordinate to the District Judge of Pabnā : on its transfer to the Nadiā district in 1871, the Munsif's Court was abolished.

The town was constituted a Municipality in 1869, with 6 Commissioners, all appointed by Government : the number of

Commissioners was increased to 9 in 1875: in 1884 the privilege of the elective system was conferred upon the town, and since then there have been 15 Commissioners, of whom 10 are elected and the remaining 5 nominated.

The population in 1901 was 4,584, as compared with 6,165 in 1891, and 5,251 in 1872. The present (1901) population is made up as follows:—Hindus, 3,242, and Muhammadans, 1,342.

The only public building is the Municipal Office. The average annual income and expenditure of the town during the quinquennium ending with 1894-95 were Rs. 4,064 and Rs. 4,415 respectively, and during the next quinquennium, Rs. 5,836 and Rs. 6,215: there has been but little variation since, and in the year 1908-09 the income was Rs. 6,131, and the expenditure Rs. 6,583.

Kushtiā Subdivision.—The northernmost subdivision of the district, lying between 23° 42' and 24° 9' N., and 88° 44' and 89° 22' E., with an area of 596 square miles. It is bounded on the north by the Padmā, and on the south-west by the Mātā-bhāngā which separates it from the Meherpur and Chuādāngā subdivisions: on the south and east it is bounded respectively by the Jhenidah subdivision of the Jessore district, and the Goalundo subdivision of the Faridpur district. The subdivision is a wide alluvial plain of great fertility and densely populated. The population, which had increased by 6·4 per cent. in the decade ending in 1891, gained a further slight increase of ·71 per cent· during the following decade, and, in the census of 1901, was returned at 468,368, which gives a density of 816 persons to the square mile. The variations in the decade ending in 1901 ranged from an increase of 7·19 per cent. in the Kushtiā thānā to a decrease of 4·69 per cent. in the Kumārkhāli thānā. The density of the population in these two thānās is extraordinarily high, being 923 and 997 persons to the square mile, respectively. The subdivision contains two towns, viz., Kushtiā (population 5,330) and Kumārkhāli (4,584); and 1,011 villages. For police purposes it is divided into four thānās, viz., Kushtiā, Kumārkhāli, Nāopārā and Daulatpur.

Kumārkhāli was at one time the headquarters of a subdivision of the Pābnā district; it included the thānās of Kumārkhāli and Pāngsā. On the formation of the Goalundo subdivision of Faridpur district in 1871, Kumārkhāli thānā was transferred to the Kushtiā subdivision, and Pāngsā thānā to the Goalundo subdivision.

Kushtiā.—Headquarters of the subdivision of the same name, situated in 23° 55' N. and 89° 9' E., on the right bank of the

Garai, not far from the point at which that river leaves the
Padmā. The Subdivisional headquarters were originally located
at old Kushtiā, which is about 3 miles from the two villages of
Bahādurkhāli and Mahājbampur, which form the town now
known as Kushtiā. It lies on the Porādah-Goalando branch of
the Eastern Bengal State Railway, and has a flag station opposite
the Subdivisional offices, and a station in the town, about 1½ miles
further on. It is the centre of a considerable trade in rice,
pulses, molasses and jute. The Mobini Cotton Mills, established
in Kushtiā by a retired Deputy Magistrate as a *Swadeshi* enterprise, have not met with much success. During the rains the
town is connected by river-steamer with Pābnā, but soon after the
advent of the cold weather this service has to be stopped owing to
the fact that sufficient water does not remain in the mouth of the
Garai to afford a passage for the steamer. The population in
1901 was 5,330, as compared with 11,199 in 1891 and 9,245 in
1872. The large decrease in population is due mainly to a
revision of the area within Municipal limits. The present (1901)
population is made up as follows:—Hindus, 3,066; Muhammadans,
2,235; and Christians, 29. The town was constituted a Municipality in 1869, with 12 Commissioners, 8 of whom are elected and
the remainder nominated.

The income and expenditure of the town remained at about
Rs. 6,000 till the year 1898-99, when, with the introduction of
Part IX, it rose to about Rs. 9,000. In the year 1908-09 the
income was Rs. 13,683, and the expenditure Rs 10,513.

Kushtiā contains the usual public offices of the headquarters
of a subdivision. Sugar-cane crushing mills of the well known
Bihia pattern are manufactured here. The Church Missionary
Society has a branch in the town. There is a cemetery here
which was consecrated by the famous Bishop Cotton in 1866. It
was on the very day on which this ceremony took place that he
lost his life. Returning to the river steamer for the night, he
had to embark by a slippery plank; his feet gave away, and he
fell into the flowing stream never to be seen again. The accident
was regarded as a public calamity. A special notice was published in the *Gazette of India* in the following terms:—" There
is scarcely a member of the entire Christian community throughout India who will not feel the premature loss of this Prelate
as a personal affliction. It has rarely been given to any body
of Christians in any country to witness such depth of learning
and variety of accomplishment, combined with piety so earnest,
and energy so untiring. His Excellency in Council does not
hesitate to add the expression of his belief that large numbers,

N

even among those of Her Majesty's subjects in India who did not share in the faith of the Bishop of Calcutta, had learned to appreciate his great knowledge, his sincerity, and his charity, and will join in lamenting his death." The Secretary of State, in acknowledging the receipt of the despatch announcing the Bishop's death, recorded that "the loss of a Prelate who discharged the duties of his high office with such zeal, devotedness, charity and sound judgment, cannot fail to be sensibly felt both by the Government with which he was connected, and by the Diocese over which he presided ; and I have to express my entire con-currence in the sentiments recorded by your Government."

Meherpur Subdivision—Forms the north-western portion of the district, and lies between 23° 36′ and 24° 11′ N., and 88° 18′ and 88° 53′ E., with an area of 632 square miles. The subdivision is bounded on the north-west by the Jalangi, on the north-east by the Mātābhāngā, on the south-east by the Chuādāngā subdivision, and on the south by the headquarters subdivision. It is a deltaic tract with a considerable portion of low-lying black clay soil, on which *aman* rice alone can be cultivated. It is divided from north to south by the dead river Bhairab. The population, which suffered a small loss of ·5 per cent during the decade ending in 1891, increased by 3·39 per cent during the following decade, and, in the census of 1901, was returned at 348,124, which gives a density of 551 persons to the square mile. The variations in the decade ending in 1901 ranged from a decrease of 5·53 per cent in the Karimpur thānā, to an increase of 8·52 per cent in the Gāngni thānā. The subdivision contains one town, viz. Meherpur, with a popu-lation of 5,766, and 607 villages. For police purposes, it is divided into four thānās, viz., Meherpur, Karimpur, Gāngni and Tehatta.

Meherpur.— Headquarters of the subdivision of the same name. It is situated iu 23° 47′ N. and 88° 38′ E. on the silted up Bhairab river. It covers an area of about 7⅓ miles, and in 1901 had a population of 5,766, as compared with 5,820 in 1891 and 5,562 in 1872. The present (1901) population is made up as follows :— Hindus, 3,968 ; Muhammadans 1,787 ; and Christians, 11. The town lies 18 miles from the nearest railway station, Chuādāngā, with which it is connected by a metalled road, interrupted by two unbridged rivers.

Meherpur was constituted a municipality in 1896, with 9 Commissioners, of whom 6 are elected and the remainder nomi-nated. The income of the town has steadily risen during the last twenty years. It was Rs. 2,059 in 1890-91, and Rs 4,754 in

1908-09. The expenditure has followed the income. It is more an aggregation of rural villages than a town, and it seems probable that it would not have been constituted a municipality, had it not been for the fact that it is the site of the headquarters of the subdivision.

The town contains the usual Subdivisional offices, Munsif's Court, Municipal office, Sub-jail, hospital and District Board inspection bungalow. The Church Missionary Society has a branch here. The only manufacture is brass-ware.

Murāgāchhā—Village in the Nakāsipārā thānā of the head-quarters subdivision, about 12 miles north-west of Krishnagar. It is now a station on the Rānāghāt-Lalgola branch of the Eastern Bengal State Railway. The population is close on 600, about two-thirds being Hindus, and the rest Muhammadans. The village has two temples, one dedicated to the god Siva, and the other to the goddess Sarvāmangalā; the latter is said to have been built in 1870 by Devi Dās Mukhopādhyāy, a salt Dewān of Hijli, who also established a High English School in the village. A fair is held in honour of the goddess on the day of the full moon in Baisākh: it lasts for three days, and is attended by one to two thousand pilgrims The importance of the village dates from the time of Dewān Devi Dās, whose family, known as the Dewān family of Murāgāchhā, is still one of the most respected in the district.

Nadiā or Nabadwip.—The town from which the district derives its name. It lies in 23° 24′ N. and 88° 23′ E., on the west bank of the Bhagirathi, opposite the confluence of the Jalangi with that river: it covers an area of 3½ square miles, and has a population (1901) of 10,880, as compared with 13,384 in 1891 and 8,863 in 1872. The present (1901) population is made up as follows:—Hindus, 10,416; Muhammadans, 457; and Christians 7. This great preponderance of Hindus over Muhammadans in a district in which the latter form 59 per cent. of the total population, is remarkable.

There are three different traditions as to the origin of the name Nabadwip: the first is that the town originally stood on an island, which was called Nabadwip (i e., new island), to distinguish it from Agradwip (former island) which lies about 15 miles up the Bhagirathi from Nabadwip; the second is that it was formerly the resort of a recluse who used to practise his religious rites at night surrounded by 9 lights, whence it came to be called 'Nava-dip' or 'nine lights,' but this derivation, as will be observed, does not account for the letter 'w' in the last syllable; and the third is that it formed one of a group of nine

N 2

islands (Nava-dwip), an account of which is given by Narahari Dās in his ' Nabadwip Prikrama Paddhati.'

Navadwip is a very ancient city, and is reputed to have been founded in 1063 A.D. by one of the Sen kings of Bengal, who is said to have been induced to transfer his capital there from Gaur, on account of its superior sanctity owing to its position on the sacred Bhāgirathi ; and also, probably, because it was considered less liable to Mughal raids. On the east bank of the river, immediately opposite the present Nabadwip, is the village of Bāmanpukur, in which are to be found a large mound known as ' Ballāldhibi,' said to be the remains of the King's palace, and a tank called ' Ballāldighi.' These names go to prove that Ballāl Sen had some connection with the place, though it is not universally admitted that the actual capital was transferred there from Gaur.* It is clear, however, that it was the constant resort of the kings of Bengal until 1203 A.D., when it was captured by Muhammad Bakhtiār Khilji, and the foundation stone of the conquest of Bengal by the Muhammadans was laid.

The following account of the capture and sack of Nabadwip is taken from the Riāzu-s-Salātin, as translated by Maulvi Abdus Salām (Calcutta, 1904).

"That year Malik Bakhtiar, bringing to subjugation the Subah of Behar, engaged in introducing administrative arrange- ments, and the second year coming to the kingdom of Bengal he planted military outposts in every place, and set out for the town of Nadiāh, which at that time was the capital of the Rājāhs of Bengal. The Rājāh of that place, whose name was Lakh- mania, and who had reigned for eighty years over that kingdom, was at the time taking his food. Suddenly Muhammad Bakh- tiar, with eighteen horsemen, made an onslaught, so that before the Rājāh was aware, Bakhtiar burst inside the palace, and unsheathing from the scabbard his sword that lightened and thundered, engaged in fighting, and put the harvest of the life of many to his thundering and flashing sword. Rājāh Lakhmania getting confounded by the tumult of this affair, left behind all his treasures and servants and soldiers, and slipped out bare-foot by a back-door, and, embarking on a boat, fled towards Kamrup. Muhammad Bakhtiar, sweeping the town with the broom of devastation, completely demolished it, and making anew the city of Lakhnauti, which from ancient times was the seat of Government of Bengal, his own metropolis, he ruled over Bengal peacefully."

---

* In the Ain Akbāri it is noted that in the time of Lakshman " Nadiā was the capital of Bengal, and abounded with wisdom."

For many centuries Nabadwip has been famous for its sanctity and learning. From its earliest days the patronage of the Hindu kings and the sanctity of its site attracted, from far and near, erudite scholars, who taught Sanskrit philosophy to thousands of students. Of such were Halāyudha, Pasupati, Sulapāni and Udāyanachārya, who are believed to have flourished there during the reign of Lakshman Sen, and also Abdihodha Yogi, a Pandit from the upper country, who is said to have been the first scholar to set up a school of logic in Nabadwip. The most celebrated of the native savants of the place were Bāsudev Sarbabhauma, who, while a pupil of Pakshādhar Misra, the first logician of Mithilā, is said to have learnt by heart the whole of the treatise on logic; and his distinguished pupils, Raghunāth Siromani, the author of the Didhiti and the commentary on the Gautam Sutra ; Raghunandan Smarta Bhatachārya, the most renowned Pandit of Smriti, whose school is followed even today throughout the whole of Bengal ; Krishnananda Agambagis, whose work on Tantra philosophy is the standard book on the subject; and Gauranga, or Chaitanya, the great Vaishnava reformer of the 16th century. Chaitanya was the son of Jaganāth Misra, and was born at Nabadwip in 1485 A.D. He was undoubtedly a man of great intellect, but the key-note of his philosophy was universal love, and he is||still spoken of as the ' Apostle of Love.' He was the founder of the Vaishnava sect, and has still a very large following throughout Bengal.

The present Nabadwip still continues to be famous for its Sanskrit teaching. The indigenous Sanskrit schools known as *tols*, in which Smriti (Hindu social and religious law) and Nyāya (logic) are taught, form the principal feature of the town. A valuable report was submitted upon them by the late Professor E. B. Cowell in 1867. This report contains a full account of the schools, the manner of life of the pupils and the works studied. Mr. Cowell describes the *tol* as consisting generally of a mere collection of mud hovels round a quadrangle, in which the students live in the most primitive manner. Each student has his own hut with his brass water-pot and mat; few have any other furniture. A student generally remains at the *tol* for 8 or 10 years according as he is studying Smriti or Nyāya. No fees are charged, and, until comparatively recent years, the pandit even provided his pupils with food and clothing. He himself makes his living by the presents which his fame as a teacher ensures him at religious ceremonies.

The following extract is taken from Professor Cowell's report :—
" I could not help looking at these unpretending lecture halls with a deep interest, as I thought of the pandits lecturing there to generation after generation of eager inquisitive minds. Seated on the floor with his ' corona ' of listening pupils round him, the teacher expatiates on those refinements of infinitesimal logic which make a European's brain dizzy to think of, but whose labyrinth a trained Nadiā student will thread with unfaltering precision. I noticed during my visit middle-aged and even grey-haired men among the students of the celebrated tols."

Sir William Hunter remarks : " The sole end of the Nadiā scholastic training is Vichāra, i.e., to win the victory at a festival by adroit arguments, which silence the opponent for the time being. According to the established rule in Hindu dialectics, the disputant first presents his opponent's views, and exhausts whatever can be adduced in their favour, and then proceeds to overthrow all that he has just brought forward, and to establish his own opinion. The pandits, therefore, come to a discussion with a store of plausible arguments on both sides, and love to oppose a popularly received opinion in order to win credit by successfully supporting an apparently hopeless cause. The very form of Hindu logic involves error, and it is so bound up with technical terms, that it is apt to degenerate into a mere play of words. This tendency reaches its climax in the Nadiā schools. Mr. Cowell in three of the tols listened to the students exercising themselves in such discussions. He noticed the intense eagerness of the disputants, as well as the earnest sympathy of the surrounding students and pandits. A successful sophism was responded to by a smile of approval from all."

In 1829 Professor Wilson found between 500 and 600 pupils studying at the tols. In 1864 Mr. Cowell found 12 tols attended by about 150 pupils. In 1881 there were 20 tols with 100 pupils, in 1901, 40 with 274 pupils, and in 1908, 30 with 250 pupils. Mahārājā Krishna Chandra instituted a monthly allowance of Rs. 100 for the maintenance of the tols. This grant was confirmed by the Committee of Revenue in 1784, but was stopped in 1829 on the ground that no mention had been made of it in the correspondence relating to the Decennial Settlement. However, in the following year, on a remonstrance from the Nabadwip students, and on the recommendation of the Murshidābād Commissioners, the grant was renewed and has since been raised to Rs. 300 per month: in addition to this, Government now awards stipends of Rs. 100 and Rs. 60 per mensem to the First

and Second Professors of Nyāya, and Rs. 50 to the First Professor
of Smriti. Mathematics, Astronomy, and Philosophy (other than
Nyāya) are not regularly taught here. About 1870 a Professor
of Philosophy, by name Kāshināth Sāstri, a native of Orissa, set
up an unsuccessful *tol*, and during the last few years a pandit
from the North-West has been teaching Darsan and Vedānta to a
few pupils. Formerly the almanacs of Nabadwip were of great
repute, and their meteorological predictions were held to be
infallible; but the Achārya (astrologer) class has become nearly
extinct.

Sir William Hunter remarks: "The past of Nadiā raises
very high expectations, but its present state is disappointing. It
is not an ancient city with venerable ruins, crowds of temples,
a great population and time-honoured *tols* in every street, with
numbers of learned pandits, such as one might expect from its
antiquity. All that meets the eye is a small rural town with little
clusters of habitations, and a community of Brahmans, busied
with earning their bread, rather than in acquiring a profitless
learning. The caprices and changes of the river have not left
a trace of old Nadiā. The people point to the middle of the
stream as the spot where Chaitanya was born. The site of the
ancient town is now partly char land, and partly forms the bed of
the stream which passes to the north of the present town. The
Bhāgirathi once held a westerly course, and old Nadiā was on the
same side with Krishnagar, but about the beginning of this (19th)
century the stream changed and swept the ancient town away."

The town, being situated on the bank of the holy Bhāgirathi, is frequented by pilgrims from all parts of Bengal, chiefly
those of the Vaishnava sect, who bathe in the sacred waters, and
at the same time pay their homage at the shrine of Chaitanya.
The concourse of pilgrims is very large at the time of the full
moon in the months of Baisākh, Kārtik and Māgh. In order to
enable the Municipality to make better conservancy and sanitary
arrangements for these large gatherings, the Pilgrims' Lodging-
house Act IV (B.C.) of 1871 was extended to the town of Nadiā
by Government Notification dated 8th August 1891, and the
annual income from this source is now above Rs. 3,000.

Nabadwip was constituted a municipality in the year 1869
with 12 Commissioners, of whom 8 were elected and the remainder nominated. In January 1904 the Commissioners were
superseded by Government for contumacy, but the municipality was re-established in March 1905 with 9 Commissioners
nominated by Government, though the elective system was not
restored till September 1907.

The principal industry of the place at present is the manufacture of brass utensils. It was, in former times, noted for its manufacture of conch-shell bracelets, and one of the streets is still known as San-kāri Sarak. The East India Company once had a cotton spinning factory here, the site of which is pointed out by old inhabitants.

The present site of the town is not satisfactory: it lies below the level of the river when in flood, and is full of pits and hollows where water stagnates during the rainy season. At one time it was protected all round by embankments, but these have been suffered to fall into bad repair. The cost of restoring them satis-factorily was estimated at Rs. 10,000, and Sir John Woodburn, while Lieutenant-Governor of Bengal, offered a Government contribution of Rs. 5,000 provided that an equal amount were raised locally : advantage was not, however, taken of the offer, and nothing has yet been done to restore the embankments. Under such circumstances it is remarkable that the health of the town does not compare more unfavourably than it does with that of other towns in the district.

That the climate of Nabadwip was at one time considered beneficial, or at any rate less unhealthy than that of Calcutta, is clear from the following extracts which have been taken from the " Diary and Consultations Book of the United Trade Council of Fort William in Bengal":—

" 673. The Governor goes for a change of air.

The Governor having for Severall Months been very much Indisposed and being advised by the Physi-tians to go up to Nuddea for change of Air, as the only means left for the Recovery of his health—Agreed That during his absence the Worshipful Robert Hedges Esq. act as Chief and Transact all affairs with the rest of the Councill, and allso take charge of the Cash—Ordered that the Doctor go with the Governour, and considering the troubles in this Country, that Captain Woodvill with 50 Soldiers go as a Guard."

January 3rd, 1713.

" 688. Return of the Governor

This day the Governour returned from Nuddea, where he has been some time for the Recovery of his Health."

February 17th.

" 691. The Governor has a relapse.

The Governor not being perfectly recovered of his Illness and beginning to relapse which the Doctors impute to the difference between the air of this place and Nuddea, where he has been lately for the Recovery of his health, and therefore advise him to go up thither again, Agreed that Mr. Hedges act as Chief during his absence.

February 23rd.

"Ordered that Thirty Soldiers do go up with the Governor as a Guard, also that Severall of the Company's Servants who are now indisposed go up with the Govr. for the Recovery of their Health."

The change does not appear to have afforded any permanent benefit to Mr. Russell, for his health became hopelessly impaired, and he was forced to leave India for good at the close of the year.

Plassey.—Village in the head-quarters Subdivision, situated in 23° 47′ N. and 88° 16′ E, on the east bank of the Bhāgirathi, near the point at which that river first impinges upon the district. It is famous as the scene of Clive's victory over Sirājud-daula, Nawāb of Bengal, on 23rd June 1757. After the capture of Calcutta by Sirājud-daula in June 1756, Clive was despatched with a force from Madras, and he recaptured Calcutta in January 1757. After prolonged negotiations he succeeded in gaining over Mir Jafar, the Nawāb's general, whom he promised to instal as Nawāb in place of Sirājud-daula. In March Chander-nagore was taken from the French, and on the 13th June a fresh advance was made; Katwa (on the west bank of the Bhagi-rathi in the Bardwān district) was captured on the 18th, and on the 22nd the troops marched to Plassey, where Sirājud-daula was encamped with an army of 50,000 foot, 18,000 horse and 50 pieces of cannon, mostly 24 pounders and 32 pounders drawn by oxen. To oppose this army Clive had a force of 900 Europeans, of whom 100 were artillery men, and 50 sailors, 100 Topasses or Portuguese half-castes, and 2,100 sepoys; the artillery con-sisted of 8 six-pounders, and 2 howitzers. Clive encamped in a mango-grove, the greater part of which is believed to have since been cut away by the Bhāgirathi, and the enemy were entrenched on the river bank to the north of him. At daybreak on the 23rd the enemy advanced to the attack, enveloping Clive's right, Mir Jafar being on the extreme left of the line. Both sides maintained a vigorous cannonade until 2 o'clock, when Sirājud-daula returned to his entrenchments. At this Mir Jafar lingered behind on the left, and eventually joined the British. Clive advanced and cannonaded the Nawāb's entrenchment, and entered his camp at 5 o'clock after a slight resistance, Sirājud-daula having already fled to Murshidābād. This decisive victory was won with only a small loss, but it made the British masters of Bengal. In 1883 the Bengal Government erected on the spot a somewhat meagre monument to commemorate the battle: the inscription upon it is simple, but dignified, and consists of the one word "Plassey." During the last few years the Imperial

Government has erected an obelisk on a black marble base, and 36 masonry pillars have been set up to indicate the supposed positions of the different troops engaged in the battle on both sides. Up till 1905 the site of this famous battle was very inaccessible, being 34 miles from the nearest railway station, but in that year the Rānāghāt-Lālgola branch of the Eastern Bengal State Railway was opened with a station only 2 miles south-east of the place, and a metalled road now runs from the station to the furnished Dāk Bungalow which has recently been constructed on the field by the Public Works Department. Cannon-balls have constantly been found by the cultivators while tilling the soil, and the writer was presented with two, one large and one small, when visiting the village in 1897. The place is of no importance, except as being the site of the famous battle.

Porādah.—A village in the Nāopārā thānā of the Kushtiā subdivision. It is a station on the Eastern Bengal State Railway and the junction from which the Porādah-Goalundo extension branches off from the main line.

Rānāghāt Subdivision.—The southernmost subdivision of the district, lying between 22° 53′ and 23° 20′ N., and 88° 20′ and 88° 45′ E., with an area of 427 square miles. The subdivision is a deltaic tract, bounded on the west by the Hooghly, on the south by the Barasat subdivision of the 24-Parganas district, on the east by the Bangāon subdivision of the Jessore district, and on the north by the Krishnagar subdivision. It contains much jungle and numerous marshes and backwaters, and the whole tract is malarious and unhealthy. The population, which had decreased by 4·6 per cent. in the decade ending in 1891, suffered a further decrease of 5·63 per cent in the following decade, and, in the census of 1901, was returned at 217,077, which gives a density of 508 persons to the square mile. The variations in the decade ending in 1901 ranged from a decline of 1·5 per cent. in the Rānāghāt thānā, to a decline of 8·16 per cent. in the Sāntipur thānā, which suffered a greater loss than any other thānā in the district. The subdivision contains four towns, viz., Rānāghāt (population 8,744), Sāntipur (26,898), Chākdaha (5,482) and Birnagar (3,124) ; and 568 villages. For police purposes it is divided into three thānās, viz., Rānāghāt, Sāntipur and Chākdaha. The head-quarters of the subdivision was originally at Sāntipur, but was transferred to Rānāghāt in the year 1863.

Rānāghāt.—Head-quarters of the subdivision of the same name. It is situated in 23° 11′ N. and 88° 34′ E., on the Churni river : it covers an area of about 2½ square miles, and in 1901 had a population of 8,744 as compared with 8,506 in 1891 and 8,871 in 1872. The present (1901) population is made up as follows : Hindus, 7,405 ; Muhammadans, 1,268 ; and Christians, 71. The town contains the usual subdivisional offices, Munsif's Court, Municipal office, Sub-Jail and hospital. It has been the headquarters of the subdivision since 1863, before which year the headquarters was at Sāntipur. It was constituted a municipality in 1864 with 14 Commissioners, 5 of whom were appointed *ex-officio*, and the remaining 9 nominated by Government. When Act III (B.C.) of 1884 came into force, the number of the Commissioners was increased to 18, of whom 12 were elected and 6 nominated : there has been no change since. The income and expenditure of the municipality during the first 20 years of its existence averaged Rs. 6,933 and Rs. 6,907 per annum, respectively ; there was but slight variation during the next ten years, but, with the introduction of Part IX, both income and expenditure increased to over Rs. 10,000 per annum during the quinquennium ending with the year 1899-1900. In 1907-08 the income was Rs. 14,128, and the expenditure Rs. 15,004.

Rānāghāt carries on a large river traffic, and is one of the principal seats of commerce in the district. It is an important railway junction, as here the Jessore and Khulnā branch, and the Rānāghāt Lālgola branch meet the main line of the Eastern Bengal State Railway. There is also a light railway connecting the town with Krishnagar *vid* Sāntipur.

The Rānāghāt Medical Mission was established here in 1893 by Mr. J. Monro, C.B. : the head-quarters of this Mission has since then been moved to a site just outside the limits of the town. An account of the Mission will be found in Chapter XIV of this volume.

Very little seems to be known of the early history of this place. It is said to have been originally called Rānighāt after the Rāni of the famous Krishna Chandra, Mahārājā of Nadiā. It is on record that dacoits swarmed here in 1809 when Mr. Tytler was Magistrate.

The town is the seat of the Pāl Chaudhuri family of Rānāghāt referred to by Bishop Heber in his journal. The family was founded by Krishna Chandra Pānti and Sambhu Chandra Pānti, two brothers who were originally petty traders in the place. It is said that their wealth originated in the fortunate purchase from Ganga Rām Dās Mahanth, the founder of the Jugal Kishwar temple at Aranghātā, of a large store of grain, which appeared to have been hopelessly damaged by insects, and was to have been thrown away, when Krishna Chandra appeared on the scenes and offered a small sum for it, which was accepted. When the grain came to be removed, it was found that only the outer layer had been damaged, and it was sold at an enormous profit. This occurred in 1780, and with the capital thus amassed, which was increased by judicious trading, the brothers became great merchants, and almost monopolized the trade in salt, which at that time was sold by auction by the Board of Reyenue. The family were most munificent in charity and works of public utility, and it is said that the Marquis of Hastings offered Bābu Krishna Chandra the title of Rājā when he visited Rānāghāt in the course of a tour ; but, being of a modest and retiring disposition, he declined the offer, preferring to retain merely the title of " Pāl Chaudhuri," which had been conferred upon him by the Mahārājā of Nadiā, and has been borne by the family ever since. For the two succeeding generations the family were deeply involved in the famous Pāl Chaudhuri suit in the Supreme Court, which lasted from 1821 to 1850, being carried four times in appeal to the Privy Council, and which cost them an enormous sum of money. Bābu Sri Gopāl Pāl Chaudhuri, the great-grandson of one of the founders, was a very public-spirited zamindar ; he subscribed largely to many works of public utility, and founded the Rānāghāt High English school, which has since been mainly supported by his descendants. The present head of the family, Babu Nagendranāth Pāl Chaudhuri, served Government for 21 years in the Provincial Civil Service, and now, in his retirement, is Chairman of the municipality. The family now own zamindāris in the districts of Nadiā, Khulnā and Jessore, the Government revenue of which aggregates about Rs. 53,000.

Ratnapur —This village has been a centre of Church Missionary Society work since 1840, and is now the head-quarters of the Ratnapur Parish, and has a population of 627 Protestant Christians. It is in the Meherpur thānā of the Meherpur Subdivision, and about 11 miles from the Darsana station on the Eastern Bengal State Railway. There is a fine church in the village, and a boarding-school for boys, which was established in 1842. The Zenānā Mission have here a hospital, dispensary and home for converts.

Sāntipur.—A town in the Rānāghāt subdivision, situated in 23° 15′ N. and 88° 27′ E., on the left bank of the Hooghly. The town covers an area of about 7 square miles, and its population in 1901 was 26,898, as against 30,437 in 1891, and 28,635 in 1872. Though there has thus been a decline, it is still the most populous town in the district. The present (1901) population is made up as follows:—Hindus, 18,219; Muhammadans, 8,672; Christians, 6; and other religions, 1. Sāntipur is about equi-distant from Krishnagar and Rānāghāt, and is connected with each of these towns by a good metalled road, and also a 2 feet 6 inches gauge light railway. The road between Krishnagar and Sāntipur is believed to have been originally constructed by Rudra Rai, the Mahārājā of Nadiā, who is reputed to have given its present name to the former of these two towns. Sāntipur is also connected with Calcutta by a steamer service on the Hooghly.

Very little information is forthcoming in connection with the ancient history of this town. It can be gathered, however, that Sāntipur was in existence at the time of Rājā Ganesh, who ruled Bengal in the 12th century. It is said that forts were at one time erected at Sāntipur by the Mughal Emperors. The names of Sutrāgarh, Sāragarh and Top-khānā, which are attached to certain portions of the town, support the popular view, but no trace of the alleged fortifications can. now be found. In the latter part of the 15th century, Adwaitachārya, who was supposed to be an incarnation in one person of both Vishnu and Siva, flourished here: it is said that Chaitanya took his initiation from Adwaitachārya, who, afterwards, himself became a disciple of Chaitanya. Ever since then the place has been held sacred. In the time of Rudra Rai, Mahārāja of Nadiā, it was a populous town and a celebrated cloth-mart. In the old days of the East India Company it was the site of a Commercial Residency, and the centre of large Government cloth factories. The Government purchases of Sāntipur muslin, which then had a European reputation, averaged over 12 lakhs during the first 28 years of the nineteenth century. None of these factories are still in existence, the last ruins having been pulled down and sold between 1870 and 1880; only the name of the suburb Kuthirpārā remains to indicate that there were once rows of kuthis or factories in the neighbourhood. It is said that the Commercial Resident enjoyed an annual salary of over Rs. 42,000, and lived in a magnificent house with marble floors, built by himself at the cost of a lakh of rupees: the Marquis of Wellesley spent two days there in 1802: the ruins of the house were finally sold for Rs. 2,000.

Holwell was landed at Sāntipur as a prisoner on his way to Murshidābād, after having survived the misery of the Black Hole: he was marched up to the Zamindār of Sāntipur "in a scorching sun near noon for more than a mile and a half, his legs running in a stream of blood from the irritation of the irons." From thence he was sent in an open fishing boat to Murshidābād, " exposed to a succession of heavy rain or intense sunshine." It is stated that in the early part of the 19th century no place was so infested with dacoits as Sāntipur, until the appointment of a resident Deputy Magistrate, and the provision of swiftly sailing guard-boats which put a great check on river dacoity.

There are many mosques and temples in the town. The oldest mosque is in Topkhānā; it was erected by one Yār Muhammad in the year 1115 Hijri, during the reign of the Emperor Aurangzib : it is now in a very dilapidated condition. Of the temples, the three most famous are that of Syāmachand, built in 1726 at the reputed cost of two lakhs of rupees, by one Rām Gopāl Khān Chaudhuri, whose family is still one of the wealthiest in Sāntipur; that of Gokulchand, built about 1740 ; and that of Jaleswar, said to have been built by the mother of Mahārājā Rām Krishna of Nadiā about the beginning of the 18th century.

Sāntipur was constituted a Municipality in 1865, with 24 Commissioners (of whom 16 were elected and the remainder nominated), and an *ex-officio* Chairman in the person of the Subdivisional Officer of Rānāghāt. The Commissioners were superseded by Government in 1903 for contumacy in the matter of the introduction of Part IX: the Municipality was, however re-established in September 1904, with 9 Commissioners appointed by Government, and the same *ex-officio* Chairman as before, but the elective system has not up to date (1909) been restored.

The average annual income has been steadily rising during each quinquennium since that ending with the year 1889-90, when it was Rs. 20,892 as compared with Rs. 30,786 in the quinquennium ending with 1904-05: there has been a further large increase since then, chiefly owing to the introduction of Part IX, and in 1908-09 the income was Rs. 48,514. The expenditure has varied with the income from Rs. 22,722 in the quinquennium ending with 1889-90 to Rs. 41,519 in 1908-09.

The major buildings belonging to the Municipality are, (1) the Municipal office with outhouses, tanks and garden, covering about 2 acres, (2) the Municipal school building with out-houses, etc., also covering about 2 acres, and (3) the charitable hospital and dispensary with a compound surrounded by brick walls, covering a little less than one acre.

The manufactures of Sāntipur are in a decaying condition. The cloth industry has been practically killed by the competition of machine-made goods, and the weavers are no longer prosperous.

The East India Company once had a sugar manufactory in the town, but this has met with the same fate as the cloth factories; however, there are still some native refineries in which date-palm molasses, imported from the neighbouring district of Jessore, is refined. There is a certain amount of local trade in other articles.

The town is visited by a large number of pilgrims at the time of the full moon in the month of Kārtik, when the Rāsh Jātrā festival lasts for two days and ends with a procession in which the idols of the Gosains are carried about on elevated wooden platforms. Sāntipur is also a celebrated bathing place.

The town suffered severely in the earthquake of 1897: many of the largest buildings were destroyed, and the impoverished owners have been unable to restore them.

Sibnibās.—A village on the bank of the river Churni, nearly due east of Krishnagar, in thana Kissengunge of the Headquarters Subdivision: the name of this village has been taken for the station upon the main line of the Eastern Bengal State Railway which was formerly called Kissengunge, the change being necessitated by the fact that there are at least two other railway stations in India named Kissengunge, whereby confusion was caused in the booking of parcels and goods.

Sibnibās was established as a country seat in the first half of the 18th century by the great Mahārājā of Nadiā, Krishna Chandra. Two accounts are given of the reason why he selected the place. The first is that, while out hunting, he casually came upon it and was so struck with its beauty and pleasant situation on the banks of the Churni, that he built a palace there for his occasional residence. According to the second account, the place was selected because it was surrounded on three sides by the Churni and thus afforded a comparatively safe and easily-defended retreat from the incursions of the Mahrattas who were giving much trouble in those days. It is said that through the bounty of the Mahārājā no less than 108 temples were constructed in the place. Sibnibās was deserted by Mahārājā Shiv Chandra, son of Krishna Chandra, and now only five temples survive in a more or less dilapitated condition. Of these three are of fair size, standing about 60 feet in height; two contain images of Siva, 9 feet and 7½ feet high, and the third contains an image of Rāmchandra, about 4 feet high. A fair is held here on the *Bhumi Ekadashi* day, and is visited by about 15,000 persons. The village was purchased in 1860 by one Swarup Chandra Sarkār Chaudhuri, whose son, Babu Brindāban Sarkār Chaudhuri, is said to have done much to improve its material condition.

In 1824, Sibnibâs was visited by Bishop Heber on his way by
boat to Dacca and the following account is taken from his Journal
(London, 1828). The gentleman with whom he had an interview may have been a descendant of Krishna Chandra, but he
was certainly not the then Mahârâjâ of Nadia—
"We landed with the intention of walking to some pagodas
whose high angular domes were seen above the trees of a thick
wood, at some small distance, which wood, however, as we
approached it, we found to be full of ruins, apparently of an
interesting description. . . . As we advanced along the
shore, the appearance of the ruins in the jungle became more
unequivocal, and two very fine intelligent looking boys, whom we
met, told me, in answer to my enquiries that the place was really
Sibnibashi, that it was very large and very old, and there were
good paths through the ruins. . . . We found four pagodas,
not large but of good architecture, and very picturesque. . .
The first (temple) which we visited was evidently the most
modern, being, as the officiating Brahmin told us, only fifty-
seven years old. In England we should have thought it at
least 200, but in this climate a building soon assumes, without
constant care, all the venerable tokens of antiquity. It was very
clean however, and of good architecture, a square tower, surmounted by a pyramidal roof, with a high cloister of pointed
arches surrounding it externally to within ten feet of the spring-
ing of the vault. The cloister was also vaulted, so that, as the
Brahmin made us observe with visible pride, the whole roof was
"pucka" or brick, and "belathee" or foreign. A very handsome
gothic arch with an arabesque border, opened on the south side,
and showed within the statue of Rama, seated on a lotus, with a
gilt but tarnished umbrella over his head, and his wife, the
earth-born Seeta, beside him. From hence we went to two of
the other temples, which were both octagonal, with domes not
unlike those of glass-houses. They were both dedicated to Siva
and contained nothing but the symbol of the Deity, of black
marble. . . . Meantime the priest of Rama, who had
received his fee before, and was well satisfied, came up with
several of the villagers to ask if I would see the Rajah's palace.
On my assenting they led us to a really noble gothic gateway,
overgrown with beautiful broad-leaved ivy, but in good preserva-
tion, and decidedly handsomer, though in pretty much the same
style with the "Holy Gate" of the Kremlin in Moscow.
Within this, which had apparently been the entrance into
the city, extended a broken, but still stately, avenue of
tall trees and on either side a wilderness of ruined buildings,

overgrown with trees and brush-wood. I asked who had destroyed the place and was told Seraiah Dowla, an answer which (as it was evidently a Hindoo ruin) fortunately suggested to me the name of the Rájá Kissen Chand. On asking whether this had been his residence, one of the peasants answered in the affirmative, adding that the Rájá's grand children yet lived hard-by . . . Our guide meantime turned short to the right, and led us into what were evidently the ruins of a very extensive palace. Some parts of it reminded me of Conway Castle, and others of Bolton Abbey. It had towers like the former, though of less stately height, and had also long and striking cloisters of Gothic arches, but all overgrown with ivy and jungle, roofless and desolate. Here, however, in a court, whose gateway had still its old folding doors on their hinges, the two boys whom we had seen on the beach came forward to meet us, were announced to us as the great-grandsons of Rájá Kissen Chand, and invited us very courteously in Persian to enter their father's dwelling. I looked round in exceeding surprise. There was no more appearance of inhabitation than in Conway. Two or three cows were grazing among the ruins, and one was looking out from the top of a dilapidated turret, whither she had climbed to browse on the ivy. The breech of a broken cannon, and a fragment of a mutilated inscription lay on the grass, which was evidently only kept down by the grazing of cattle, and the jackals, whose yells began to be heard around us as the evening clossd in, seemed the natural lords of the place. Of course I expressed no astonishment, but said how much respect I felt for their family, of whose ancient splendour I was well informed, and that I should be most happy to pay my compliments to the Raja, their father. They imme-diately led us up a short steep straight flight of steps in the thick-ness of the wall of one of the towers, precisely such as that of which we find the remains in one of the gateways of Rhuddlan Castle, assuring me that it was a very " good road " and at the door of a little vaulted and unfurnished room like that which is shown in Carnarvon Castle, as the queen's bed chamber, we were received by the Raja Omichand, a fat shortish man, of about 45, of rather fair complexion, but with no other clothes than his waist cloth and Brahminical string, and only distinguished from his vassals by having his forehead marked all over with alternate stripes of chalk, vermilion and gold leaf. . . . . I confess I was moved by the apparent poverty of the representa-tive of a house once very powerful, and paid him more attention than I perhaps might have done had his drawing room presented a more princely style. He was exceedingly pleased by my calling

o

him "Mahárájá," or Great King, as if he were still a sovereign like his ancestors. . . . The news had probably spread through the village that a "burra admee" (a great man) had come to see the Raja, with divers account of our riches and splendour, and about one o'clock an alarm of thieves was given by my sirdar-bearer, who happening to look out of one of the cabin windows, saw three black heads just above the water, cautiously approaching the sides of the vessel. His outcry of "Dacoit, Dacoit" alarmed us, but also alarmed them; they turned rapidly round, and in a moment were seen running up the river banks. Thus we had a specimen of both the good and evil of India."

Swarupganj.—A village on the south bank of Jalangi at its junction with the Bhágirathi. It was at one time an important mart, and centre of river trade, but with the opening of the railways it has lost its importance. It is a station for the collection of Nadiá Rivers tolls.

INDEX.

198

Municipalities, 124 to 129.
Murāgāchhā, 179.
Murshid Kuli Khān, 104, 120.
Mutiny, the; 31, 32, 172.

N

Nabadwip, description of, 179 to 185.
Nabadwip, capture of, 24, 25.
Nabadwip hospital, 64.
Nabadwip, Municipality, 126.
Nadiā Fevers Commission, 59.
NADIĀ RĀJ, 149 to 163.—
"Nadiā Rivers," account of, 6 to 17.
"Nadiā Rivers," revenue of, 13, 14.
"Nadiā Rivers," Division, 12.
Nakāsipārā dispensary, 65.
Namasudras, 43.
Natnda dispensary, 65.
Natural configuration, 2 to 4.
NATURAL CALAMITIES, 74 to 81.

Newspapers, 135.
Nischintapur, 172.

O

OCCUPATIONS, MANUFACTURES AND
TRADES, 91 to 96.
Occupations, 91, 92.
Opium, 118.

P

Padmā river, description of, 4.
Patni Taluks, 111, 112.
Parganas, Headquarters Subdivision, 83.
  Ditto, Chuādangā Subdivision, 84.
  Ditto, Rānāghāt Subdivision, 84.
  Ditto, Kushtia Subdivision, 85.
  Ditto, Meherpur Subdivision, 86.
PEOPLE, THE, 39 to 56; material condi-
tion of, 88 to 90.
Permanent Settlement, 107.
PHYSICAL ASPECTS, 1 to 21.
Plague, 64.
Plassey, 185, 186.
Pods, 46.
Police, 119, 120.

Porādah, 186.
Postal communications, 103.
Potatoes, 72.
Pounds, 124.
Pratāpāditya, 26, 151.
Prices, 87, 88.
Primary Education, 133.
Projects, railway, 101.
PUBLIC HEALTH, 57 to 66.

R

Rabi crops, 72.
Railways, 100 to 102.
Railway projects,'101.
Rainfall, 21, 72.
RĀJ, NADIĀ, 149 to 163.
Rām Prasād Sen, 38.
Rām Saran Pāl, 47, 48.
Rānāghāt, description of, 186 to 188.
Rānāghāt Subdivision, 186.
Rānāghāt Municipality, 126.
Rānāghāt-Krishnagar Light Railway,
  101.
Rānāghāt hospital, 64.
Rānāghāt Medical Mission, 65, 145 to
  147, 187.
Ratnapur dispensary, 64, 188.
Registration, 118.
Religions, 44.
RENTS, WAGES, AND PRICES, 82 to 90.
Rents, 82 to 87.
Rental of district, 116.
Resumption proceedings, 110.
Reui, 174.
Revenue, land, of district, 105, 106,
  111, 116.
Revenue of district, 115.
Revenue of "Nadiā Rivers," 13, 14.
Rice, varieties, of, 69; prices of, 87.
Rice, autumn or aus, 69.
Rice, winter or aman, 70.
Riyazu-s-Salatin, quoted, 27, 180.
Road cess, 116.
Roads, 102, 103, 123.
Roman Catholic Mission, 147, 148.
Routes trade; 96.